CURRICULUM AS INSTITUTION AND PRACTICE

Essays in the Deliberative Tradition

Studies in Curriculum Theory
William F. Pinar, Series Editor

CURRICULUM AS INSTITUTION AND PRACTICE

Essays in the Deliberative Tradition

William A. Reid

LEA LAWRENCE ERLBAUM ASSOCIATES, PUBLISHERS
1999   Mahwah, New Jersey   London

Lawrence Erlbaum Associates, Inc., Publishers
10 Industrial Avenue
Mahwah, New Jersey 07430

Cover design by Kathryn Houghtaling Lacey

Library of Congress Cataloging-in-Publication Data

Reid, William Arbuckle.
   Curriculum as institution and practice: essays in the
deliberative tradition / William A. Reid.
      p.   cm.
   Includes bibliographical references and indexes.
   ISBN 0-8058-2981-4 (cloth: alk. paper)
   1. Education—Curricula—Philosophy. 2. Curriculum planning—
Philosophy. 3. Teaching—Philosophy. I. Title.
LB1570.R373 1998
375'.0001—dc21   98-39832
                                                       CIP

Books published by Lawrence Erlbaum Associates are printed on acid-free paper,
and their bindings are chosen for strength and durability.

Printed in the United States of America
10 9 8 7 6 5 4 3 2 1

Intellect itself moves nothing, but only the intellect which aims at an end and is practical—**Aristotle**

Contents

Preface

The appearance of this volume of essays is due to the kindly prompting of Bill Pinar. Coincidentally, the span of time they cover—the last 20 years—parallels the period over which I have enjoyed intermittent friendly meetings and discussions with him. Our engagements with curriculum have, at first sight, followed rather different tracks. He long ago established himself as a leader of the movement known as *reconceptualism*, which has set out to reorientate curriculum studies away from its preoccupation with the design of school programs and toward a focus on curriculum as a reflection of individual biographies. I, on the other hand, while sharing much of his impatience with the soulless reiteration of models and paradigms into which curriculum theory was descending in the 1970s, have preferred to stay close to the work of schools and ask "Do paradigms have to be soulless?" While he was reading Virginia Woolf, I was reading Joseph Schwab—though I did take time off to contemplate the spot where Virginia consigned herself to the waters of the Sussex Ouse in January 1941, and he, for his part, has recently written an essay that speaks well of Joseph. I like to feel that, in some respects, we have shared elements of a common enterprise.

That curriculum and biography are intimately connected is certainly a true observation. As has been wisely remarked, "Curriculum is one of those places where we have told ourselves who we are"; but, where curriculum studies is concerned, is this foreground or background? Our answer to that question marks one of the great divides in the modern literature of curriculum. I know that the coalescence of two apparently disparate themes in the essays collected here—pursuit of the Aristotelean notion of "the practical" and a nagging preoccupation with the history of the English public school in the 19th century—is biographically determined, and that if, as I believe, they do mutually illuminate each other, it is because they share common meaning in my own experience. But, for me, this is means, not end: In so far as our biographies lead to what may be illuminations of the significance of educational practice, this becomes something to be used, hopefully, for the improvement of practice, and the institutions that support practice, not something to be celebrated simply for its own intrinsic interest. The public and the private is another theme for curriculum theorists to contemplate.

Personal debts for friendship and discussion, connected to the production of these essays, are also due to Joseph Schwab, Ian Westbury, Maurice Holt, Janek Wankowski, John Olson, James Dillon, Bjørg Gundem, O. L. Davis, Jr., and many others who have written and thought about curriculum as institution and practice.

I am grateful to Naomi Silverman, Kate Graetzer, Lori Hawver, and Robin Weisberg at Lawrence Erlbaum Associates for their support and advice during the preparation of this volume.

The essays chosen for inclusion have all been reviewed in detail and, where appropriate, reworked or revised, although in most cases, the changes are of a minor nature.

"The Idea of the Practical" appeared in *Curriculum Work and Curriculum Content: Theory and Practice, Contemporary and Historical Perspectives*, edited by Bjørg B. Gundem, Britt Ulstrup Engelsen, and Berit Karseth (Pedagogisk Forskningsinstitutt, University of Oslo, 1991). "Practical Reasoning and Curriculum Decisions" formed chapter 4 of *Thinking About the Curriculum: The Nature and Treatment of Curriculum Problems*, which I published with Routledge & Kegan Paul (London) in 1978. "The Method of the Practical" is extracted from *Curriculum Planning as Deliberation*, published by Pedagogisk Forskningsinstitutt, University of Oslo, in 1994. "Curriculum Research Within a Practical Perspective" appeared in *Curriculum Work and Curriculum Content* (1994). "Schwab's Conception of Liberal Education" is reproduced from "Democracy, Perfectability, and the 'Battle of the Books': Thoughts on the Conception of Liberal Education in the Writings of Schwab," published in volume 10 (1980) of *Curriculum Inquiry*, and "Does Schwab Improve on Tyler?" first appeared in volume 25 (1993) of *Journal of Curriculum Studies*.

"The Institutional Context of Curriculum Deliberation" was published in *Journal of Curriculum and Supervision*, volume 4 (1988). "The Problem of Curriculum Change" was chapter 5 of *Thinking About the Curriculum*. "Curricular Topics as Institutional Categories" was contributed to *Defining the Curriculum: Histories and Ethnographies*, edited by Ivor Goodson and Stephen Ball (Falmer Press, 1984). "Curriculum Change and the Evolution of Educational Constituencies" appeared as "Curriculum Change and the Evolution of Curricular Constituencies" in *Social Histories of the Secondary Curriculum: Subjects for Study*, edited by Ivor Goodson (Falmer Press, 1985). "On the Origins of the Institutional Categories of Schooling" was published as "Strange Curricula: Origins and Evolution of the Institutional Categories of Schooling" in *Journal of Curriculum Studies*, volume 22 (1990), and "The Institutional Character of the Curriculum of Schooling" is extracted from *Curriculum Planning as Deliberation* (1994).

I am grateful to the University of Oslo Institute for Educational Research, Routledge & Kegan Paul, Blackwell Publishers, Taylor & Francis, The Association for Supervision and Curriculum Development, and Falmer Press for permission to reprint this material.

Introduction

What should be taught in our schools, by what means, to whom, under what circumstances, and with what end in view? These are the central questions of curriculum that are endlessly debated by politicians, administrators, educators, and, not least, the public at large. But what is *curriculum*? Unless we have a clear and realistic conception of what this thing is, which is at once a focus for dispute and a vehicle for idealism, our arguments, proposals, and policies risk being poorly targeted, and the bright hopes of visionary aims risk ending in disillusionment.

It is not my claim here that there is only one clear and realistic conception of what curriculum is—indeed I argue that a search for such a thing is one of the obstacles that lie in the way of sensible curricular policies. What is at issue is not some physical object that can be measured, analyzed, experimented on, but a human construct, subject to all the uncertainties, ambiguities, and revisions that attend such things. My concern is to put forward one conception of curriculum that is, I hope, friendly and flexible enough to live alongside others, yet, at the same time, sufficiently coherent and focused to be describable and identifiable.

The conception I shall put forward has two sides to it, which are interrelated yet conceptually distinguishable: from one point of view, curriculum is to be understood as *practice*, and from another as *institution*. Perversely, in view of my title, *Curriculum as Institution and Practice*, I shall first of all talk about practice. *Institution and Practice* may sound better, but, logically and sociologically, practice has to come first.

The overall mode of thought, which I apply to curriculum in order to reveal its two sides of practice and institution, I refer to as the *deliberative tradition.* The choice of words is suggestive of its character as capacious yet principled, friendly to other conceptions yet sure of its own distinctiveness. Deliberation connects with cognate ideas such as *practical reasoning* and *inquiry* to define a tradition of thinking about human institutions within their socio-political settings. The language of deliberation is found in many contexts, notably in the writings of Aristotle and, in the educational field, those of Dewey and Schwab. Deliberation implies the careful weighing of possibilities, which may relate to what we are to do, or what we are to believe, in the light of available evidence, without the expectation that what we decide will be the only possible thing to do or believe, or the only correct thing to do or believe. This tradition of thinking finds itself opposed to those which claim to operate on principle. Principled thinking attempts to found conclusions on logical processes that show them to be necessarily entailed by indubitable premises, or by demonstrable facts. Upholders of deliberative thinking are inclined to doubt whether premises are ever as sound as they are claimed to be, or whether facts are ever a faithful reflection of reality: their mode of thinking tends to be psychological rather than logical.

Of course, both approaches have their strengths and weaknesses. It would be futile to engage in deliberation about whether (given Euclid's premises) the square on the hypotenuse of a right angled triangle is or is not equal to the sum of the squares on the other two sides. Demonstrably, it is (though there could be deliberation about the advantages and disadvantages, for particular purposes, of proceeding from different premises). Equally, it would be futile to try to prove, through the application of logic, that there is one best way to teach children to read and write (though the attempt has been made).

What is it that distinguishes the two situations? In the first, what is being reasoned about is an abstract concept, a puzzle that we delight in solving, though there is nothing to compel us to do it. The answer can be thought about without reference to human preferences, traditions, or ambitions. In the second, what is being reasoned about is a practical problem that demands a solution and that is intrinsically bound up with human preferences, traditions, and ambitions. Confronted with decisions to be made, our difficulty is to decide which kinds of problems we are dealing with. Problems of what to teach in our schools, by what means, to whom, under what circumstances, and with what end in view are problems that, I hold, demand deliberation.

But while this contrast between deliberative thinking and principled thinking is illuminating, it is also problematic. Are we to conclude that deliberative thinking is unprincipled? That what we are substituting, however well meaningly, for the attempt to be logical is mere opportunism or compromise? One of my main objectives in this book is to show that this is not the case. Though deliberation takes the position that, often, arguments from premise are simplistic, this does not mean that principle is to be thrown away. It is possible to treat a problem as too complex and multifaceted to be amenable to some kind of calculation, yet at the same time apply standards of inquiry in the same way that standards of inquiry are applied to the solution of logical puzzles.

The particular complexity of curriculum as a field for decision making that stands in need of a deliberative approach resides, as I have suggested, in the sometimes awkward relationship between its two main elements: its character as a practical endeavor, and its character as a human institution. On the one hand, curriculum consists of particulars. As Schwab put it, of "this student, in that school, on the South Side of Columbus, with Principal Jones during the present mayoralty of Ed Tweed and in view of the probability of his reelection."[1] Particulars, such as those enumerated here, are complex, multifarious, and subject to change. They are what practitioners— and principally teachers—have to deal with most of the time. But dealing with them means more than managing or coping: practitioners, while confronted by ever-changing circumstance, strive to pursue ideals of practice. The practice of teaching, like the practice of medicine, or the practice of law, assumes a relationship of trust and responsibility between practitioner and client.

So here we have a partial answer to the question "What is curriculum?". It is a multitude of encounters between teachers (practitioners) and students (clients) in circumstances of great individuality, where outcomes are seldom predictable.

But curriculum is also, necessarily, an institution. We could have a situation where those with things to teach and those willing to learn came together without the idea of curriculum being necessary or appropriate. This, in fact, was the state of affairs that, in varying degrees, existed before the invention of modern schooling systems. But today schooling systems are pervasive: we can and must talk of curriculum because the student in Schwab's classroom, as well as being in the situation of uniqueness that he described, is also in a situation of generality. He or she is now in a particular grade, let us say the sixth, having completed the curriculum of the fifth grade, and is looking forward to entering the seventh grade. He or she is studying a subject (geography, perhaps) in a program of specified content, with a beginning and an end, which is to be successfully completed. All of this is possible because both the school authorities, including Principal Jones, and, more importantly, the public at large, have a conception of curriculum as *institution*, which includes notions of "gradedness" (what it means to be a sixth grader), notions of "subjectness" (what it means to study sixth-grade geography), and so on.

Thus particularity and generality coexist and intertwine: out of the multiplicity of contexts that thousands of idiosyncratic teachers and students inhabit emerge universal categories of career and achievement that define them to each other and to the world at large; out of the universal prescriptions of ministries and accrediting agencies emerge the variegated classrooms of nations in which teachers and students pursue their unique ambitions.

But it was practice, and the particularities of practice that came first. So it is to these that we turn in the first part of this book.

NOTE

1. Schwab, J. J. (1978). The practical: A language for curriculum. In I. Westbury & N. J. Wilkof (Eds.), *Science, curriculum, and liberal education* (p. 289). Chicago: University of Chicago Press.

I

CURRICULUM AS PRACTICE

The deliberative tradition, which is concerned with how problems about action should be confronted and resolved, has a long history. Its philosophical origins are usually traced back to Aristotle, who, in his *Ethics* and *Politics*, set out to provide a theoretic basis for linking thought to action. Such Aristotelean concepts informed much of European teaching in the Middle Ages, and were at the heart of the "arts and methods" that formed the substance of the academic work of the medieval universities. After the Renaissance, a preoccupation with the methods of science led to the eclipse of the "old" ideas of Aristotle in favor of the "new" thinking of philosophers such as Descartes, Hume, and Hobbes, and the success of scientific thinking in solving theoretic puzzles led to its extension into the practical areas of decision making that had been the natural home of deliberation.

Thus, when national education systems began to flourish in the 19th century, the spotlight in Europe and North America was turned toward proposals for scientific curriculum planning due to followers of Herbart and Spencer. The deliberative tradition was, however, kept alive in the writings of Dewey, and its modern elaboration as means of dealing with questions of curriculum is due mainly to the work of scholars standing directly in the line of succession to Dewey, such as McKeon and Schwab. The main focus of their work has been to resurrect and explicate, in terms of modern dilemmas about what should be taught in schools and colleges, Aristotle's understanding of how thought should be connected to action, and the leading idea around which they have woven their arguments has been that of The Practical. A revived notion of "method" has been invoked to show how, confronted by the need to take action over issues of education and curriculum, we can proceed to identify problems and move them toward resolution. The first six chapters in this book are devoted to consideration of practice and the practical along the lines advocated by McKeon and Schwab.

Chapter 1, *The Idea of the Practical*, draws on the work of Schwab to illustrate the distinctiveness of the flavor that deliberative thinking brings to the idea of practice, emphasising how far it goes beyond the idea of practice as simply "what works."

Next, in chap. 2, *Practical Reasoning and Curriculum Decisions*, I examine the nature of the practical problems that curriculum makers must solve and show how this determines the kind of reasoning that should be brought to bear on them.

This argument is carried further in chap. 3, *The Method of the Practical*, which considers the strengths and weaknesses of a practical reasoning approach to curriculum making, as compared and contrasted to those of other planning perspectives.

In chap. 4, *Curriculum Research Within a Practical Perspective*, I consider how ideas of what we should research, and how research should be conducted, would be modified within a conception of curriculum that views it as a practical art.

The implications of the deliberative paradigm for how we conceive the nature of education form the subject matter of chap. 5, *Thoughts on Schwab's Conception of Liberal Education*, where I argue that, far from being neutral in its implications for educational outcomes, the application of practical reasoning to the resolution of curriculum problems necessarily points us toward aims that are inherent in the idea of liberal education.

Finally, chap. 6, *Does Schwab Improve on Tyler?* sets out to explain the essential difference between educational theorists who adopt a "practical reasoning" approach and those who have constituted the mainstream of curriculum theorists and have concerned themselves with the planning of school programs—proponents of what Philip Jackson called the *dominant perspective*. This returns us, in a different context, to the distinction between practice and the practical with which we began.

1

The Idea of the Practical

This chapter first appeared, under the same title, in B. B. Gundem, B. U. Engelsen, and B. Karseth (Eds., 1991), Curriculum work and curriculum content, *Report No. 5, Institute for Educational Research, University of Oslo. It had previously been presented at the Conference on Curriculum Work and Curriculum Content held at the University of Oslo, October 10–12. Scholars at the Oslo Institute, in recent years and under the leadership of Gundem, have been very friendly to the deliberative tradition of curriculum, and have usefully confronted it with the interestingly similar, yet also profoundly different tradition of German didactics.[1]*

Any consideration of practice in relation to curriculum must begin with a reading of Schwab's series of practical papers, which he published over the period 1969–1983. This chapter deals with three specific obstacles that, in my experience, tend to hinder engagement with the ideas that Schwab put forward in these seminal papers.

This chapter discusses the notion of the practical as laid out by Schwab in a series of papers published between 1969 and 1983. It is important, however, that these be seen against the background of many other papers that Schwab published over a much longer period, mainly addressing issues in science education and liberal education.[2] The thinking behind all of them represents a coherent philosophy of social action generally, including the planning and provision of curricula and stemming from a close acquaintance with the work of a number of philosophers, of whom Dewey and McKeon are the most important. Central to this philosophy of social action is the idea of the practical. Rather than attempt to offer a full discussion and explanation of this idea, I shall here try to exemplify its character by talking about three particular difficulties that it raises (see Fig. 1.1).

What these difficulties have in common is that they all relate to fundamental differences between commonsense notions of what practice is, and the conception of practice as it appears in Schwab's account of the practical. They are all obstacles to our understanding of what the practical is.

The first difficulty is that, within any philosophical perspective, conceptions of practice are determined by conceptions of theory. In education, theory, as opposed to practice, tends to be thought of as abstract and refined in nature, and, the more theory is characterized in this way, the more practice is conceived of as concrete and mundane: practice is simply what people do in schools and classrooms. In contrast to this position, although the theory–practice opposition is central to the idea of the practical, the kind of opposition that Schwab had in mind was very different.

The second difficulty arises from the fact that practice is conventionally thought of as the deployment of resources and the application of skills, so that if, for example, we discuss how the practice of teaching (as opposed to the theory of teaching) is to be improved, we would most likely engage in consideration of needed resources of buildings and materials and of requisite skills of management and presentation. However, viewed within the perspective of the practical, practice depends primarily not on resources and skills, but on tradition and character and, therefore, discussion of the improvement of practice needs primarily to be discussion of how tradition is to be shaped and how character is to be formed.

The third difficulty is that practice tends to be seen as value-free. Good practice is simply that which works. The idea of the practical, on the other hand, represents practice as deeply implicated with considerations of a social, cultural, and political nature, and implies that as we confront problems of practice, we also confront problems of moral choice.

I will discuss each of these difficulties in turn and, in doing so, will hope to convey my own understanding of what Schwab meant when he talked about the practical.

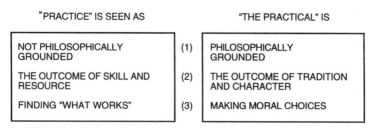

FIG. 1.1. Practice and the practical.

THE FIRST DIFFICULTY: THE PRACTICAL
AND THE THEORY–PRACTICE DISTINCTION

It is fundamental to the notion of practice that it is contrasted with theory. But the contrast that Schwab talked about in his practical papers is not between theory and practice, but between *the theoretic* and *the practical,* and he was as much concerned to point to what they have in common as to what separates them. What they have in common is that they are both forms of inquiry. There is theoretic inquiry and there is practical inquiry, but both are philosophically conceived means of treating problems or puzzles. We could, if we liked, remove the labels theoretic and practical, and talk simply about inquiry, but that would obscure the very important point that Schwab wanted to impress on us: The form of inquiry that we use has to be adapted to the kind of problem that our inquiry is intended to resolve.[3] There is, in fact, no universal recipe for conducting an inquiry, and by making the wrong choice we risk reaching the wrong conclusions. In the case of curriculum, the choice to which we have to be particularly sensitive is that between inquiry suited to problems arising from states of mind and inquiry suited to problems arising from states of affairs.

In the first case, we need to apply the methods of theoretic inquiry: in the second, the methods of practical inquiry. Schwab believed—and there is a good deal of evidence to support his belief—that many mistakes are made because designers of curricula neglect to observe this distinction and try to use theoretic methods when they should be using practical ones. For this reason—a very practical reason—he chose to compare and contrast the theoretic and the practical. In doing so, he used a rhetorical device intended to persuade his readers that the process of inquiry contains pitfalls of which they need to be aware. By talking about the theoretic and the practical, he provided them with a way of thinking about this problem and a way of avoiding it.

Schwab contrasted his two forms of inquiry in terms of (a) the kinds of problems they deal with, (b) the subject matters they seek out, (c) the methods they apply to this subject matter, and (d) the kinds of outcome to which they lead (see Fig. 1.2).

The theoretic addresses itself to perceived deficiencies arising from states of mind. That is, problems or puzzles about things we do not understand, but would like to understand. For example, why something predicted by theory fails to occur. In order to solve the problem, we look for data of a general nature, and we analyze them according to disciplinary principles (for example, the principles of inquiry in quantum dynamics). Solving the puzzle means coming up with an explanation for what was discrepant or not understood.

PRACTICAL INQUIRY   THEORETIC INQUIRY

STATE OF AFFAIRS	PROBLEM	STATE OF MIND
PARTICULAR	SUBJECT MATTER	GENERAL
DELIBERATION	METHOD	DEDUCTION/ INDUCTION
ACTION	OUTCOME	EXPLANATION

FIG. 1.2.   Practical and theoretic inquiry.

The practical mode of inquiry, on the other hand, treats states of affairs—human or social conditions that we believe should be improved, or aspirations that we would like to translate into concrete proposals. In this case, the route to the resolution of our problem lies through knowledge particular to the situation for which a resolution is sought: knowledge of persons, of places, of actions, and of consequences of actions. There is no general principle that allows us to weigh and interpret particular knowledge of this kind. As Schwab said, the practical has no rule or guide.[4] For knowledge to point us toward a resolution, it has to be deliberated upon. That is, arguments have to be made, by individuals or by groups, to which judgment, individual or collective, is applied. As a result of the application of judgment, a resolution is reached. This is not an explanation, but a decision to follow a course of action.

Thus Schwab was enabled to speak of the radical difference of the practical from the theoretic. The practical is different, he said, "not only in one aspect but in many: it differs . . . in method. Its problems originate from a different source. Its subject matter is of a different kind."[5] But while these differences need to be pointed out, they are not fundamental. The distinction that Schwab was making was not between theory, which treats problems in a philosophically grounded way, and practice, which deals with them in an ad hoc, rule-of-thumb fashion, but between two kinds of inquiry, both philosophically grounded, but adapted to the investigation of different kinds of problems. Moreover, the findings of the theoretic are necessary, though not sufficient, for the resolution of certain kinds of practical problem. While Schwab warned against the use of overriding principles to guide practical inquiry, he did not deny that principled, theoretic inquiry can furnish materials to help in the resolution of practical problems. In practical inquiry, however, the incorporation of such materials, along with other relevant data, must be controlled by deliberation, which is the method of the practical. Thus, if we are designing curricula, the findings of, say, cognitive psychology or social anthropology are not irrelevant to our endeavor, but their relevance, along with that of many other kinds of data—knowledge of specific children and teachers, knowledge of specific communities and settings—has to be a matter of judgment. Moreover, the form in which theoretic arguments enter into practical judgments also has to be determined according to the demands of the deliberative process. Decisions about form and relevance are reached through what Schwab refers to as "arts of eclectic": these, he says, are "arts by which we ready theory for practical use (and) by which we discover and take practical account of the distortions and limitations which a theory imposes on its subject matter."[6]

THE SECOND DIFFICULTY:
THE PRACTICAL AS THE PRODUCT
OF TRADITION AND CHARACTER

Contrasting practical inquiry with theoretic inquiry can lead to undue emphasis on negative aspects of its nature:

1. It does *not* deal with well-defined problems ("Practical problems do not present themselves wearing their labels around their necks."[7]).
2. Its subject matter is *uncertain*. Which matters are relevant to the resolution of the problem and which are not? How do we know where to look for evidence, or when we have enough?
3. There is *no* definite guide or rule that can be applied to the weighing of evidence, or to the movement from evidence to conclusion.
4. There is *no* way of knowing whether a course of action is the best available one (or, retrospectively, was the best).

It is very easy for us to think about the practical in this negative way—to see it as offering nothing but confusion and uncertainty—because the things that make it strong and purposeful are not things that currently attract the attention of theoreticians or researchers. Currently, faith tends to be put in procedures that are clearly specifiable, learnable, and capable of exact evaluation. These characteristics are associated with the methods of the theoretic: with induction and deduction according to disciplinary principles. But they cannot assure the strength of the practical, since that is concerned with a different kind of inquiry, adapted to a different class of problem. What lends strength and purpose to the practical is not the dependability of rule-governed procedure, but the less fashionable resources of tradition and character. Deliberation, as the method of the practical, is more purposeful if it takes place within a well-cultivated tradition of how particular classes of practical problems are to be dealt with. Tradition differs from procedure in that it cannot be specified by rules. Tradition evolves in the minds of people who learn from precedent and adapt to circumstance. Tradition is kept alive in, and by practice. Of course, theoretic problems too can be said to be treated within living traditions of which practitioners are the inventors and bearers, but our attention is not drawn to this fact: the rhetoric of science leads us to believe that method, abstracted from tradition, is paramount in the solution of theoretic problems, and that method does indeed inhere in specifiable rules of procedure. Thus, when we propose to treat practical problems, we are more conscious of what we cannot have in the way of resources—a set of definite rules of procedure—than what we can have, a tradition of how problems are to be confronted and resolved. Within such a tradition, there can be confidence that what we are doing is not ad hoc and confused, but reasoned and methodic. The sight of experts in particular kinds of practice operating in this way can be impressive. This is the case, for example, in the arts when actors deliberate on how to play a scene, or musicians on how to interpret a piece of music. Arguments do not have to be elaborately developed: participants in the deliberation get the point quickly because tradition provides a shared repertoire of moves, ideas, techniques, and criteria of judgment.

As well as depending on collective tradition, the practical also relies on individual character. There are techniques of deliberation, but it is never entirely clear which technique is needed at that moment of the process. Judgment is required, and the ability to exercise judgment depends not only on tradition but also on traits of character that are best described in the language of virtue. For example, in the exercise of individual judgment, patience is an important virtue. In practical situations, where there is no rule or guide to make error obvious, it is easy to rush to judgment on the basis of little evidence. People possessing patience are likely to make better judgments because they review more evidence and weigh it more carefully. Or, in the exercise of collective judgment, humility is an important virtue. Without humility, we believe that our own opinions are correct and do not listen to, or try to understand those put forward by others. But if the decision of the group is to be better than those that might be reached individually by its members, all contributions have to be brought to bear on the process of judgment.

THE THIRD DIFFICULTY: THE PRACTICAL AS MORE THAN "WHAT WORKS"

Raising issues of tradition and character enables me to move more easily to my third and final difficulty about the nature of the practical: the idea that it consists simply of discovering "what works." In this view, the practical is simply a matter of technical know-how: there are various means of accomplishing certain kinds of purposes—for example, increasing the amount of learning that takes place in classrooms—and the choice between them turns on the question of which practices are most effective. But if tradition and character are important factors in the successful conduct of practical inquiry, then we have to reflect that tradition and character are more than the product of extensive experience of what works. Tradition and character support or sympathize with certain kinds of practice on the basis of what communities or individuals value. And these valuations depend on the perceptions they have of their histories and their destinies, of what is moral and what is virtuous.

This brings me to one of the most important and least obvious aspects of Schwab's account of the practical. As far as I know, he does not state in his practical papers that what he is talking about is one of several possible conceptions of the character that practical decision making might assume (see Fig. 1.3). Nor does he make it clear that his choice of a character for the conduct of practical affairs is a moral choice.

In fact, it would have been perfectly possible for Schwab to have presented an account of practical activity that was *not* dependent on tradition and character. He might, for example, have offered a discussion of how to establish what works. Such an explanation—one with which Schwab was

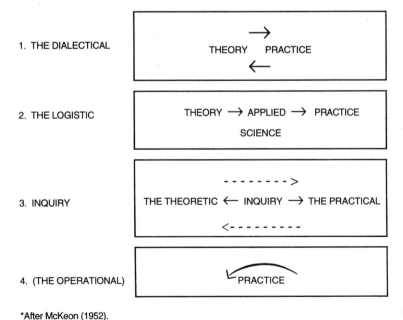

*After McKeon (1952).

FIG. 1.3. Forms of theory–practice relationship.

thoroughly familiar—is to be found in Richard McKeon's 1952 paper in *Ethics* entitled "Philosophy and Action."[8] McKeon calls it the "operational" conception of practice. Neither did Schwab choose to subscribe to two other conceptions of the theory–practice relationship discussed by McKeon in the same paper: the "dialectic" and the "logistic." Schwab's choice (following Dewey) of an account of the theory–practice relationship based on inquiry stemmed from moral and ethical considerations. Like McKeon, he saw the operational as simply expedient and lacking in any moral character. The dialectic he rejects because he sees it as politically restrictive. To be self-consistent, a dialectical view of practice has to be guided by some specific account of social evolution. It will therefore cater to one possible conception of history and destiny to the exclusion of others that participants in judgment might hold. The logistic he rejects because it implies a different kind of restriction. In the logistic mode, practice is guided by theoretical knowledge that is the province of experts. Expert knowledge is therefore elevated to a level of importance far exceeding that of the knowledge of particulars that others can bring to practical decision making. For Schwab, a theory–practice relationship based on inquiry reflects and supports what he considers to be the best kind of society—one that respects the theoretic, but that understands the different requirements of the practical and involves, directly or indirectly, the whole community, not a subgroup of dialecticians or experts, in the resolution of practical problems. From this morally motivated choice of an inquiry-based conception of theory and practice all the rest followed—his account of the practical as a language for curriculum, his discussion of the eclectic, his proposal for the conduct of curriculum planning groups, his conception of liberal education, and so on.

CONCLUSION: CHOOSING A CONCEPTION OF THE THEORY–PRACTICE RELATIONSHIP

Thus the practical appears not just as an account of how courses of action can be decided on and justified, but as a vision of a particular kind of moral world with implications, not only for the design of curricula, but also for the organization of schools, for the character of communities within which schools are set, and for the whole society within which communities are embraced. The practical is emphatically not another version of the administrative or managerial account of curriculum practice. Nor, as a humanistic account, does it refer solely to the nature of individuals, or the nature of schools and classrooms. Its vision, as I hope I have shown, is much broader than that, and it is in the broad vision that the strengths and weaknesses of the practical lie.

If we share the vision, the technical problems involved in the work of deliberating groups seem not so important. In fact, they appear not so much as problems as opportunities. But if we do not share the vision, or fail to see it, then we wonder why such an elaborate account of curriculum as practice is necessary, and why we should not prefer some other scheme—the operational, perhaps—that seems, on the face of things, to be easier to understand and simpler to use. As Schwab made his choice, so we make ours: Is practice more than what works? And if it is more, what kind of moral society should it reflect?

NOTES

1. See, for example, Hopmann, S., & Riquarts, K. (1995). Starting a dialogue: Issues in a beginning conversation between Didaktik and the curriculum traditions. *Journal of Curriculum Studies, 27*, 3–12.
2. For a collection of Schwab's major papers, see Westbury I., & Wilkof, N. J. (Eds.). (1978). *Science, curriculum, and liberal education.* Chicago: University of Chicago Press. The final practical paper is published in *Curriculum Inquiry, 13* (1983), 239–255.
3. I choose to say "resolve" rather than "solve" because within a practical perspective, problems are not regarded as solved in any final way. What is reached is an acceptable resolution of a difficulty, rather than a unique answer to a puzzle.
4. Westbury and Wilkof, *op. cit.*, p. 290.
5. *Ibid.*, pp. 288–289.
6. *Ibid.*, p. 323.
7. *Ibid.*, p. 316.
8. McKeon, R. (1952). Philosophy and action. *Ethics, 62*, 79–100.

CHAPTER

2

Practical Reasoning and Curriculum Decisions

My first attempt to work out the meaning of the concept of the practical for curriculum grew out of a study leave spent at Stanford University in the Summer of 1975. Case studies in curriculum change,[1] *which I co-edited with Decker F. Walker of the Stanford School of Education, had just appeared, conveying a critical message about currently popular ways of setting about curriculum design. So what could be offered as a better alternative? "Practical reasoning and curriculum decisions," which grew out of discussions with Walker and Elliot Eisner, and later with Ian Westbury of the University of Illinois, and went through several revisions over the next 3 years, was an attempt to answer that question. It finally appeared as chap. 4 in* Thinking about the curriculum[2] *published by Routledge & Kegan Paul in 1978. It is reproduced here, in a marginally revised form.*

In spite of over fifty years of curriculum theorizing on the part of those who have consciously set out to develop curriculum theory, and centuries of thought devoted to wider problems of the nature of education, fundamental questions of the purposes and concepts that should characterize curriculum theory are still matters of lively contention. That this is the case is a cause of concern not only to philosophers and theoreticians, but also to all those responsible for and affected by practical decision making on the curriculum. At a time when, all over the world, there is massive intervention on the part of governments in the shaping of school curricula, questions of how we conceptualize curriculum tasks assume a special importance: intervention is never atheoretical; it always implies some view of what the curriculum is and what theories and metaphors should guide its planning. The theory of rational curriculum design expounded by Tyler and others is, perhaps, the outstanding example of a conceptualization that has exerted, and continues to exert, a profound and worldwide influence on the nature of curriculum decision making.

But what do we mean by curriculum theory? We may mean a set of propositions about what the curriculum is or how it changes, but, most centrally, we mean theories about how to plan, implement, and evaluate curricula. It is in order to arrive at these theories of practice that we interest ourselves in inquiries of a more strictly theoretic nature. Good practice turns on good decision making, and decision making in its turn is a kind of problem solving. So we can say that curriculum theories are theories about how to solve curriculum problems. Probably few would be found to dispute this conclusion.[3] But now we come to the critical issue: What kind of a problem is a curriculum problem? Those who support planning by objectives would say that it is a procedural problem—a problem we solve by applying a uniquely suitable formula or technique. Quite another view is put forward by Schwab who denies that curriculum problems are of such a nature that they can be solved procedurally, and argues that solutions to them must be found by an interactive consideration of means and ends. The process through which this is achieved is called *deliberation* or *practical reasoning*. What is proposed here is that, generally speaking, curriculum problems relate most closely to that class of questions that are referred to in some philosophical writings as uncertain practical questions.[4]

We encounter uncertain practical problems as a regular part of everyday life. "How shall I redecorate the living-room?", "Where shall I go for my holidays this year?", "Which party should I vote for at the next election?" But there are also questions of great public importance that have the same character. "Should we build a third London airport, and if so, where?", "Should Scotland and Wales have their own national assemblies?", "Should worker directors be on the boards of all public companies and, if so, how should they be elected?" Questions of this type, whether they be everyday ones, or questions of national importance, have many features in common. First of all, they are questions that have to be answered—even if the answer is to decide to do nothing. In this they differ from academic, or theoretic questions that do not demand an answer at any particular time, or indeed any answer at all. Second, the grounds on which decisions should be made are uncertain. Nothing can tell us infallibly whose interests should be consulted, what evidence should be taken into account, or what kinds of arguments should be given precedence. Third, in answering practical questions, we always have to take some existing state of affairs into account. We are never in a position to make a completely fresh start, free from the legacy of past history and present arrangements. Fourth, and following from this, each question is in some ways unique, belonging to a specific time and context, the particulars of which we can never exhaustively describe. Fifth, our question will certainly compel us to adjudicate between competing goals and values. We may choose a solution that maximizes our satisfaction across a range of possible goals, but some will suffer at the expense of others. Sixth, we can never predict the outcome of the particular solution we choose, still less know what the outcome would have been had we made a different choice. Finally, the grounds on which we decide to answer a practical question in a particular way are not grounds that point to the desirability of the action chosen as an act in itself, but grounds that lead us to suppose that the action will result in some desirable state of affairs. The goal of our solution is not to vote for the party, but to bring about a situation where the party has power, not to give Scotland and Wales their own assemblies, but to create, through the setting up of assemblies, new political, social, and economic contexts in those countries.

Uncertain practical problems, then, present many kinds of complexity. As Gauthier remarks "the sphere of the practical is necessarily the sphere of the uncertain." A practical problem he says, is "a problem about what to do . . . whose final solution is found only in doing something, in acting."[5] Yet practical problems are the kinds of problems that we face most of the time and, in fact, people are quite good at solving them. It is difficult to evaluate solutions to problems that present severe uncertainty, but in conditions where solutions have to be found within known parameters, such as in games of chess, we find that the lesser computing ability of the expert player is sometimes better able than a computer to answer the question, "What move should I play next?" or "What kind of overall strategy will give me the the best chance of success in this position?" Where such limiting parameters do not exist, and judgments must be embedded in a wider context, one would assume that the human practical reasoner would definitely show superiority.

PRACTICAL PROBLEMS AND THEIR SOLUTION

The method by which most everyday practical problems get solved has been variously called deliberation or practical reasoning. It is an intricate and skilled intellectual and social process whereby, individually or collectively, we identify the questions to which we must respond, establish grounds for deciding on answers, and then choose among the available solutions. But, because it is an everyday activity, we tend to undervalue it, and to make little effort to understand it.[6] Some writers, indeed, would have us believe that the whole class of practical problems is of little interest. Science, it is claimed, shows us how to treat them by procedural means, and makes them easy to solve. Only theoretical questions are really challenging. Of course, there are practical problems, or parts of such problems, that are not complex or uncertain and may have answers that can be reached by procedural means. If we have decided where to spend our holidays, then the practical problem of how to get to the place we have chosen may turn out to be purely procedural. We check the route maps or timetables and find the solution that fits our already-established requirements. When we have decided to decorate our living room walls and know what kind of wallpaper we want, appropriate calculations and measurements will tell us how much to buy. If a problem can be solved by research or calculation it can be classified as *procedural*. The answer to our request for help in solving it would be an indication of a known procedure to be followed, and we would make the request in some form such as "What must I do?" or "Show me what to do." The mark of the uncertain problem, on the other hand, is the question "What should I do?" or "Tell me what I ought to do." But because this is a more difficult question to answer, there is a strong temptation to try to reduce uncertain problems to procedural ones. Ethical prescriptions try to do this for problems of moral behavior, books on etiquette try to do it for problems of social conduct, axiomatic philosophical systems try to do it for general questions of action and belief, and political ideologies try to do it for questions of public policy.

The reduction of the uncertain to the procedural can be attempted in two ways. One is to tackle the problem at its root and to say that what is needed is a method that, routinely applied, will yield suitable solutions. For example, to say that if we want to know where to put a third London airport we should do a cost–benefit analysis. The other is to declare a goal or principle, on the assumption that, if the end is agreed, the search for means is relatively simple. For example, if we agree that the end of all political action should be the establishment of the dictatorship of the proletariat, then, it might be supposed, the nature of that action will not be open to major dispute. In some respects, it could be said that the invention of principles and procedures represents progress. Culture and civilization advance by moving things that yesterday were in the province of doubt and anxiety to the realm of the routine, leaving the mind free to turn to different and higher things. But what constitutes progress, and what represents decline in the application of principle and procedure is a matter of controversy, for both methdology and ideology may turn out to be false or misguided.

Pressures for the implementation of procedural methods of problem solving become especially strong where the practical questions concern matters of great public moment, and large political, administrative, or economic commitments have to be made. Yet, as Gauthier points out, it is precisely in this area that we can be sure that problems do not admit of procedural solutions. He subdivides uncertain practical problems into the prudential and the moral. Prudential reasoning, he suggests, "may be considered to be that part of practical reasoning in which the reasons for acting are restricted to the wants, desires, needs and aims of the agent."[7] Hence, any problem the solution of which will affect the "wants, desires, needs, and aims" of a wider population must certainly have moral aspects, and, although the boundary between prudential and procedural problems may sometimes be obscure, the one between moral and procedural problems is not. The attempt to deny the need for moral reasoning by setting up prespecified objectives or procedures must fail.[8]

The preceding discussion enables us to form a hierarchy of problems (see Fig. 2.1). The first division of the tree is into the practical and the theoretic. The second, within the practical, is into the procedural and the uncertain, and the last, within the uncertain, is into the moral and the prudential. It is not claimed that every problem can be neatly slotted into one or other of these categories. In some instances, especially where the problem is vaguely felt, or of a complex nature, and not easily translated into specific questions, we may be unsure where to place it: in others we may face a family of problems, some of which belong in one category and some in another. Perhaps, even, the solution will come through shunting the problem back and forth, looking at it now in one light, then in another. The chess player may begin in procedural fashion by calculating variations according to the rules by which pieces move. This may lead to ideas about how certain kinds of advantage may be secured, or disadvantage avoided. These considerations will become the grounds for a process of prudential reasoning about losses and gains that are beyond the reach of procedural analysis, or not capable of being procedurally considered in the time avail-

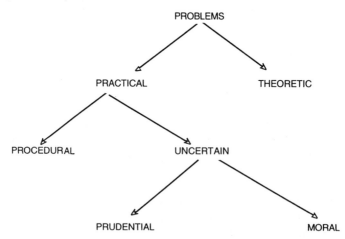

FIG. 2.1. A hierarchy of problems.

able. Finally, when a provisional choice of a course of action has been made, there may be a return to the procedural mode to verify that it does not contain some tactical flaw. In this way, by appeals to different types of practical reasoning, the player hopes to bring about a state of affairs that is as satisfactory as possible, given the starting position.[9] However, the diagram does provide us with a useful heuristic device that will help us to decide what kind of problem we are dealing with, and what kind or kinds of reasoning should be applied to it. It suggests that a guide to making this sort of decision will be a careful attempt to translate our problem into accurately phrased questions. If the question asks for a description or explanation, then it is theoretic—about knowing or understanding. "What is being taught to eighth graders in our high schools?" or "How do young children learn?" are theoretic questions. But questions about what to do, or how to do it: "What ought we to be teaching to eighth graders?" or "How can we help young children to learn?" are practical questions. If they ask for suggestions about established methods, they are procedural: "What must I do?" If they ask for adjudication about preferences as well as about procedures, they are prudential: "What should I do?" If they require the use of words like "ought," then this adjudication has to take into account moral, ethical, as well as prudential considerations. This last distinction is difficult to make: when we use words like "should" and "ought," it is not always clear whether we are asking prudential questions or moral ones.[10]

THE NATURE OF CURRICULUM PROBLEMS

This discussion of the nature of practical problems clears the way for a closer consideration of the central issue to which curriculum theorists and practical educators need to address themselves: what kind of a problem is a curriculum problem? Curriculum problems inhere in the practical concerns of a particular task area. The task is to solve a primary set of questions about *what* students should learn, and a secondary set of questions about *how* decisions on desirable programs of learning should be taken and *how* they should be implemented. Our conclusions about what kinds of questions these are will determine our views on what kind of strategy we should adopt when we attempt to solve them.

A consideration of curriculum problems suggests that they have all the characteristics of uncertain problems. First, they pose questions that have to be answered. Something is going to be taught in the eighth grade. Second, the grounds on which we have to make decisions are unsure. We can see that, if someone says, "But why do you teach that?", the request is not for a formal proof that what we are doing is what *must* be done, but a justification, a reasoned argument to show that what we are teaching is the outcome of a rational consideration of a range of possibilities. In practice, of course, the questioner may get a different type of response, one that disclaims responsibility, and points to constraints that preclude choice: "Because that's what the district mandates." However, our concern here is with the expectations within which the question is framed rather than with the range of possible answers. These will be considered later. Third, we already teach something and that something is a necessary point of departure for any fresh process of decision making. Existing resources, expertise, and expectations have to be taken into account. Fourth, we have to make our decisions relative to a unique context. Fifth, we have difficulties with conflicting aims and how to adjudicate between them. We may want our students to enjoy themselves, but not so much that they forget what they are supposed to be learning; to obey instructions, but also to think for themselves; to work quickly, but also to be accurate. Sixth, we know that, whatever we decide to do, the outcome will be, to a degree, unpredictable. Finally, the justification of an act of teaching lies not in the act itself, but in the desired ends we intend to achieve by it.

This characterization of the nature of decisions about teaching is put forward as self-evident and unproblematic because it is likely that teachers would agree with it. But perhaps this agreement would be based on a limited and partial view of what such decisions entail? And why, in any case, should we suppose that the question of what to teach is all pervading in curriculum decision making? Is this not to oversimplify or even to preempt the question of the nature of curriculum tasks? Evaluation certainly, implementation possibly, and perhaps even design could be seen as essentially procedural matters. Indeed, they have been seen as procedural matters by many curriculum theorists. Tyler's rationale for curriculum planning clearly points the way to a concept of curriculum design based on procedural principles. It can be argued that this was not how Tyler himself saw it, and that his concern was more to show how some parts of the deliberative process could be brought within procedural rules.[11] However, theorists of a more technological bent have developed rational curriculum planning to the point where the deliberative elements are relegated to insignificance, so that agreement on ends is treated as totally unproblematic and is separated off from agreement on means, which is to be arrived at through the application of a programmed sequence of moves.

As I suggested earlier, there will always be those who think, for one reason or another, that the ends of education are fixed, whether these be the teaching of so-called basic skills, initiation into existing modes of social behavior, or preparation for some utopian state of affairs that is just around the corner. Study of curriculum practice, however, suggests that ends are never fixed, and that this is not due to some temporary difficulties that will be cleared up when we have more knowledge, more resources, or better means of enforcing an officially approved ideology. Even in totalitarian states there can be sharp disagreements about which proximate ends are in tune with ultimate ideals, and controversies over which means are implied by the chosen ends. Does one, for example, best induce conformity by repressive authoritarianism—the imposition of values—or by forcing people to seek their own sources of stability through group processes—Reisman's "other directed man?"[12] But even if values are in dispute, should there not be, at least in the realm of major decision making on the curriculum, the possibility of some kind of scientific procedure for problem solution? At this level, the pressures are great to arrive at effective and efficient decisions, and there is also the opportunity to develop special expertise that could not be available to every curriculum designer in every curriculum project. The analogy might be between the householder deciding where to put a garden shed, and the government where to put the third London airport. In the second instance a huge investment of money is at stake, and there are vast implications for housing, for industrial development, and for the creation of ancillary transport services. Surely experts who can offer methods and procedures will earn their keep, however expensive that turns out to be.

The Roskill Commission on the third London airport undertook the most thorough cost–benefit analysis ever attempted in England. The Commission's inquiry was hailed as "the most rational, dispassionate procedure that good minds could devise." Allied to the expertise of the cost–benefit analyst was the experience in weighing evidence of a High Court judge. When the report appeared it immediately aroused such a wave of protest that its recommendation for an inland site was set aside in favor of a decision (never carried through) to develop a coastal site at Foulness that the Commission had ruled out at a very early stage in its proceedings.[13] The lesson of Roskill is that public decisions affecting large numbers of people in such a way as to influence the nature of the lives they lead must be moral and political decisions. A rational model of inquiry assumes some limited and predetermined view of human wants and desires, but wants and desires are always various and contradictory. As McKeon suggests, logistic solutions to practical problems "stand in need of a science of human action to guide the uses of the sciences" because "when it is proposed to apply science to practical problems, the conception of the practical is determined by the conception of scientific method which is employed."[14] Landing a probe on Mars is a practical problem to which, once the project has general approval, scientific procedures can and should be applied, both in producing the necessary hardware and setting up the social systems to operate it. Those immediately involved can be fitted into the technology, whereas the remote public participate only as taxpayers—a simple role that can be encompassed by a simple theory of human nature. But, in cases where decisions have to be taken that affect intimately the ways of living of whole communities, it seems highly unlikely that any scientific approach could be found that would reflect such a complex and varied conception of human nature that the procedure could cater for all wants and all values. The distinction, as Daniel Bell has it, it between "games against nature" and "games between people."[15]

But what of the objection that, in any case, too much prominence is being given to the question, "What should be taught?" It is true that many curriculum problems and tasks do not involve us in asking such a fundamental question. Nevertheless, when translated into question form, they present us with decision situations to which the same kinds of characteristics apply. If, for example, we are asked to evaluate a curriculum, "What should I do?" is a more appropriate way to request help than "What must I do?"—and this is not simply because we have not yet found the time or the ingenuity to devise the method that must be employed because it is the right one. The answer must be "It all depends—on the context, on the ends in view, on who wants the evaluation, and for what purpose." If we agree with Hampshire that "there is no means of establishing a *universal* connection between a specific action, and the reasons for and against performing it, in virtue of which certain reasons *must* be accepted as good reasons independently of everything else,"[16] then the evaluation procedure must always be contingent. Our practical reasoning about it will lead us to prefer one procedure or set of procedures to another, and at that point our style of reasoning will shift to the logistic mode. But an immediate decision to apply a given technology imposes a solution dictated by logistics rather than by the situation to which it is applied and runs the risk of sponsoring an irrelevant action.

To sum up the argument: it is claimed (a) that problems can be divided into two basic categories of theoretic and practical, and that curriculum problems can be seen as falling within the sphere of the practical (This is not, of course, to say that answers to theoretic questions are not helpful for the solution of curriculum problems; only that the practical sets the context within which such questions are raised.); (b) that there are various ways in which practical problems can be solved, depending on the extent to which they must be regarded as uncertain on the one hand, or procedural on the other; (c) that problems are uncertain when the grounds for decision are unclear, when there are conflicts of aims, when the problems relate to unique contexts, or when people with varying wants and desires are affected by the solutions to them—any one or more of these features points to the existence of an uncertain problem; and (d) that curriculum problems present all of these features, first because they relate to a fundamental question, "What should we teach?", that exhibits them, and second because curriculum tasks, though they may be suited to some kinds of procedural treatments, are embedded in unique contexts that must be deliberatively appraised before these treatments can be chosen. The conclusion is that the main instrument for the solution of curriculum problems must be deliberation, or practical reasoning.

Is this the same thing as saying that, on the whole, logistic methods are inapplicable to curriculum problems and that, as a result, we should leave the practitioners to find solutions by whatever means common sense would seem to dictate? This would be a totally wrong conclusion. Practical reasoning is not the same thing as common sense, though it may owe a great deal to it, as do all kinds or reasoning.[17] First of all, conceptions of the practical, though they do not treat of theoretical questions, are not on that account to be regarded as untheoretic. As McKeon points out, "the expression of practical philosophies depends, despite their quest for concrete foundations, on the formulation of a theory that takes its place among other theories."[18] Second, the skills of the practical rest on the identification and refinement of a stock of knowledge that is the result of artful practice and contemplation. To return to our analogy with the game of chess, the superiority of some players over others is not just a matter of ability to act procedurally in analyzing lines of play, but of applying practical reasoning to the evaluation of positions.[19] It is clear that these practical reasoning processes have been improved over a long time by expert players and that they can be described and taught. A tradition of practical reasoning is built up through extending, elaborating, and refining the criteria by which actions are to be justified, and showing how these criteria are to be weighed in practical situations. The growth of the tradition is made possible by the collation and discussion of examples of practice, by the insights of gifted individuals, and the discovery of new possibilities through experimentation. The result is a formal and accessible body of knowledge, not of a commonsense nature, about how to engage in effective deliberation.

CURRICULUM TASKS: RESEARCH AND ANALYSIS

Returning to curriculum tasks, we can equally well suppose that ways can be found of improving the kind of practical reasoning that their performance requires and, in this instance, of also creating the kinds of contexts within which they can best be deployed by people working both individually and in groups. That this has not occurred, or has occurred only to a limited extent, can be attributed to a number of facts—that performance is not easy to evaluate, that practice is less visible (in some areas hardly visible at all), and that experimentation has tended to be conducted on the assumption that what is needed is not a way of treating curriculum problems as uncertain practical problems, but of reducing them to procedural ones.

Some work has, however, been done in the area of curriculum decision making that helps us to see how notions of practical reasoning can be applied to it. Scheffler, in his article "Justifying curriculum decisions," characterizes them as "controllable acts," what he calls "moves."[20] Moves, he says, imply responsibility, so that justification for them must be based on practical reasoning, not on rational or scientific deduction, for that would mean that we could somehow prove that what we had done was logically inevitable—"we consider decisions on educational content to be responsible or justifiable acts with public significance."[21] In such situations, many things are justifiable though some are more justifiable than others. But clearly some things are not justifiable and claims of constraint are not, by themselves acceptable reasons for actions. We may say "I teach it because it is in the official curriculum that I am legally obliged to implement," but implied in that response is also "and it accords with the moral obligations of my practice." Disclaimers of responsibility would certainly not be acceptable from those who create constraining contexts—national parliaments, state boards of education, or examining authorities. Justifications for what they propose must be related to the fundamental purposes of schooling and education.

Scheffler gives us ways of thinking about how, and to what extent, practical reasoning may enter into decisions by distinguishing three levels of justification. As well as the "forced move"—what I must do because it is mandated, for example—he discusses moves with "relative justification" and moves with "general justification." Relative justification involves showing that what is done, while not compelled, fits in with existing policies and preferences. At some point, we suppose, fundamental questions have been confronted and solutions found and we have no reason to believe that these are not still acceptable. General justification implies expansion of the scope of practical reasoning to its fullest extent. What is done, we claim, follows from a wide-ranging deliberation embracing all the various kinds of evidence that can be brought to bear on solving the problem we faced. The three levels can be compared to the three types of question previously discussed: questions of what *must* be done, what *should* be done, and what *ought* to be done.

Scheffler's analysis also suggests that the three levels can, to some extent, be associated with levels of organization and that, therefore, people operating at these various levels will have different attitudes toward the nature of the process that should guide curriculum tasks. Classroom teachers will feel themselves to be the most constrained, and will show the least interest in theory and data because they are not often called on to justify their actions in general terms. Administrators will be concerned with relative justifications—accepting policy frames and determining what actions fit those frames, while those responsible for producing ideas and innovations will have the greatest concern with the appeals to full deliberation, embracing theory and data, that general justification implies. This dispersal of the focus of argument and justification is exemplified in studies of curriculum innovation such as Shipman's *Inside a Curriculum Project*, or Smith and Keith's *Anatomy of Educational Innovation*.[22] This situation is not likely to change dramatically. The sheer size of the educational enterprise makes it certain that a large part of curriculum decision making will always be, in one way or another, routinized. Otherwise the decision making capacities of the system will be overloaded. Protests about "too much innovation" can be protests about the strain of having to justify things.

Scheffler's analysis helps us see how various modes of practical reasoning might be related to a range of practical tasks. A closer examination of how practical reasoning might be applied to a more specific kind of decision making situation is offered by Schwab in his article "The practical: Translation into curriculum."[23] His main concern is with processes of deliberation in small groups gathered together to design curricula. The point of departure of his argument is that group deliberation is essential to curriculum making because only the group can gather together all the kinds of evidence and expertise that are needed. Schwab's intention is to suggest what the nature of curriculum design, as a task, demands in the way of processes of deliberation. He distinguishes five sources of expertise that are essential to curriculum making and three kinds of process that must be engaged in. The sources of expertise are: disciplines, learners, milieus, teachers, and curriculum making. The processes are: discovery, coalescence, and utilization. He suggests that the group should consist of 10 or 12 people, so that the sources of expertise can be represented without creating a group so big that it is too formal. Informality is important because, without it, discovery of relevant knowledge is made difficult: people are afraid to risk assertions or, on the other hand, to contest them—their concern may be more with defending positions than discovering wants, aims, and possibilities. This emphasis on discovery echoes the views of both Hampshire and Gauthier on the nature of deliberation. "Coming to know what one wants is partly a decision and partly a discovery," and "Only as we consider what we can do or not do, can we determine what wants and desires, aims and ends, may be effected by our action. As a result of this inquiry we establish practical judgments."[24] Discovery of other people and their wants and desires leads us to an amalgamation or coalescence of aims, data, and judgments. The knowledge and awareness thus produced must then be creatively used to arrive at a curriculum design. But Schwab sees these processes as alternating rather than sequential: "The process is carried forward in a spiral movement toward a body of generated educational alternatives and choices among them." Also, he considers the process to be intrinsically educative. Good decisions will be made because they will be taken in view of an exhaustive and honest appraisal of needs, possibilities, and criteria for choice. However, he realizes that this is an ideal that curriculum groups frequently fail to achieve. Most often, he thinks, this will be because discussion is dominated by scholars—disciplinary experts—who present subject matter as a model rather than a source, preempting many possible solutions. Equally bad, however, is the opposite problem that arises when the task is construed as "How can we use science (etc.) to achieve x, y, or z? Where the x, y, or z originate the deliberation and the scholarly materials are dragged in by the heels."[25] These are all aspects of a wider problem that he expresses as follows: "It is 'normal' for men to treat their own values as if they were well examined, to ignore contrary or different values utilized by others, and, most of all, to elevate automatically the area of their own expertise to the role of ultimate arbiter of matters under consideration."[26]

The role in the group of the curriculum specialist should be that of a countervailing force. Presumably, though he does not say so, Schwab envisages this person as chairing the discussion, on grounds of an ability, as a disinterested party, to guide the process of mutual discovery. The curriculum specialist, on this view, would be more a person skilled in managing groups than someone with factual knowledge of curriculum construction.

Deliberation in its purest form is likely to be found in situations where there is consciousness of the need to justify decisions in general terms, and where group members are in sufficiently prolonged contact to be able to engage in the discovery process. Such conditions are encountered in curriculum project teams. Several studies have been made in such groups, one of the most detailed being that carried out by Walker.[27] His curiosity was aroused by the fact that groups in which he had participated had never operated on the procedural basis advocated by the exponents of rational theories of curriculum planning.

> I had come West to study education in hopes of learning how curricula should be developed. I had seen what seemed to me to be an inordinate amount of fumbling around, false starts, uncoordinated effort, misunderstandings of purpose, failures to sustain an agreed-upon directness across long units of work and just plain mistakes of conception and execution. I thought there must be a body of lore somewhere that would enable curriculum makers to profit from the insights and mistakes of their predecessors. Surely others with more experience who have been able to give the problem more thought would have written of these things? But when I began to read in curriculum I found advice that seemed appropriate to another activity altogether. "First state your objectives."[28]

So he set out to find an answer to a theoretic question that might help to solve his practical problem. To see how curricula should be planned, he tried to discover how they *are* in fact planned. How do design teams arrive at a common understanding of the purpose and direction of their work? How do they organize their tasks? How do they use their understanding of the purpose and direction of the work to produce plans and materials? To do this he made a case study of an art project at Stanford University directed by Elliot Eisner. He listened to discussions and made and analyzed tape recordings of them. At first, the talk seemed random and ill-directed. But the more he studied it, the more functional and purposeful it began to appear. Drawing on a number of writers, including Gauthier and Toulmin, he devized a scheme for analyzing the discussions of the project group. First, he located what he called *episodes*—sequences that were given unity through the treatment of some single theme in a uniform style of discourse. Then, within the episodes, he tried to find a finer structure. This led him to propose six kinds of deliberative move: proposals, arguments for, arguments against, clarifications, instances, and a miscellaneous other category. The terms are self-explanatory. Proposals for action are put forward (though they may be implicit rather than explicit in what is said). Points are made for and against such proposals. Attempts are made to clarify a point, to clear up misunderstandings about it, and instances are quoted to illustrate what is being conveyed through proposals or arguments. Walker found that observers could be trained to produce analyses along these lines with a good degree of reliability. He then went a stage further, and asked about the actual content of deliberative moves. What kinds of data did they draw on and what were the data about?

His work establishes two main points. First, that curriculum deliberation as it is customarily practiced is not random. It is structured and task-relevant. This suggests that it can be studied with a view to establishing principles and methods for raising the capacity of groups for effective problem solving.[29] Second, that it is possible to characterize the nature of any piece of deliberation in terms of the data on which it draws. Thus we can evaluate it by studying how effectively data were used to state problems, to define the area within which solutions could be sought, and to justify the arguments and judgments that guided choice between possible solutions.

Walker's conclusions did not cast doubt on the intrinsic value of the deliberation process, but they did show that the database on which it proceeded was rather slight. He found that rather more than half the arguments he analyzed were based on experience, conventional wisdom, or speculation rather than observation; that, where observations were quoted, about half were made within the project rather than outside it; that most of the observations quoted had been made personally by team members and did not result from a search for research evidence, and that the majority were made incidentally and not purposefully. In terms of Schwab's categories, there was fairly frequent reference to disciplines and learners, but other categories, and especially data from beyond the school and the classroom, tended to be ignored. Walker comments:

> There is [an] almost complete lack of talk about society, about the world outside the school. Traditionally this source of information has been regarded, along with the student and the subject matter, as one of the three factors that should always be considered in developing a curriculum. Some writers have gone so far as to subsume the others under this one, since many characteristics of students and presumably all characteristics of subject matter are socially determined. Yet virtually none of the arguments in this sample of the deliberations of three projects appealed to data about the society.[30]

NATIONAL DECISION MAKING ON THE CURRICULUM

Curriculum decisions, other than those of a very trivial kind, are, in the words of Scheffler already quoted, "responsible or justifiable acts with public significance." Though they may have some unique features, curriculum questions at a high policy level seem not to be intrinsically different from question of the type suggested earlier in this discussion: "Should we build a third London airport and, if so, where?" "Should Scotland and Wales have their own national assemblies?" "Should trade unions appoint directors to the boards of public companies?" We can recognize these as the kinds of practical problems that, in Scheffler's terms, require solutions having a general justification, and that Gauthier would classify as uncertain. Attempts will be made to treat them as procedural—as in the case of the Roskill Commission—or as questions requiring only relative justification. But we feel, rightly, that only some of the factors involved in such decisions can be handled procedurally, and that, although major decisions should be compatible with established policy, they are also in need of general justification.

How, in fact, we deal with practical questions at the national level and how we should deal with them is the theme of Vicker's book, *The Art of Judgment*.[31] The analysis he gives of the process of decision making suited to the solution of national policy questions closely follows that suggested for a different level by Schwab. Five stages of decision making are defined although, as in the case of Schwab's stages, they are not necessarily sequential. The stages are: appreciation—how the problem is to be defined; reality judgment—what the relevant facts are; value judgment—what solutions would be acceptable; generation of alternatives—what might be done, and proposals—what should be done.

The concept of appreciation relates to the fact that important questions of policy do not present themselves in clear and unambiguous terms. We start from a feeling that a problem exists and that action should be taken to solve it. We probably also have some notion of what the problem might be about and how it could be framed in terms of specific questions. But, if we rush too quickly to an assumption that the problem has been adequately stated, we may waste time and resources on trying to solve the wrong problem, or a problem that is not within our capacity to treat, or can only be treated at great expense. Vickers quotes the example of problems about traffic in towns. In England in the early 1960s this tended to be construed as a problem of how to enable city roads to carry heavier traffic loads. The Buchanan Report of 1963 came to a quite different conclusion. It construed the problem not as one of road development, but of traffic regulation, and it drew attention to the fact that even this problem could not be solved unless it was seen as part of a wider problem "of relating the needs of transport in and through an area with the needs of life within that area; and this is a problem of town planning in three dimensions."[32] Finding out what the problem is entails the participation of a variety of people having a wide range of expertise and viewpoints. This conclusion parallells Schwab's point about sources of expertise. At the national level, royal commissions are examples of bodies appointed not necessarily to recommend action, but to "appreciate" a situation. They expose what they regard as the relevant facts, make clear their value judgments on these facts, and describe the processes by which they have connected facts and values in order to reach conclusions. Thus they provide the authority that appointed them, and also anyone else who reads their report, with a common basis for forming their own appreciation. Vickers sees appreciation as a two-way process. Facts and opinions interact. Appreciation is educative in the way that deliberation is seen by Schwab as generally educative. People's minds are changed by the act of appreciation. They come to see things in new ways and therefore change their views on what constitutes the body of facts relevant to judgment. Since appreciation is educative, it is a worthwhile activity in its own right, even if recommendations for action are ignored. Commenting on the Gowers Report of 1953 on capital punishment, Vickers observes:

> If all the recommendations for action had been ignored, the major importance of the report as an appreciative judgment would have remained the same. The state of the commissioners' minds on the subject of capital punishment, after they had made this appreciation, was different from what it was when they began: and this change, communicated through the report, provoked change, similar or dissimilar, in greater or less degree, in all it reached, from serious students to casual readers of newspaper paragraphs; and this released into the stream of events and into the stream of ideas an addition to the countless forces by which both are moulded.[33]

If he is right, then the time spent on such activities is to be seen as an investment and not just a cost.

The next two categories both contain the key word judgment. However thorough and educative our appreciation of a situation, what we eventually do is a matter of judgment—judgment about what knowledge is of relevance to a decision (reality judgment), and judgment about what courses of action might be possible (value judgment). Judgment is the companion of justification and therefore of responsibility. "Judgment," says Vickers, "is an ultimate category, which can only be approved or condemned by a further exercise of the same ability."[34] In legal affairs this is plainly true; a lower court gives a judgment, a higher court confirms or reverses it.[35] But these are both judgments; we do not know that one is better than the other, only that one is more authoritative than the other. In all situations where we must face practical problems of an uncertain nature we have to make judgments and be held responsible for them. We cannot escape by saying that because we adopted an approved method, formula, or procedure, what we did must have been right.

Reality judgments are made difficult by the fact that what is the case may be a matter of dispute, and by the difficulty of deciding what, in the light of our appreciation of the problem, constitutes relevant information among the facts and opinions advanced by various interested parties. Where part of the reality judgment concerns what people feel, value, or believe, then the problems of exercising judgment are magnified. The making of reality judgments is, therefore, "a critical and an integrating mental activity,"[36] not just a matter of routine fact gathering. Value judgments connect facts to possible actions, inferring implications for beneficial or disadvantageous outcomes. Some actions might be excluded on moral grounds, some because of unwanted side effects they might entail, and some because they might be expensive or ineffective. Value judgment on possible actions lays the ground for making sets of alternative proposals that can be compared and evaluated. From these will emerge a final set of proposals—a plan for action. But the categories may interact with one another: the realization of the implications of some possibility for action may lead us to reexamine our appreciation of the problem, or an insight in the reality judgment phase may directly suggest a definite plan of action.

Vickers does not deal in any detail with the composition of deliberative bodies on major national issues, but his analysis of process would lead us to suppose that his recommendations would not be very different from those offered by Schwab. Large groups will find it difficult to engage in an honest and open interchange of ideas; people who represent constituencies may impair deliberation by acting in a political way; exclusion of important sources of data and opinion will lead to faulty judgments. (McKie quotes the case of an interdepartmental committee on the third London airport that sat from 1961 to 1963 and demonstrated the classic dangers in determining membership. Of its 15 members, 13 were from aviation).[37] A further problem in the case of committees and commissions is that of deciding on terms of reference. Vicker's conception of the process of appreciation demands that there should be a very broad freedom to define the nature of the problem to be answered. Yet the terms of reference often do not allow for this (the various airport commissions were not permitted to suggest that growth of air traffic should not be allowed, or that it should be catered to in some other way than by building a third airport in southeast England).[38] We might deduce that the personal qualities demanded of those who participate in the processes described by Vickers will be much the same as those required of members of Schwab's deliberative groups.

IMPLICATIONS FOR THE PRACTICE
AND THEORY OF CURRICULUM

If we accept that decision making on the curriculum at all levels is a matter of solving uncertain practical problems, and that the kind of reasoning required is of the type described by writers such as Gauthier, Schwab, Scheffler, Walker, and Vickers, what conclusions should we draw? First of all, there are implications for curriculum theory. With a few exceptions, some of which have already been discussed, curriculum theorists have assumed that curriculum problems are theoretic problems in need of procedural or logistic solutions. If, however, they are seen as requiring practical reasoning, to which logistics and procedure are subordinate, then a number of deficiencies in the current state of curriculum theory become apparent. It has failed to provide us with understandings of the nature of deliberation, and especially of the ways in which curriculum deliberation may exhibit unique features not shared by other forms of deliberation. Through concentrating on method, it has neglected to show how method is to be translated into practice through human agency or social system, and, through concentrating on selection of content, it has overlooked the need for the products of design to be governed by understandings of the milieus within which they are to be enacted. Design theory has grown up in isolation from implementation theory, which is an essential input to all stages of deliberation.[39] An overcommitment to the rationalist approach has encouraged a search for *the* theory of the curriculum, when an understanding of the nature of deliberation suggests that there must be multiple theories for multiple contexts. It has encouraged an erroneous belief that curriculum theory can, in some way, point to a value-free method of reaching curriculum decisions, whereas it is of the essence of the deliberative approach that values are central to decision making, and not to be denied. It suggests the possibility of final solutions when, in fact, changing situations constantly raise new problems and call for new appraisals. Deliberative problem solving is called for precisely when the process to be engaged in is a cyclical one, leading from old problems to new. Finally, by adopting a narrow frame of reference for the statement of problems, conventional curriculum theory has drawn attention away from the need for careful appreciation, in the sense in which Vickers uses the word, and presented problems as reducible to questions of appropriate objectives, content, and method. The deliberative approach demands that we test such assumptions, and inquire whether curriculum problems may not sometimes be problems of administration, of personal relationships, of ideologies, of community life, or of democratic participation.

If we accept the arguments in favor of seeing curriculum problem solving as an exercise in practical reasoning, then there are consequences both for the conduct of curriculum tasks and for the skills demanded of those who undertake them. The two are essentially interdependent. Unless there is a belief that it is possible for decision makers to act other than as representatives of constituencies of one kind or another, unless there is confidence that time spent in exploratory and appreciative discussion is well-invested, unless it is accepted that better data lead to better decisions, then the opportunity for people to gain the skills of deliberation will not exist. The unfortunate truth is that, over a long period of time, these skills have been declining. This is true in fields other than that of curriculum decision making; in many areas of public policy, expediency, procedure, majority votes, and authoritative pronouncements have gradually usurped the place of appreciation, deliberation, and judgment. Generally, this can be attributed to the increasing rate of decision making that has to be sustained. Specifically, it has resulted from a desire to achieve greater efficiency by seeing ends as unproblematic and using science to solve problems through the application of increasingly sophisticated means. Scientific management, cost–benefit analysis, and management by objectives are all, within certain limited spheres, useful techniques for problem solving; all have been stretched far beyond their range of convenience in the belief that they can save us from having to adjudicate between competing and incompatible goals, and have led us into situations where problems get treated not because they are the problems that matter, but because they are the problems for which some procedural technique exists. At the same time, the social systems on which decisions have to be made have become more complex, bureaucratized, and routinized. The purposes for which they exist tend to be obscured under the administrative apparatus, and, when problems arise, they are apt to be construed as being due to "operating difficulties" rather than to a need to rethink basic strategies.

In the case of curriculum, the problem of the last 100 years has been one of access; the objects of policy have been the building of larger and more unified systems for delivering a curriculum to more and more students for a longer period of time. The very success of the vast mobilization of resources this has entailed has distracted attention from questions of the value of what the system is supposed to deliver. In terms of the data available for appraising the system, we have leaned heavily in the direction of information on inputs rather than outputs. We have even been distracted from studying what is supposed to be happening within the system in our pursuit of fixed goals relating to the provision of places and equipment and to the encouragement of an ever-rising rate of enrollment. The virtual realization of these goals, far from bringing us to a point of total problem solution, has left us facing crucial issues about what the curriculum should consist of, an almost complete absence of means for resolving them, and a vast inertial education system that would be desperately hard to reform, even if we knew how.

The problem is not just that curriculum questions are badly handled, but that the means of handling them well are being steadily eroded, for the exercise of practical reasoning depends on the existence of a living tradition. Once we have found ways of treating procedural questions, they will continue to be available to us; formulae and techniques, once discovered, stay discovered, short of natural catastrophe. But the methods of practical reasoning have to be learned through experience and involvement, and live and die with the individuals who exercise them. Vickers puts it as follows, "Those who are engaged in a course of decision making soon become aware that each decision is conditioned not only by the concrete situation in which it is taken but also by the sequence of past decisions; and that their new decisions in their turn will influence future decisions not only by their effect on the history of events but also by the precedents which they set."[40] Thus, the context within which initiative can be exercised is constantly changing and "scope for initiative is created and preserved largely by the way in which it is exercised. It follows that good judgment can be recognised only over a span of years. Tomorrow is already committed; but how varied, today, are the possibilities for ten, twenty, thirty years hence!"[41]

Seeing curriculum problems as uncertain practical problems that have to be treated by the exercise of practical reasoning has a number of healthy results for curriculum theory and practice. From the point of view of theory, it saves curriculum thinking from the blind alleys of unwarranted seeking after science on the one hand, and denial that it can be anything more than common sense on the other. It allows curriculum theory to cohere around a special set of problems that demand a knowledge of specific kinds of contexts, data, and understandings, but which, at the same time, can be seen as part of a wider group of uncertain practical problems with social and moral significance. The curriculum thinker and the curriculum maker are not cut off from others who should contribute to the solution of curriculum problems, as they are when curriculum theory is construed as a special kind of applied technology available only to initiates.[42] From the point of view of practice, we benefit through the acknowledgment that curriculum problems do not admit of ideal solutions, through the return to a central place in decision making of commitment and responsibility, and through the realization that the exercise of practical reasoning is only to be justified in *action*. Too often, curriculum decision making has suffered from the illusion that there must be a uniquely "right" answer to a problem. The search is conceptualized as an attempt to discover what already exists. If it cannot be found, the problem is: (a) left unsolved, (b) is "solved" by setting up a treatment with the same name as the problem, or (c) is handed over to the "technical experts."

An example of the first type of outcome was the treatment of the problem of the upper secondary curriculum by the Schools Council for England and Wales in the 1960s and 1970s. A 10-year search for a uniquely "right" formula stifled the possibility of progress and students were therefore condemned to a set of outdated learning experiences, even though a great deal might have been done to improve the curriculum within its existing framework.[43] An example of the second outcome was the attempt by the Council to treat the problem of the relation of the curriculum to industry by having an "Industry" project, on the supposition that giving the right name to the remedy is equivalent to solving the problem.[44] The third type of outcome is illustrated by the initiative of the Department of Education and Science in solving the problem of the adequacy of basic skills learning by setting up an Assessment of Performance Unit to produce basic skills tests.[45]

A further weakness in decision making has been the flight from values and commitment. Partly this has resulted from a praiseworthy desire to save education from becoming indoctrination, but greater significance is to be attached to two further factors: first, a decline in the wish and the ability to engage in debates on values resulting from a narrow definition of the range of those deemed competent to take part (since it is an invitation to outsiders to join in), and second, a belief that the need to take up and defend value positions has somehow been reduced by the development of technical and procedural expertise. But technique and procedure are not, in their application, value free, and to believe that they are is to abandon the exercise of responsible choice that is inseparable from the justification of curriculum decisions. When expertise in solving curriculum problems is seen as part of a wider range of expertise in which all are to some degree competent, then the way becomes clearer to making curricula responsive to varied and changing social needs. If curriculum problems are thought of as technical problems that can be solved only by those with inside knowledge of schools or of curriculum design, then it is hardly surprising that outsiders are found to have little to contribute. But if the scope of appreciation and judgment is set up to be intrinsically educative, then the obstacles to breadth of participation seem not so daunting.

Finally, the realization that practical problems are solved only in action puts into a new light questions of why decisions are not effectively implemented, or why curriculum materials fail to get adopted. The technical model of treating curriculum problems suggests that failure must lie in the schools—"Let's go and see why these people are not doing what they should be, or what we hoped they would." The practical reasoning model suggests that if the problem is not being solved in action, then the process through which the action was decided on was perhaps at fault. Why should we suppose that setting up a curriculum project will solve a curriculum problem? Perhaps a more adequate problem appreciation would have indicated other possible courses of action. And whatever action we choose should be chosen through a deliberative process that takes account of data and judgments on the likely *effects* of the various courses we might pursue, not just through looking at their procedural feasibility.[46]

Apart from these directly instrumental advantages, the practical reasoning approach can provide a wider range of benefits than the approach through technique and procedure. The latter offers advantage only through its products, and if these are unsuccessful the gains of using it are confined to the experts who were hired to carry out the work. The former yields advantages that accrue from the process as well as the product. The process educates the participants and improves the general level of problem appreciation, even when solutions are elusive or ineffective. It develops skills of general, not merely specific use, and thereby increases the ability of the educational system and the wider community to be sensitive to and to treat curriculum problems. By stressing key words like "action," "judgment," "deliberation," "appreciation," "criticism," "responsibility," "argument," and "justification," it introduces a fresh and more appropriate climate of metaphor into curriculum theory and practice, which may help us to avoid the kinds of errors into which we are led by thinking in the imagery of engineering and design. We may draw a parallell with Kaplan's observation that "Aesthetics does not produce art, but it may free both artist and audience from constraints that stand in the way of its creation and appreciation."[47] In this way too, practical reasoning may justify itself through the process of its application and not merely through its immediate and visible products.

NOTES

1. Reid, William A., & Walker, Decker F. (Eds.). (1975). *Case studies in curriculum change: Great Britain and the United States*. London: Routledge & Kegan Paul.
2. Reid, William A. (1978). *Thinking about the curriculum: The nature and treatment of curriculum problems*. London: Routledge & Kegan Paul.
3. An alternative view is that expressed by Kallós and Lundgren: "Curriculum studies cannot primarily be focused on *how* a curriculum should be constructed or developed, but must primarily explain the determinants of the curriculum" (Kallós, D., & Lundgren, U. P. (1976). An enquiry concerning curriculum: Foundations for curriculum change (mimeo). Gothenburg: University of Gothenburg, Pedagogiska Institutionen). Much hinges on the word

"primarily." If what is being said is that an understanding of how a curriculum can change must precede any attempt to change it, then there is no serious disagreement with the position I am taking here. It seems more likely, however, that what is being claimed is that the major focus of curriculum studies should be on the theoretic rather than the practical. If so, it has to be shown that the social and political determinants of the curriculum are significantly different from those that shape other human activities. If they are not, then their study should form part of the social sciences generally. Any significant uniqueness of curriculum as an activity is more likely to lie in the tasks it proposes than in the forces that determine its nature.

4. Schwab, J. J. (1978). The practical: A language for curriculum. In I. Westbury & N. J. Wilkof (Eds.). *Science, curriculum, and liberal education* (pp. 287–321). Chicago: University of Chicago Press. For a philosophical discussion of 'uncertain practical questions' see Gauthier, D. P. (1963). *Practical reasoning: The structure and foundations of prudential and moral arguments and their exemplification in discourse*. Oxford: Oxford University Press.

5. *Op. cit.*, pp. 1 and 49.

6. "Where logic and strategy have received large and successful study down the ages, yielding the most powerful canons and instructions for their use, the more particular arts of deliberation and tactics have been given little more than honor for their function. From Aristotle to Dewey and Pierce, they have been recognized for what they do, honored for their contribution to our lives, but given little or no attention in their own right" (Schwab, J. J. (1975), foreword to Reid, William A., & Walker, Decker F. (Eds.). *Case studies in curriculum change: Great Britain and the United States*. London: Routledge & Kegan Paul, p. viii).

7. *Op. cit.*, p. 24.

8. Powerful arguments have been made on moral grounds against the supposition that ends can justify means. "[T]o manipulate men, to propel them towards goals which you—the social reformer—see, but they may not, is to deny them their human essence, to treat them as objects without wills of their own, and therefore to degrade them" (Berlin, Isaiah (1958). *Two concepts of liberty*. Oxford: Oxford University Press, p. 22). These are matters of faith and feeling on which curriculum theorists should declare their position.

9. See, for example, Kotov, A. (1971). *Think like a grandmaster*. London: Batsford.

10. And confusion can be deeper still. What are we make of "a curriculum theory ought to be a rational explanation of why a certain content shall be taught and why activities shall be used?" (Lundgren, U. P. (1972). *Frame factors and the teaching process: A contribution to curriculum theory and theory on teaching*. Stockholm: Almquist & Wiksell, p. 38). Is this a question about prudential action or theoretic understanding?

11. I am indebted to Ian Westbury for this conception of Tyler's contribution to curriculum theory. As I have said elsewhere, "Tyler's work was more important for the logical extensions which it invited than for what it specifically recommended, and for what was conspicuously omitted than for what was included" (Reid & Walker (1975). *Op. cit.* , p. 243).

12. Reisman, D., Glazer, N., & Denney, R. (1950). *The lonely crowd*. New Haven, CT: Yale University Press.

13. See McKie, D. (1973). *A sadly mismanaged affair: A political history of the third London airport*. London: Croom Helm.

14. McKeon, R. (1952). Philosophy and action. *Ethics, 62*, p. 84.

15. Bell, Daniel (1974). *The coming of post-industrial society: A venture in social forecasting*. London: Heinemann, p. 336.

16. Hampshire, S. (1959). *Thought and action*. London: Chatto & Windus, p. 151. Compare, also "there is no way of considering the nature and quality of the act intended except by comparing it with more and more groups of other actions, and by describing it in different terms and by drawing attention to different features of the surrounding situation" (*Ibid.*,

p. 218), and "One does not in general need to consider the occasion on which a belief was formed in somebody's mind in order to decide upon its truth, in the same way that one generally needs to consider the occasion upon which an action was performed in order to decide upon its rightness" (*Ibid.*, p. 150).

17. See, for example, Popper, K. R. (1972). *Objective knowledge: An evolutionary approach.* Oxford: Oxford University Press. "Science, philosophy, rational thought, must all start from common sense" (p. 33).

18. McKeon. *Op. cit.*, p. 79.

19. De Groot was able to show through empirical research that, although players at the master level tended to analyze more deeply, they were less likely than grandmasters to find the best move in a given position (De Groot, A. D. (1965). *Thought and choice in Chess.* The Hague: Mouton).

20. Scheffler, I. (1958). Justifying curriculum decisions. *School Review, 56,* 461–472.

21. *Ibid.*, p. 116.

22. Shipman, M. (1974). *Inside a curriculum project,* London: Methuen. Smith, L. M., & Keith, P. M. (1971). *Anatomy of educational innovation: An organizational analysis of an elementary school.* New York: Wiley.

23. Schwab, J. J. (1978). The practical: Translation into curriculum. In Westbury & Wilkof, *op. cit.*, 365–383.

24. Hampshire. *Op. cit.*, p. 105. Gauthier. *Op. cit.*, p. 4.

25. Schwab, J. J. (1978). The practical: Translation into curriculum. In Westbury & Wilkof, *op. cit.*, p. 377.

26. *Ibid.*, p. 381.

27. Walker, D. F. (1975). Curriculum development in an art project. In Reid & Walker, *op. cit.*, 91–135.

28. *Ibid.*, p. 92.

29. The studies that have been made of working groups have (a) tended to direct attention toward general rather than specialist problem solving and (b) often used specially constituted rather than already established groups. There is a need for more studies of the Walker type that take actual working groups and look at them in terms of the unique features of the tasks they have to carry out (see Bales, R. F. (1951). *Interaction process analysis: A method for the study of small groups.* Cambridge, MA: Addison-Wesley, and McGrath, J. E., & Altman, I. (1966). *Small group research—A synthesis and critique of the field.* New York: Holt Rinehart).

30. *Op. cit.*, p. 92.

31. Vickers, G. (1965). *The art of judgment.* London: Chapman & Hall.

32. *Ibid.*, p. 28.

33. Vickers, G. (1968). *Value systems and social process.* London: Tavistock, p. 146.

34. Vickers, *op. cit.* (1965), p. 62.

35. Just as in curriculum evaluation, those who are not satisfied with what one inquiry produces set up another. This has happened, for example, in the case of the National Foundation for Educational Research (NFER) evaluation of the teaching of French in English primary schools that came to largely unfavorable conclusions.

36. Vickers, *op. cit.* (1965), p. 62.

37. McKie, *op. cit.*, p. 74.

38. Interestingly, much of the growth in air traffic that a third London airport might have created has been taken up by Schipol, the Amsterdam airport—a possibility that none of the commissions considered.

39. For amplification of this point, see Reid, William A. (1975). The changing curriculum: Theory and practice. In Reid & Walker, *op. cit.*, 244–247.
40. Vickers, *op. cit.* (1965), p. 15.
41. *Loc. cit.*
42. McKeon, *op. cit.*, p. 92.
43. See Reid, W. A., & Holley, B. J. (1974). The factor structure of teacher attitudes to sixth form education. *British Journal of Educational Psychology, 44,* 65–73.
44. This project was set up in 1976, apparently as a political initiative, and with minimal consideration of what problems it was to address, or in what ways. The syndrome is described by Wise (Wise, A. E. (1977). Why educational policies often fail: The hyper-rationalization hypothesis. *Journal of Curriculum Studies, 9,* 43–57).
45. *Times Educational Supplement,* October 1, 1976, p. 2.
46. Gauthier (*op. cit.*, pp. 4–7) distinguishes between the "solution" of a practical problem and its "resolution." The decision about what to do is a resolution, but the solution is an action. Resolution does not necessarily imply solution.
47. Kaplan, A. (1964). *The conduct of enquiry: Methodology for behavioral science.* San Francisco: Chandler, p. 24.

CHAPTER

3

The Method of the Practical

"Practical reasoning and curriculum decisions" set a broad framework for thinking about curriculum as practice. This is, in a way, an easier task than working onward from that framework to make suggestions for how curriculum workers should go about their business: difficult because the concept of practical reasoning presents a paradox. Although, on the one hand it implies a definite view on how the work of curriculum should be thought about, on the other it denies that such work can ever be a matter of prescribed procedure—those who would support the idea of practical reasoning have to become comfortable with a conception of "method" that defines something very different. This chapter is a recent attempt to explicate that difference. It is extracted, with some revisions, from Curriculum planning as deliberation, *which appeared as Report No. 11, Institute for Educational Research, University of Oslo, 1994.*

In recent years, citizens of many countries in Europe, America, and Australasia have seen an outpouring of documents on schooling and the curriculum. These have covered an impressive range of issues: the relationship of curriculum to social and economic problems, the need to devise curricular means of raising levels of skills and achievement, the reform of school organization, of subject matter, of systems of assessment, of teacher preparation, and so on. The media are full of statements, reactions, critiques emanating from people and organizations of all kinds. But discussion of one issue is conspicuous by its absence: how are all these claims and counterclaims, remedies and reforms to be translated into curriculum plans? "America 2000,"[1] for example, sets goals such as "by the year 2000 U.S. students will be first in the world in science and mathematics achievement," or "the high school graduation rate will increase to at least 90%." But it has nothing to say about what kind of curriculum planning could produce such results. Most of the time, reform proposals are put forward on the assumption that someone, somewhere, knows what to do, that the question of how to make a curriculum does not need to be addressed, and that discussion can be confined to the definition of desired states of affairs.

But, it may be objected, surely we are right to assume that somebody, somewhere knows? People gain degrees and diplomas in curriculum planning, and then deploy their skills in ministries, state departments, and school districts. However, curriculum planning as a subject of study has tended to be mainly about the administrative approach to curriculum. It assumes, as do the many current reports and proposals, that we can think about schools and classrooms as relatively unproblematic delivery systems for curriculum, and that what we have to be concerned about are the procedures necessary for maintaining and improving the system. Up to a point, this is a reasonable assumption. Schools and classrooms, like any enduring institution, incorporate ways of getting the job done, and these often seem to be a matter of implementing standard procedures. But the complaints we hear today are not simply about needed adjustments to standard procedures. The changing context of curriculum, both as practice and institution, raises demands that go far beyond what can be delivered by approaches designed to fine-tune systems that are already functioning well.

DEFICIENCIES OF PROCEDURE

As an answer to the question of how fundamental exercises in curriculum planning should be approached, the administrative model suffers from several major defects that the deliberative model claims to remedy.

First of all, to conceive of curriculum making as a procedural matter is to mistake the character of the problems it has to resolve. The deliberative model considers curriculum problems to be moral practical problems, and proposes as the means to their resolution the employment of the method of the practical. The shift from procedure to method may not seem large, but it is critical. A method, like a procedure, is a way of adapting means to ends. But, unlike procedure, it need not treat means as a prespecifiable sequence, it need not treat means as separate from ends, and it need not treat ends as being fixed. The essence of methodic inquiry is to initiate and sustain a process through which the nature of a problem is exposed, and a resolution converged upon. Each step is contingent on preceding steps: at each moment, method and subject matter interact. At every point the use of method is subject to the judgment of individuals, and only retrospectively can its course be charted because its logic is continuously reconstructed as it interacts with its subject matter.

The method of the practical begins, not from some prespecified statement of the problem to be addressed, so that deliberation is confined to means, but from the feeling that some state of affairs is unsatisfactory, and that it is constituted of conditions that we *wish* were otherwise and that we think *can be made* to be otherwise. The first state of deliberation, then, is the search for the problem, and it is the problem discovered and possessed by the deliberating group that then controls the inquiry process, rather than the imperatives of political or administrative agencies who have already defined the problem and claimed ownership of it.

Since it is the nature of the problem that controls the process, no item of information has an automatically privileged status in providing answers to the questions that inquiry has raised. It is the deliberative process that assigns authority to facts and opinions. They do not enjoy status simply because of the perceived expertise of the source from which they come.

As subject matter is gathered and deliberated on, the focus of practical inquiry shifts from the search for the problem, and the search for information, to the search for proposals. Of course, some proposals will have suggested themselves at an early stage of the process—possibly were there before it started—but these will not have priority. Successful practical inquiry will *invent* proposals in the course of deliberation, and will have available to it a variety of them, old and new, that can be examined for their relevance to the problem that has been defined. An essential element in this state of inquiry is the effort to trace out the consequences of actions, and this will, almost certainly, entail yet more data gathering. The final state of inquiry is the process of resolving the problem, which means choosing a course of action through consideration of all available proposals. Unlike theoretic problems, practical problems are never in any definite sense solved, and therefore inquiry must attend closely to all possible consequences of the course of action it proposes.

A second deficiency of procedure that the method of the practical claims to remedy is that it lacks a historical perspective. Problem definition, judgments about the relevance of data, and decisions on courses of action take place not just in relation to prevailing states of affairs, but with reference to the historical conditions that gave rise to them. Administrative perspectives evince little interest in such matters. Since their procedures are treated as universally relevant, the facts of the problem to be solved are regarded as immediately available, and as requiring no retrospective investigation.

However, the character of practices, such as curriculum and teaching, is defined by their histories. However much we may wish that their characters were otherwise, initiatives to change them will not succeed if we do not appreciate their origins and development. Deliberation recognizes this to be the case. Understanding of what led up to unsatisfactory states of affairs, and access to personal experiences of prior states of affairs, are regarded as essential to the treatment of the kinds of problems with which curriculum planning must concern itself.

Historical understanding is also prerequisite to the task of conceptualizing the institutional role of curriculum. Administrative models of planning tend to work with simplistic conceptions of the function of institutions, or to consider them simply in their manifestations as forms of organization, and, as a result, assume an elementary causal relationship between inputs of content and teaching and outputs of skill and knowledge. Deliberation, on the other hand, assumes that institutions achieve their effects in much more subtle and less predictable ways.

A third merit of the method of the practical is its ability to confront moral aspects of the question of how apparently conflicting interests, both as they affect individuals and groups and as they affect the institutional character of curriculum, are to be resolved. Administrative models assume that interests can be subsumed within procedures that lay claim to neutrality, but this aspiration is theoretically and practically flawed. Determinations about social action cannot masquerade as exercises in pure science, neither, in practice, do they succeed in doing so.

POLITICS AND THE PRACTICAL

The agendas on which administrative planning procedures are brought to bear are politically determined, and their outcomes require political will for their implementation. Deliberation recognizes this as a self-evident fact. The question for those who meet in deliberation is: how far can the political process be improved upon? The art of politics, like the practice of deliberation, aims to find common ground on which varied people and differing interests can stand. Politics proceeds by defining issues that can lead to the construction of political platforms attracting more or less unanimous support. The search for the problem can also be thought of as the search for the platform. But throughout the searches for data, for proposals, and for resolution, reconsideration of the platform will be required, as inconsistencies, contradictions, and inadequacies are revealed. For some purposes, we may need to be content with this kind of metaphor. At the highest level of generality, and even at lower levels, curriculum questions inevitably have political aspects to them. However, the aspiration of curriculum deliberation is to draw out those aspects of curriculum making that go beyond the establishment of platforms by political means. A purely political interpretation of accommodation between interests would emphasize avoidance of conflict, trade-offs based on relative power, and reconciliation between people who are representative of positions. This kind of accommodation will sometimes, and to some degree, be necessary in order to manage the boundaries between the curriculum process and the political milieus within which it has to take place. But, in so far as it is possible, the values internal to curriculum making demand that higher goals be set.

THE MORAL CHARACTER OF DELIBERATION

Deliberation is a process through which planners begin to discover *themselves*—their values and their projections into educational intentions—begin to discover their colleagues, and arrive at a collegiality in pursuing the task in hand. In other words, discovery, in the context of deliberation, is a moral rather than a technical process, and its successful pursuit depends on qualities of character, rather than mastery of technique.

The process of deliberation enables knowledge possessed by various individuals and interests to become a group possession. The possibility of the creation of a unified and virtuous process, rather than one driven by specialization of knowledge or interest is offered by the sense of a clear focus on a problem that is a problem for all. Curriculum deliberation identifies problems that are not about the improvement of teaching, or about the welfare of students, or about the refurbishment of subject matter, or about the furthering of special interests, but about the creation of a curriculum. Faced with such problems, no one person or group has the knowledge to find resolutions single-handedly, but all of them, deliberating collectively, have a unique capability for resolving them. Deliberation is the *practice* of the identification and resolution of curriculum problems, and, as a practice, takes on a virtuous character.

DELIBERATION AS A PRACTICAL ART

On the one hand, then, deliberation is a virtuous process that has to be fostered through such apparently esoteric activities as self-discovery, purposing in common, and the cultivation of qualities of character. But, on the other side of the picture, it also depends on technical resources. If practice, as understood within a deliberative context, has a side to it that looks almost existential, this is complemented by another side that is clearly hard-headed and task-focused. We cannot expect that virtuous habits will arise from good intentions, or qualities of character from exhortation. Technique plays an important part in the creation of circumstances under which humble, patient, courageous, or honest behavior becomes natural rather than unnatural. The quality of deliberation depends on its resourcefulness in creating settings conducive to the display of such qualities—informal settings will probably prove to be more productive than formal ones. Technique also plays its part in ensuring that the conduct of deliberation favors virtuous behavior. For example, without technical intervention, the knowledge that is contributed to deliberation is associated with the person who owns it. In these circumstances, critical or dismissive responses are seen as damaging to the bearer of ideas, information, or proposals. But this need not be the case. It can be arranged for knowledge to be effectively disassociated from persons, so that it can be treated in a more objective way.

Another important technical question is how resolutions of curriculum problems are to be communicated to those who are affected by them, but are not members of the deliberating group. When deliberation is about problems at the institutional level, it is inevitable that the deliberating group will include only a tiny number of those who will be affected by its workings.

How, then, are the products of deliberation to be presented to the many who have no direct knowledge of the processes that led to them? On the one hand, curriculum making has to contribute knowledge of what has to be known, and how sufficient knowledge of the right kind can be conveyed, so that intentions are translated into action, but, on the other hand, curriculum making also has to judge what gaps in interpretation it is best to leave, so that general intentions can be adapted to the circumstances of particular districts, schools, and classrooms.

In all these ways, curriculum making is a practical art, but the techniques that it possesses are subordinated to the requirements of a methodic process, dependent on virtue and character. Technique does not appear as the answer to the question, "what must we do?", but is invoked, when required, as part of a methodic search for an answer to the question "what ought we to do?". In keeping with this conception of the role and status of technique, curriculum making will see its products not as authoritative, but as persuasive. Proposals for new contents and practices must not be simply directives about what expertise deems to be necessary activity, but also representations of the values that these contents and practices are supposed to embody.

CURRICULUM DELIBERATION AND THE CLASSROOM

Administrative models of planning stand outside the order of classrooms, and frequently offer products that are ill-matched to their natural constraints and resources. However, it is intrinsic to the character of curriculum deliberation that it is not seen as a specialized piece of the curriculum process, whose nature and function is distinct from those of other parts of the process. This is most clear when we consider the relationship of deliberation to the realization of curriculum in the classroom.

Curriculum making as practice, and teaching as practice share common forms and purposes. Both are concerned with the interests of individuals and groups, and with how these are to be creatively reconciled. Both use techniques for fostering qualities of character in order to encourage purposing in common. Both see process and product, ends and means, as inextricably linked. From a classroom perspective, deliberation, in terms of its style if not its range, is relatively easy to understand. Teachers not only feel competing pressures, but know that the resolution of them has to be found through their own practical action. They also know that the outcomes of this action are not entirely predictable. They are therefore conscious of the need to search for the problem, search for information, search for proposals, and search for a resolution. And they understand that none of these searches can be conducted through the application of explicit rules, and that resolutions are unlikely to take the form of clearcut formulae that solve the problem for good. Teaching creates a context within which the deliberative consideration of ends and means is a totally natural way of dealing with the problems of practice.

We can therefore discern a useful reflexivity between the practice of curriculum deliberation and the practice of the classroom. Each is, in important ways, a reflection of the other. This ensures a compatibility in values between the one and the other, and makes it more likely both that teachers and students will readily enter into curriculum deliberation, and that proposals emerging from curriculum deliberation will be communicable to the settings where they have to be translated into action.

CURRICULUM DELIBERATION
AND THE PUBLIC INTEREST

While curriculum as it relates to the classroom can be appropriately characterized as the method of the practical, as it relates to the society at large it presents another face: that of an institution. Just as the classroom can be seen as a kind of microcosm of the deliberative curriculum-making process, so curriculum making itself can be seen as a microcosm of arenas where the values of the broader field that encompasses institutions such as curriculum have to be formed. Here too there is an equally important, though less immediately apparent reflexivity, which is lacking in administrative models of planning. The curriculum of schooling, as an institution, is dependent for its vitality on the widespread recognition of common values, of agreed upon culturally significant content, of civic aspirations that it can embody. But those who are to be the practical reformers of curriculum (as opposed to the enunciators of global goals and ill-defined concerns) are confronted with a multiplicity of fragmented interests, and have to try to take on themselves the task of distilling from them some version of public interest that has to inform the institution of schooling. Increasing specialization of interests in society generally deprives curriculum making of the natural focus that it requires for confronting the problems of the schools. But, by the same token, curriculum making itself has been under pressure in many parts of the world to become a narrowly specialized field. First of all, the knowledge appropriate to the field has been narrowly defined. This has had two undesirable results. The kinds of knowledge that have been certified as appropriate to the curriculum expert have been almost exclusively of a procedural nature. Indeed, much effort has been invested in devising approaches to curriculum that take as their starting point psychometrics, and related branches of psychology, and then elaborate theories of planning based on specifications of objectives, forms of objective evaluation, and systematic implementation of curriculum protocols. None of this sits well with the idea of curriculum making as an exercise in the arts of practical inquiry.

Curriculum making has come to be seen as subservient to the activities of political and administrative agencies that set reform agendas having little to do with the practicalities of curriculum inquiry. This results in much busy activity of producing schemes for upgrading and evaluating programs that suggests that a great deal is happening, while the problems of the practical curriculum in classrooms are ignored, or even exacerbated. To remedy this, a new emphasis is needed in the preparation of those who will present themselves as expert in the field of curriculum, an emphasis that diminishes specialization and focuses on broad issues of the nature and direction of society and its institutions. This would represent a return to the practice of an earlier epoch, when educators concerned themselves with the problems of society, approaching them from moral and philosophical perspectives, and striving to find practical solutions within the constraints of schooling, rather than claiming to apply a neutral technology to the vaguely stated concerns of politicians and interest groups.

Deliberation, by its nature, is conducive to efforts to articulate a public interest and does not encourage the belief that such efforts can be replaced by specialized and technical planning procedures. Deliberation, by example, encourages the search for common values and common aspirations among apparently conflicting interests.

VIRTUES OF DELIBERATION

The proposition that curriculum planning should be understood as a morally directed process can be seen as more realistic than the idea that it should be thought of as a matter of technique. It is hard to argue with the assertion that the question, "What *ought* we to do?" is the one that curriculum planners typically have to answer. So why would one suppose that a moral question—which this is—can be treated through technique, which is designed to deal with the question, "What *must* we do?" with its implication that the materials to be acted on and the means for doing it are totally certain and fully understood? In spite of the best efforts of the technical experts, curriculum questions continue to be moral questions, which is why technical measures so often result in inferior plans and poor decisions. Where the curriculum of schooling is concerned, to talk the language of virtue is to be realistic. Why should we not believe that planners are capable of developing and fostering qualities of character, as much as they are capable of acquiring skills and techniques? The curriculum of schooling, obstinately, continues to be about the development of character, and the idea that those who plan for it should themselves be concerned about qualities of character is entirely logical. Discussion of how to plan curriculum, through applications of the method of the practical, should be discussion of the uses of virtue before it is discussion of the uses of technique.

NOTES

1. United States Department of Education. (1991). *America 2000: An educational strategy.* Washington, DC: US Department of Education.

CHAPTER

4

Curriculum Research
Within a Practical Perspective

Practical problems relate to unique settings, and the method of the practical gives priority to personalized, contextualized knowledge. But it also allows an important place to theoretic knowledge, which is traditionally yielded through research. But should research be thought of solely as an exercise in the theoretic? Might not the conception of the practical be able to accommodate activities that we could and should recognize as research? This chapter attempts to deal with that question. It was first given at the Conference on Curriculum Work and Curriculum Content held at the University of Oslo, October 10-12, 1990, and was subsequently published under the title 'The character of curriculum research within a practical perspective' in Gundem, Bjørg B., Engelsen, Britt Ulstrup, and Berit Karseth (Eds.), Curriculum work and curriculum content, Report No. 5, Institute for Educational Research, University of Oslo, 1991.

It is a commonplace of writing on curriculum research that it should become more practical. There is a sense that Schwab was right when be claimed that the problems of the curriculum field stemmed from "inveterate, unexamined, and mistaken reliance on theory."[1] There is also a sense that what researchers do is not valued by teachers. Remedies for this have been proposed that envisage either the adoption of new, more naturalistic research methods, or the establishment of new kinds of relationships between practitioners and researchers.[2] I do not see in many of these proposals an appreciation of the kind of distinction Schwab was making when he spoke of the practical and the theoretic, or, consequently, of the difference between practical as a commonsense notion and the practical as a philosophical idea. As a result, attempts to change the character of research tend to be cosmetic rather than fundamental. This chapter explicates Schwab's practical–theoretic distinction, and examines what consequences an appreciation of the nature of the practical, as he described it, would have for ways in which research is conducted. I pursue this as a self-contained exercise, leaving it to others to speculate on questions of how far, if at all, such a conception of research may already be embodied in current modes of inquiry with claims to practicality, such as action research.

AN EXAMPLE

Let me begin my explanation by considering a passage from *Running a School*, a book of advice to school principals.[3] It confronts us with a practical problem—that is, one that occurs in unique circumstances, and that demands action. As I read this story it seems to me that it encapsulates, rather neatly, the conflict between theoretic and practical ways of conceptualizing school situations that require a practical response. First, the reader is plunged into the problem:

> Mr. Walton, your music specialist, and only teacher of music, is a friendly, willing but now ineffectual colleague of 49. He is completely incapable of maintaining discipline in any class owing to his extreme diffidence, much of which is believed to stem from a severe mental illness from which he suffered, several years ago, before you came to the school . . .
>
> The present standard of music teaching is very poor. Much inconvenience has been caused by noise and indiscipline in the music room, and by the difficulty of persuading classes to settle down for their next period, when they have just come from the music lesson. (p. 1)

So here you are, a unique school principal, in a unique setting, about to tackle the problem of the unique Mr. Walton. And, at the outset, the authors do indeed show an impressive concern to stick with the particulars of the situation and with the moral and prudential issues that it raises:

> To begin with, you are bound to be concerned for Mr. Walton himself. He has been teaching for nearly thirty years, and he was clearly, at one time, a competent teacher of music. His present inability to maintain even a modicum of discipline is evidently, at least in part, a consequence of a nervous breakdown he suffered several years ago. He is, therefore, fully entitled not only to your sympathy and concern, but to your professional support and protection. The more closely you have identified yourself with Mr. Walton and his problems, however, the more forcefully you have been reminded that you cannot consider his difficulties in isolation. You have a concurrent responsibility for all his colleagues, whose work is being continuously disrupted, as well as for the children in the school, whose discipline is being undermined, and who are

being almost entirely deprived of the contribution which music should make to their general education.

Inside school, therefore, it is clear that Mr. Walton and his personal and professional problems arouse many conflicting interests and loyalties. But, however much you may wish it could be so, these loyalties cannot be confined to the internal running of the school. (p. 2)

So far, so good. The full complexity of the problem is laid out: there is no pretence that it can be neatly bounded in terms of time, space, or personalities. And the authors acknowledge that there is no one right answer to the question of what to do in such a situation. At this point, however, having almost negotiated the course without penalty, they fall at the next fence. They have shown us the wide range of knowledge the decision maker must bring to bear; they have emphasised how uncertain some of that knowledge is, how inextricably bound up with the particularity of cases, with moral and ethical judgments, and with questions of value and purpose. But the subject of their text is "running a school," so now they face their own personal dilemma of how to make the connection between knowledge and action—between complex, uncertain knowledge on the one hand, and action affecting the lives of individuals and communities on the other. And they choose the way that many thinkers and writers in the field of education choose: they make an abrupt switch from the practical to the theoretic:

We suggest that principles are the most stable and significant factors which influence decisions. If, for example, having weighed all the conflicting claims upon your compassion and your judgment, you should decide that your obligation to the children, and to their parents is your first priority, then, inevitably, your concern for Mr. Walton will have to come second or even lower on the list . . . The identification of principles is an essential step towards the solution of any problem . . . If the analysis of a problem always follows the sequence of first identifying objectives, determining priorities, and assessing resources before taking action, then the ultimate answer is more likely to be acceptable than one reached on any other basis or by any other process. (p. 3)

This statement appears to me to be misguided, and to represent exactly the kind of confusion between "being practical" and "pursuing the practical" with which I am concerned in this paper. Let me elaborate on this.

WHAT IS MEANT BY THE PRACTICAL AND THE THEORETIC?

First of all, what did I mean when I said that the authors "make an abrupt switch from the practical to the theoretic"? As I shall explain later, I am not addressing the question of the relationship of practice to theory in a general way. I am making a particular kind of distinction that is one with a long history, beginning with Aristotle's *Ethics*, and finding its most cogent recent expression in the literature of curriculum in Schwab's practical papers.[4] Within this mode of thinking, the practical and the theoretic represent two faces of knowledge seeking and knowledge using. The practical is concerned with the finding and using of knowledge for the purpose of taking action; the theoretic with the finding and using of knowledge for the purpose of providing explanations. In the case of the practical, the situation that has to be dealt with is unique, and the action taken will also be unique, as will the ways in which knowledge of the situation is connected with the action decided upon. In the case of the theoretic, on the other hand, even if the search for explanation is triggered by a particular event, the knowledge sought, the explanation put forward, and the arguments connecting knowledge and explanation will be of a general nature.

Thus, the question of what to do about Mr. Walton is clearly "practical": it is a problem about action to be taken in a unique situation, and how that action can be justified. However, it is inevitably the case that such problems also raise questions that point us toward explanations rather than decisions. An example would be, "Why is Mr. Walton a poor disciplinarian?" Maybe if we knew the answer to that we could do something about it. The authors imply that the answer is "because he had a nervous breakdown," and, on the face of things, this seems to be a statement about Mr. Walton as an individual. But, as is unavoidable in the search for explanations, there are underlying premises that are general in nature: "and people who have breakdowns lose confidence, and loss of confidence leads to poor discipline."[5] The use of terms like "nervous breakdown" signals a move to theoretic abstraction. As an instance of nervous breakdown, Mr. Walton ceases to be unique. He joins a category, and shares in all the properties conventionally associated with that category. Note, however, that, while it is not essential to have explanations of Mr. Walton's conduct, it is necessary to make a decision on what to do about a perceived problem. We engage in the practical because practical problems have to be resolved: we engage in the theoretic because it is nice to have things explained, and because explanations can help our practical decision making. However, we can manage without explanations—and often do. What is less easy is to dispense with the *language* of explanation.

The language of explanation is attractive because it is demonstrative. At the expense of substituting universals for particulars, it moves from premises to necessary, or apparently necessary conclusions. There is, therefore, every temptation to import the language of the theoretic, which is designed to frustrate attempts to disprove the statements it contains, into the area of practical decision making, where action must be based on particulars, and must stand on criteria of justifiability, rather than on canons of experimental verification. And this is exactly what our authors have done: having launched us into a discussion of a practical problem, just at the point where a decision to act has to be made, they shift to the language of the theoretic. They begin by showing us how to establish a knowledge base for action that refers to unique people, places, and events. But then, instead of demonstrating how that knowledge of particulars can be used (aided, where appropriate, by theoretic inquiry) to resolve a practical problem, they move to talk of objectives, priorities, and overriding principles. These are abstract conceptions that cut across the uniqueness of people, places, and events. They belong with theoretic language, not the language of the practical.

So far, my argument has been a logical one, based on the idea that procedures must be appropriate to cases. But, in the practical world, is it not possible that theoretic methods may work in spite of logical incompatibilities? In the first place, I would say that there is a lot of evidence that they don't. We have quite a few studies that show that procedures for the resolution of practical problems that ignore, or relegate to a low order of priority, considerations of the particulars of situations are ineffective.[6] However, over and above such empirical considerations, there is also a moral one: unless we are able to carry through our engagement with the practical from knowledge gathering to knowledge using, expressions of concern for our children, our parents, our teachers, our Mr. Waltons, are empty gestures. Their interests and well-being may play a prominent role in the rhetoric surrounding our problem solving, but, as the decision point approaches, the focus shifts to the application of an algorithm that, once supplied with suitable data, will provide a solution through dictates of logic, rather than a resolution based on considerations of moral obligation.

ATTRACTIONS OF THE THEORETIC

I have used a particular instance to illustrate a pervasive problem: when we try to generate knowledge for the improvement of educational practice, whether in the running of schools, the design of curricula, or the training of teachers, there is a widespread failure to link knowledge to action within a practical paradigm. The improvement of practice is a practical problem. Research applied to the improvement of practice should therefore make use of the language of the practical that, as I have suggested, has no meaning or purpose except as a guide to action.

In the case I have cited, the failure occurred because of a shift to a theoretic mode that came late in the argument, following a previous attempt to consider the problem in practical terms. In curriculum research, and especially in curriculum evaluation, even an initial concern with the practical is often not felt to be necessary.[7] In these cases, at least we can say that what is done reflects a consistent technical and ideological position. But how can we account for the fact that researchers who try to shape their data gathering and analysis along practical lines frequently avoid the problem of how such knowledge should be translated into action, either by stopping short of the point of decision (effectively passing the problem to someone else), or by making a delayed transition to the language of theoretic? Is it perhaps the case that it is just not possible to find a way to apply a consistent conception of the practical to a plan for curriculum research?

The question why research is conducted in the way it is seems to me to be the easier one to resolve. The answer belongs partly in the history of ideas and partly in the contemporary evolution of social institutions. In terms of the history of ideas, intellectual activity is still overshadowed by the immense success of theoretic reasoning as it was applied to the explanation of natural phenomena by scientists in 17th- and 18th-century Europe. With the arrival on the scene of Bacon, Galileo, and Descartes, the older scholarly tradition that distinguished the arts of the practical from the theoretic sciences was doomed. Once Aristotle's *Physics* was shown to be fatally flawed, his *Politics* and *Ethics* also lay open to the incursions of "scientific" theorizers who deliberately distanced themselves from the practical and began to behave as moral judges or critics, armed with a priori principles, rather than as moral agents engaged with the particularities of cases. The writers of the Declaration of Independence could defend their political actions as based on "self-evident truths"; Bentham could advocate the application of a scientific calculus to human affairs; Comte could envision sociology as the ultimate positivist science. In the case of curriculum, this tradition has developed through Herbartianism, neo-Darwinism, and the efficiency movement to its current apotheosis in computer-based evaluation programs that aim to draw ever simpler and more definite conclusions from ever more complex data—even to the extent of trying to show, on a continental scale, which is the best type of elementary curriculum.[8] The use of theoretic reasoning is associated with the quest for certainty that obsesses those for whom tolerance of ambiguity is difficult.[9]

But, as well as this intellectually powered thrust toward the certainty, prestige, and elegance of theoretic reasoning, we also have to take into account the press toward the theoretic, which is associated with modern attitudes to the nature of authority. As we could infer from the example given in *Running a School*, use of theoretic reasoning is also intended to solve the dilemma of how to maintain control in a situation where decisions are still made through traditional structures, but the right of individuals or small groups to decide what is good for everyone is no longer automatically respected. A practical approach to this problem would be to engage all those likely to be affected by a decision in the process of arriving at it. But such a tactic would be threatening to the security of administrators who prefer to keep decision making in their own hands. An attractive way out of this difficulty is to represent the decision as coming from a scientific procedure, for which the administrator supplies only the requisite expertise, in the hope that it will be accepted as inevitable.

In spite of these twin attractions of theoretic reasoning, we do, however, encounter numerous attempts to move away from it, in search of alternative approaches to research and decision making. It is now time to provide some guidelines for assessing these against criteria we might derive from the conception of the practical with which I intend to work. What features should a practical mode of curriculum inquiry exhibit?

CHARACTERISTICS OF PRACTICAL RESEARCH

It is important at this stage to explain in more detail the philosophical nature of the practical, to contrast it with the theoretic and, in particular, to show how it differs from commonsense notions of practice.

The theory–practice conflict is one that has long dogged attempts to advance understanding within curriculum and education, as well as within similar applied fields. There are various ways in which the theory–practice dilemma can be thought about. McKeon[10] offers a scheme that identifies four modes of philosophically connecting theory and practice, one of which is not a proper mode since it effectively sidesteps the problem. The types of theory–practice connections that McKeon discusses are (a) the logistic, (b) the dialectic, (c) the problematic, and (d) the operational.

The logistic mode is described as "formal and mathematical." It keeps theory and practice apart, and can join them only through the creation of a science of human action that treats planning and decision making through the same formal principles that are applied to the understanding of the natural world. This we recognize as reflecting the research and decision-making procedures I have already identified as typical of current practice in the curriculum field.

The dialectic mode sees theory and practice as in a state of mutual interaction that is made possible by certain shared characteristics: "action, like thought, consists in reconciling contraries in dynamic organic wholes."[11] Thus, both theory and practice advance dialectically. But, also, theory is reflection on practice, and practice reflects theory in a constant cycle of disjunction and reconciliation of ideas, so that the dialectic operates at a higher level as well.

The notion of inquiry is the key to the problematic mode. This conceives of practice as a matter of "influencing and determining moral, political, and social actions" that is focused on "the process by which men come to agree on a conclusion or to acquiesce in a course of action."[12] Inquiry denotes a method that is scientific, but neither logistic nor dialectic, and that can be applied to theory as well as practice. (At this point I should note that, although the specific notion of inquiry is important to the understanding of the idea of the practical, which has strong Deweyan roots, I have not attempted within the restricted compass of this chapter to confine the word to a strict technical sense. In the following discussion, research and inquiry are used more or less interchangeably.)

Finally, the operational mode (the one that is not truly a means of linking theory and practice) proposes to start from states of affairs and "clarify and define the scientific method by reference to actual situations and practical problems"; it "applies the test of concrete action by translating ideas into processes and seeking verification in discernible results."[13] This mode differs fundamentally from the logistic, the dialectic, and the problematic in being essentially persuasive (rhetorical), rather than scientific (truth-seeking).

The theory–practice dilemma can be discussed in relation to any of these modes. For example, while staying within the logistic mode, which sees the problem as one of engineering connections between two distinct realms, we can stress the priority of practice over theory and the need to ensure that the connections that are made between them respect the nature of practice. This, however, is not to engage in the practical: the idea of the practical is associated exclusively with the problematic mode that offers its own special understanding of the nature of the link between thought and action. As McKeon makes clear, the choice of how to regard the theory–practice connection is not simply intellectual, it is also moral. In evaluating the modes that he presents, he refers to the implications they have for how social action is understood and organized. Within the logistic mode, the selection and evaluation of courses of action fall within the province of experts; within the dialectic, they are undertaken by the class that determines how dialectical necessity shall be politically interpreted; within the operational they become the prerogative of those with power to persuade, since the possibility of offering scientific grounds for action is discarded. Only within the problematic mode is the basis for social action generalized to all who are affected by it.

EXEMPLIFICATION OF PRACTICAL INQUIRY

Having established the character of practical inquiry, and distinguished it from inquiry that focuses on practice, we are now in a position to suggest what a program of curriculum research that used the method of the practical might look like.

Schwab lists the following features of practical (as opposed to theoretic) inquiry:

1. It begins from the feeling that some state of affairs is unsatisfactory, that it is "constituted of conditions which we *wish* were otherwise and we think . . . *can be made* to be otherwise."
2. Its subject matter is "concrete and particular."
3. The method of the practical is deliberation. Through application of deliberation, treatment of the unsatisfactory state of affairs is moved through three phases of search:

    (a.) The search for the problem,
    (b.) The search for data, and
    (c.) The search for solutions.[14]

Though these phases are sequential, they are not distinct and any kind of overlap may occur. For example, the search for a solution may draw attention to some way in which the search for the problem was deficient, so that this phase is now resumed.

These then are the features that will characterize an instance of practical research. It will begin from a sense of lack of satisfaction with an existing state of affairs, use deliberation as the means of defining the problem to which attention needs to be given, seek out data that enable the nature of the problem to be understood, invent possible solutions, and decide on a course of action to remedy feelings of dissatisfaction.

Some aspects of these criteria need amplification. Interest in remedying unsatisfactory states of affairs will relate to the possibilities that exist for implementing solutions. It is unlikely that great effort will be expended in deliberation on the nature of problems and the availability of solutions unless those engaging in the deliberation have some power of decision, or have influence over others who are able to take action. By deliberation, I mean face-to-face, problem-focused discussion involving, ideally, all those who would be affected by a decision to act, or who constitute important sources of knowledge relating to the problematic situation. In the event that the involvement of all is logistically impossible, deliberation should take place in a group that is representative of those affected and those with relevant knowledge. Deliberation, as the method of the practical, is not controlled by principle, but by the particulars of the case under consideration. Finally, a decision does not have to be a decision to change the existing state of affairs. As well as remedying dissatisfaction by the alteration of external conditions, it is also possible to alleviate it by the modification of desires. As Schwab points out, "practical problems intrinsically involve states of character and the possibility of change."[15]

What would this method of the practical look like if applied to research? In what ways would it differ in style and results from procedures currently employed in research into curriculum questions? What problems and opportunities would it encounter?

THE SEARCH FOR THE PROBLEM

As we have seen, the genesis of programs of practical inquiry should be brought about by feelings of dissatisfaction with current states of affairs. This criterion is quite often met by investigations at the local or national level into what are perceived as poor levels of reading skill, or poor performance in mathematics. However, these studies do not typically follow a course of practical inquiry. What happens in such cases is a familiar story. In the first place, the dissatisfaction that gives rise to research originates in, or is shaped by political and administrative interests that sharpen broad concerns into narrowly defined problems. The hastily identified problem is them handed over to the technical experts who, according to the character of their expertise, head in two main directions: amassing data to show that the issue is, indeed, serious, or experimentally implementing programs that, it is claimed, will remedy the deficiency. Finally, reports emerge that document the problem on a very general level and probably show that there is little to choose between the old and the novel ways of teaching. The question of what action should ensue is then handed back to the political or administrative authorities who commissioned the research in the first place, and who may or may not take action, depending on how their interests have moved in the meantime.

The essential difference between this way of responding to dissatisfaction and the way that would be adopted by practical research lies in the question of what controls the inquiry process. In the former case, control is exercised by political or administrative agencies who define and own the problem. Research supplies expertise for investigating an already known problematic, and yields data of a general nature that are available to decision makers, but that may not spur them to any particular action, or to any action at all. In the latter case, control is exercised by the problem itself. In the first of the three overlapping phases of inquiry, the problem is an object of search, so that it can be mapped and understood; in the second phase, it guides the quest for relevant data, and in the third and final stage, it directs the pursuit of solutions suited to the context in which it has been identified. This is the essence of McKeon's notion of a problematic mode for linking theory and practice—it regards both theory and practice as being driven by problems.

It will also be remembered that, in its practical form, problematic inquiry required that responsibility for the identification phase, as for the succeeding ones, should not be confined to a restricted group of people within a community. The translation of dissatisfaction into a well-formed problem would not, then, be the task of politicians and administrators alone. In turn, this suggests that, in practical inquiry, the translation should take place at the level of a recognizable community, small enough that there would be no need to hand over problem identification to people who would partici- pate in a merely representative capacity. With more and more diverse people directly involved, of course, the direction of inquiry would become unpredictable. Problems might disappear, leaving researchers without work, or problems might develop in unanticipated directions, burdening them with situations seen as not within their field.

This observation draws attention to another difficulty about the control of research. Moving the focus of inquiry to a more local level helps free it from one kind of control—that exercised by administrators and politicians, but may, at the same time, expose it to another—that deployed by theoretical or technical experts. Smaller scale inquiries are typically carried out by individual researchers who are already committed to a particular paradigm, whether traditional or innovative. This paradigm then controls what is done and how it is done, admitting certain kinds of problems and methods and excluding others. The initiation of a program of practical inquiry would require the presence of researchers whose commitment was to the process of identifying and solving problems, without limiting these to certain admis- sible types.

THE SEARCH FOR DATA

The search for data does not need to wait upon the clarification of the problem. Unlike theoretic research, where data are represented as materials generated exclusively by instruments or procedures shaped to the require- ments of a previously defined question, practical research uses data to establish the nature of the problem it is trying to resolve. These will usually be particular data—knowledge of the specific circumstances surrounding an unsatisfactory state of affairs—though general (theoretic) data may also be helpful. As the focus on the problem or problems becomes clearer, the role of general data will probably increase. To some extent, our local difficulty will be an example of difficulties encountered elsewhere. If we are worried about reading levels, then reading levels in other school districts are a relevant concern.

But just as practical research allows the nature of its problems to be revealed by the process of inquiry, so also it lets that same process deter- mine the status of the data that it gathers. No item of information or set of data has the privilege of providing a definitive answer to the questions that inquiry has raised. Deliberation, as the method of the practical, must decide what weight should be placed upon particular kinds of data, whether these be qualitative or quantitative, general or particular. It is the deliberative process that assigns authority to facts and opinions. They do not automatically enjoy authority because of the expertise of those who deliver them, or because of disciplinary endorsement of the theories or instruments that produced them.

THE SEARCH FOR SOLUTIONS

As subject matter is gathered and deliberated on, the focus of the practical research process moves from definition of the problem to proposals for possible solutions. But the phases of search continue to interact. The arrival of an idea about a solution may indicate where more data should be sought, or even shed new light on the nature of the problem. Contrast this with the process of research inspired by the theoretic, where analysis of data marks an end point at which the question of what the findings imply for the solution of practical problems is handed on to another agency (or sometimes the researchers themselves acting in a different role). Practical research, however, incorporates within itself the search for solutions and proceeds on the assumption that these must arise from an engagement with the problem and with its emergent subject matter. Quite different is the situation that theoretic researchers often find themselves in, of having to adjudicate between a finite number of previously determined courses of action. The final stage of a process of practical research is either the specification of a number of possible courses of action, or a decision to follow one particular course, depending on whether those conducting the research also have power of decision. An essential part of this final phase is the effort to trace out the consequences of actions, and this will almost certainly involve more data gathering. Practical research is not conclusive in the way that theoretic research is conclusive. The end point of theoretic research is the answer it produces to the question that gave rise to it (or an explanation of why the question cannot be answered, or only inconclusively answered). But the end point of practical research is a proposal for changing the circumstances of people's lives that will, in turn, lead to future frictions and dissatisfactions. Practical problems are never, in any absolute sense, solved, and practical research must, therefore, attend closely to the possible consequences of any course of action it proposes. These courses of action will, as we have noted, be specific to the problem under review. And, in considering this question of the specificity of solutions, we are driven back to the issue of the level at which problems are defined. Faith in theoretic research persuades us of the pervasive nature of problems and of data, and, therefore, of solutions. But is it likely that the problem of dissatisfaction with children's ability to read will be solved by national decisions to make universal changes in teacher training, curriculum materials, or testing procedures? Not only do these fail to address local circumstances that are important for the definition and treatment of problems, they also fail to enlist the support of those on whom the success of action depends because they deny them any involvement in the research process.

CAN THERE BE PRACTICAL CURRICULUM RESEARCH?

I have tried to describe what practical curriculum research would look like. But is such a process possible? And, if it were, would we be justified in calling it research? I believe that positive answers can be given to both these questions.

We do not have to go very far to find examples of practical inquiry. If we look into schools and study how teachers work individually and in groups, especially groups in informal settings, we will inevitably recognize the characteristics of such a form of inquiry. Studies of teacher thinking[16] illustrate how teachers use practical reasoning to guide their classroom activities. Investigations into groups set up to solve curriculum problems show how they too engage in practical inquiry.[17] Whether this everyday process engaged in by teachers and educators represents good, average, or poor curriculum research is another question. Some observers have suggested that it is generally inferior in nature, especially in its neglect to pursue data that lie beyond the classroom and the commonplaces of the subject matter to be taught.[18] But, whatever its quality, it is recognizable as an embodiment of the method of the practical. We admit the possibility of labeling work done in a theoretic mode as legitimate inquiry even when we criticize it as having been poorly conceived, poorly executed, or presenting unjustified conclusions. So why would we hesitate to use the title practical inquiry in circumstances where we can point to deficiencies in the process? The more important question, however, is whether at least some practical curriculum inquiry can be counted as curriculum *research*.

The issue here is, as I see it, partly semantic and partly cultural or sociological. First of all, if we are to work with a category called research it has to have a meaning that distinguishes it from all other categories. What I have said about teachers may make it appear that I am falling into the extreme kind of categorical conflation promoted by action researchers who claim that "all teaching is research." In terms of definitions, I would say that central to the concept of research is the idea of discovery. Research of whatever kind is directed to the uncovering of something: a fact, an explanation, a solution to a practical problem. Therefore, teachers have the opportunity, and I would say the obligation, to be researchers some of the time. They and their students can benefit from the discovery of solutions to problems, both practical and theoretic. But, for a lot of the time, teachers are doing other things. Very often they are engaged in routine activity based on what Elbaz calls "principles of practice."[19] This is fortunate for them. If teaching were nothing but discovery it would be intolerably stressful. But research has to be more than discovery. The extra meaning I would attach to the notion of research is that it is not just any process of discovery, but a process of discovery guided by a reflective use of method. Inquiry involves the making of choices: choices about what questions to ask (or what questions are worth asking), which data shall be sought, what means of evaluating and analyzing data shall be employed, how data shall be connected to conclusions, and how the trustworthiness of conclusions shall be judged. Such choices can be made by default, unreflectingly, or, on the other hand, with attention to the range of alternatives that exists, and to the criteria by which some may be judged as better or worse than others. Only when inquiry is guided by such reflection would I claim that what is being done is research. But, obviously, in terms of the arguments I have been making, this requirement could be fulfilled in a number of ways. Theoretic research carried out through use of disciplinary algorithms or paradigms is one way. But practical research, thought of in its proper Deweyan sense, can also yield canons of appropriate method and appropriate ways of connecting method to outcome.

This brings me to my second point about what we understand by research. To say that it is discovery guided by a reflective use of method is to define it semantically. But what counts as discovery, and what counts as method are matters determined at any particular time and place by social and cultural norms. Here we come to the heart of the problem of whether research within a practical perspective is possible. The answer we give to that question is ultimately dependent not on definitions of the word research, but on our perception of what it is that can lend authority to a claim that what is being done is indeed research. Here we face the difficulty that the social and cultural definitions imposed on the idea of research tend to confine it to inquiry carried out within a theoretic perspective. That is, to the kinds of research conducted in universities and government agencies, and guided by the pursuit of explanations rather than decisions on courses of action.

Theoretic inquiry addresses itself to problems arising from failures and inadequacies of theory. It searches for and analyzes data within disciplinary perspectives, and aims to produce publishable results. The main reason why it retains this character is because mastery of its methods, and opportunities to publish, lead to academic and social advancement for those who engage in it. This in turn is translated into the power to define what shall count as research, and preserves the dominance of the theoretic mode. Practical inquiry, on the other hand, evokes no such recognition. The questions it seeks to answer are seen as being of a lower order: matters of management, of the refurbishment of what already exists, or of risky ventures into the unknown. Its methods are hidden and, if discussed at all, thought of as not much more than common sense. Its outcomes are not generally considered suitable material for academic books and journals.

The power of definition that lies with the established academic institutions becomes apparent as we look at various attempts that have been made to move curriculum research away from the dominant modes of inquiry. Examples would be the "teacher as researcher" movement in the U.K., or the growth of phenomenological research in North America. Both initiatives were largely inspired by appreciation of the twin problems I raised at the outset: on the one hand, the existence of a powerful theoretic research tradition that frustrates attempts to bring inquiry to bear on the practical problems of teachers and teaching, and, on the other, the powerlessness of teachers to influence the research agenda and participate in it. Both initiatives have been successful in drawing attention to these problems and ameliorating some aspects of them. But neither has addressed the basic question of how the authority to define what counts as research might be shifted. Whatever the rhetorics surrounding attempts to make teachers into researchers or into phenomenologists, in both cases the new definition of what constitutes research has been proposed by academics who preserve their role as keepers of that definition, and as sources of the expertise needed by teachers if they are to work with it. Academics assess the work that is done, grant degrees and diplomas, and steer teachers toward the production of publishable material. The cultural definition of research is moved only a little, since power of definition remains in the same hands.

In my view, practical curriculum research becomes a possibility only when the power of definition moves into different hands. The issue, as I have tried to show, is not only one of method, but of authority. As long as we see the idea of the practical as being simply about addressing certain kinds of concerns, taking the wishes of certain kinds of people into account, or promoting styles of research that are qualitative rather than quantitative, naturalistic rather than discipline-centered, then the issue of authority is not being confronted, and confusion will persist between research that is directed to ends that are seen as, in some way, practical, and research that respects the method of the practical as I have described it. The capability of inquiry within a practical perspective for contributing to the treatment of curriculum problems can be tested only when those with authority to define the nature of research accept the imperatives implied by the basic philosophy of the practical, as opposed to embracing the ambition to be, in some way, practical. At that point, the possibility will exist for curriculum research to be undertaken that exhibits all the features of practical inquiry I have described: research that takes uncertain practical problems as a starting point, uses deliberation as a method, yields proposals for action rather than explanations as its outcome, and is guided by canons of moral conduct as well as by the dictates of procedure.

NOTES

1. Schwab, J. J. (1978). The practical: A language for curriculum. In I. Westbury & N. J. Wilkof (Eds.). *Science, curriculum, and liberal education*. Chicago: University of Chicago Press, p. 287.

2. See, for example, Short, Edmund C. (Ed.). (1991). *Modes of curriculum inquiry*. Albany, NY: SUNY Press.

3. Barry, H., & Tye, F. (1972). *Running a school*. London: Temple Smith.

4. Westbury & Wilkof, *op. cit.*

5. That is to say, in cases where the explanation sets out to be demonstrative: "This is what you would expect to happen because, generally speaking, x is associated with y," or some similar, formally structured account. Another possibility is narrative-based explanation that takes account of particulars and is therefore demanding of much more detailed research. Narrative-based explanations are what we expect to hear from great detectives who announce that "they have a theory."

6. See, for example, Hall, Peter (1980). *Great planning disasters*. London: Weidenfeld & Nicholson.

7. For a relevant critique, see Reid, William A. (1980). Making the problem fit the method: A review of *The Banbury Enquiry*. *Journal of Curriculum Studies, 11*, 167–173.

8. Abt Associates (1976/1977). *Education as experimentation: A planned variation model*. (Vols. 1–4). Boston, MA: Abt Associates.

9. Dewey, John (1960). *The quest for certainty*. New York: Capricorn Books.

10. McKeon, Richard (1952). Philosophy and action. *Ethics, 62*, 79–100.

11. *Ibid.*, p. 84.

12. *Ibid.*, p. 85.

13. *Ibid.*, p. 86.

14. Schwab, *op. cit.*, pp. 288–291.

15. *Ibid.*, p. 289.

16. See, for example, Elbaz, Freema (1983). *Teacher thinking: A study of practical knowledge*. London: Croom Helm.

17. See, for example, Walker, Decker F. (1975). Curriculum development in an art project. In William A. Reid & Decker F. Walker (Eds.). *Case studies in curriculum change: Great Britain and the United States* (pp. 91–135). London: Routledge & Kegan Paul.

18. Walker, *op. cit.*

19. Elbaz, *op. cit.*

CHAPTER

5

Schwab's Conception
of Liberal Education

So far, practical reasoning has been discussed as a way of conceptualizing and conducting curriculum planning and curriculum research. But, unlike other approaches to such activities, it does not assume a neutral stance about what kind of proposals should emerge from processes of planning and research. While it is generally true that products tend to reflect the nature of the processes that give rise to them, in most instances the connection can be seen as accidental rather than logical or intentional. In the case of the deliberative, or practical reasoning approach, however, the connection is inherent and necessary: since the process is moral in character, and since it sees means and ends as inextricably linked, its products will reflect a consistent vision of education. This vision is, perhaps, best described as that of a liberal education. Liberal education, however, is a conception that has assumed many different forms at different times and in different places. What is its essential character? And how does it relate to a practical reasoning perspective?

These questions were raised for me by the appearance, in 1978, of a collection of Schwab's essays under the title Science, curriculum, and liberal education.[1] *The result was the contribution of a paper to the symposium "Commentaries on J. J. Schwab's 'Science, curriculum and liberal education'" at the AERA Annual Meeting, San Francisco, 1979. This was subsequently revised and published as "Democracy, perfectability, and the 'battle of the books': Thoughts on the conception of liberal education in the writings of Schwab" in* Curriculum Inquiry, *10, 1980, 249–263. It is this version that appears here.*

What is a liberal education? Many educators and curriculum theorists would dismiss such a question as unanswerable; some in their zeal for positivism, would declare that the question was meaningless. Schwab is an educator and curriculum theorist who represents a diametrically opposed viewpoint. For him, the question of what constitutes a liberal education is one that should animate us at a fundamental level in our endeavors to define and solve curriculum problems: ultimately, the educator's work is always undertaken in response to questions of this order, though not in the expectation that conclusive answers can be found. The questions act rather as programmatic devices, helping to set the framework of assumptions and ambitions within which practical or theoretic problems in education should be confronted. The problems themselves will be specific in context, arising from particular sets of aims and needs. Decision making represents the attempts of moral agents to connect realities and actualities with possibilities, visions, and ideals.

The ideal that liberal education presents was first shaped in classical times when it was related to that form of education suited to free men who would be the leaders of their society. Through its subsequent development, it has continued to be guided by an image of the leader as a person having a capacity for action informed by a mind attuned to wise and independent judgment. Implied here are notions of *wholeness* and *autonomy*—wholeness because the mark of a liberal education is the ability to marry thought and action, autonomy because liberal education is education for freedom: the person who experiences it must be able to transcend the particulars of which it consists to emerge with appetites and capacities that can be turned to problems as yet unknown. The antithesis of liberal education is servile training: learning directed to the acquisition of practical skills and knowledge that can be broken down into easily assimilated packages. The approach of liberal education to teaching and learning is based on a notion of perfectability. It knows of no point at which education is complete. Satisfactory levels of performance are mediocre: liberal education seeks excellence and, beyond excellence, perfection.

These enduring ends of liberal education are reflected in Schwab's writings. In "Science and Civil Discourse: the Uses of Diversity," he examines the liberal curriculum "in terms of its traditional function—the preparation of a leadership."[2] His purpose is not to question the function, but to show in what ways the concept of leadership needs to be reformulated in order that it can take its place as an end in liberal education in 20th-century America. He retains and extends the connection of liberal education with judgment and autonomy. A liberal curriculum is one designed to help students develop "critical and organizing power and deliberative command over choice and action."[3] But this is not to be achieved by construing intellectual education as something self-contained and self-sufficient: "There are neither biological, psychological, nor philosophical grounds for isolation of the intellect as a principle of education. It is indissolubly a *part* of the learning organism."[4] The result of a liberal education is, for Schwab, "*actively* intelligent people."[5] And binding all these concerns together is a belief that an idea of perfectability can still be a key notion in liberal education: "There is considerable danger involved in (the) limitation of education to mere maintenance and further spread through the population of our present level of reasonableness. It produces and extends the sense of capacity for self-determination while effectively hiding those complexities of problems with which our present capacity for reasonableness is not prepared to deal."[6]

Schwab's contribution to the development of the conception of liberal education is marked by a reaffirmation of its central tenets, not by a questioning of them. The importance of his work consists, therefore, in his efforts to see how these central tenets can be related to means suited to their realization in a modern, democratic, industrial society. Schwab stands in the mainstream of those who, while holding fast to the vision of a liberal education, have appreciated that the means to its realization must be adapted to the social and political institutions of the age and society within which it is to be pursued. It is to the evolution of the notion of liberal education in terms of its changing sociopolitical contexts that we must turn in order to appreciate the value of Schwab's contribution.

Two important sources help us to appreciate the nature of this evolution. The first is a brilliantly argued essay on the means to a liberal education by Richard McKeon who was a colleague of Schwab's at the University of Chicago.[7] The second is a cleverly written and insightful, though sometimes tendentious review of ideas on liberal education in 18th- and 19th-century England by Sheldon Rothblatt.[8]

McKeon's analysis suggests that though the context of the debate on the means to a liberal education has changed over the centuries, the practical issues to be resolved have consistently centered around a number of major dilemmas or ambiguities. He takes as his text Jonathan Swift's satire "The Battle of the Books," an account of a "terrible fight . . . between the *Antient* and *Modern Books* in the King's Library" in which a Homeric contest takes place between the forces of the ancients on one side (led by Homer, Pindar, Euclid, Plato, and Herodotus) and those of the moderns on the other (Tasso, Milton, Descartes, and Hobbes). According to McKeon, "the ambiguities of the battle of the books are of three sorts: an ambiguity about the arts and the sciences, an ambiguity about the relation of the arts and the sciences to religion and politics, and an ambiguity about the old and the new in the knowledge most worth having."[9] The ambiguities consist not merely in the problems about what decision to make at any given time, but also in the difficulty of knowing what the implications of any decision would be for the purposes of liberal education. "The questions raised in the battle of the books were basic and therefore ambiguous questions: neither position in such a controversy is clear or demonstrable and the old and the new seem to be on both sides of all arguments."[10]

Just as McKeon shows that arguments about the means to a liberal education are not, in any final sense, logically resolvable, so Rothblatt demonstrates that they are not, in any final sense, socially or politically resolvable. Liberal education is an ideal, and precisely because it is an ideal it can never assume any permanent embodiment. In Georgian England, according to Rothblatt, "it was given the immense burden of rendering men and women sociable, tolerant, and broad-minded in situations where also every encouragement was given to the pursuit of personal advantage."[11] Later, in the Victorian epoch, its burden would be to produce leaders "who grasped the magnitude of the problems before them and by an effort of the speculative imagination, based on a solid understanding of the meaning of industrialism in the context of world history, would be able to give the turbulent society a proper sense of its character and mission."[12] Liberal education in 19th-century England had ceased to be a personal matter, dependent on books, travel, objects of art, and learned and sociable companions. Instead it became tied to institutions—the great universities of Oxford and Cambridge and, through them, the established Church.[13]

Thus, each age demands a reinterpretation of the idea of liberal education in terms of its own social and political order. Any conception of it that removes this adaptability, or refuses to raise anew the question of the means appropriate to its implementation, leads to a sterile pursuit of irrelevant goals and excessive attachment to educational forms no longer connected to living purposes. Schwab and McKeon understand from the inside the spirit in which liberal education must be conceived and applied in order for it to avoid such fates. Both grasp the critical difference between science and the liberal arts: "Science is the knowledge of truth considered speculatively, and art is the knowledge of truth considered as directive of our practice for the attaining of our true good and happiness."[14] Both see that liberal education, in its essence, relates to the second kind of truth, so that exposition or criticism of it can be entered into only from a position of personal engagement and intellectual relativism. Their conception is marked by a reimportation of that Aristotelean spirit of mind that was progressively abandoned by English educators of the 18th and 19th centuries: a mode of thought that emphasises the problems of the moral agent as against those of the moral judge or theoretician[15] and that, to use McKeon's words, sees the central problem of education as "the relation of reason and argument to social values and alternative realities."[16]

The very different path taken by most English writers on liberal education can be illustrated by reference to a widely quoted article by Hirst,[17] which is almost contemporary with McKeon's "Battle of the Books." Instead of recognizing the inherent ambiguities in the idea of liberal education, which Schwab and McKeon handle so fruitfully, Hirst suppresses them by imposing stipulative definitions that enable him to engage in an essentially axiomatic discussion of his subject. The result is an argument about the nature of knowledge only tangentially connected, it seems, with the traditional goals of liberal education. For Hirst, it is only part of an educational whole that includes, for example, "specialist education, physical education, and character training." Liberal education becomes simply "an education based fairly and squarely on the nature of knowledge itself."[18] The reductionism of Hirst's position is rooted in his conception of knowledge as a set of apparatuses that the mind applies to objective data. "A liberal education in the pursuit of knowledge is . . . seeking the development of mind according *to what is quite external to it, the structure and pattern of reality.*"[19] Yet, in spite of the divorce that is proposed between thought and action, Hirst believes that "because of the significance of knowledge in the determination of the good life as a whole, liberal education (that is, liberal education as he defines it) is essential to man's understanding of how he ought to live, both individually and socially."[20] Although his argument reduces liberal education to a positivist, intellectual education, in which truth is conceived of as being empirically demonstrable, nevertheless it is taken to be capable of including the moral and the aesthetic: "It is a necessary feature of knowledge as such that there be public criteria whereby the true is distinguishable from the false, the good from the bad, the right from the wrong."[21]

As one might expect, Hirst is critical of the Harvard Committee on General Education, whose report, published in 1945, is really about liberal education.[22] Its conclusions, he says, are based more on appeals to desirable qualities of mind than to fundamental forms of knowledge, and "the belief that in metaphysics man has knowledge of ultimate reality is ignored, if not rejected." The result, for him, is "an unsatisfactory treatment of the problem of definition and a limited and debatable treatment of the question of justification."[23] The point at issue here is basic to the conception of liberal education: is it the pursuit of unalterable realities to which education must address itself through the established disciplines? Or is it, as Schwab and the authors of the Harvard Report prefer to believe, the management of an inherently ambiguous idea in the interest of shaping engaged moral agents?[24]

Hirst's article does not stand alone. It represents an end point in a tradition of writing on liberal education in England that can be traced back for over a century. Neither does Schwab stand alone. His thought, though in many ways highly individual, is embedded in a path that stretches back through the central figure of Dewey to the late 19th-century builders of Chicago and other leading American universities. The divergence of these two traditions of thought, sharing a common European ancestry, raises profound historical questions that deserve a more detailed treatment than they can receive here.

Prior to 1776, traditions of liberal education were largely shared between England and the American colonies. The forms of scholasticism, in their declining years, "had been translated to Harvard and Yale, and at one time were as rightfully American as a first generation Puritan."[25] Even at the end of the 18th century, the content of a liberal education in an American college would not have been very different from the liberal curriculum of late Georgian England.[26] But already the decline of that curriculum in England had been set in train, as Rothblatt notes, by "the export . . . of unsettling ideas, political, social and more threateningly secularist than eighteenth-century England had known," and that "interrupted the general concern with polite behaviour."[27] In America, these ideas had done rather more than interrupt a concern with polite behavior, but England, though plunged into a period of prolonged anxiety, resisted fundamental social and political change. The hierarchical assumptions on which society rested were only superficially disturbed. The nature and composition of the social classes changed, but the regulative idea of social classes remained, so that, for example, the Taunton Commission on Secondary Education, in many ways an enlightened body, could produce in 1868 proposals that tied types of education quite specifically to the perceived needs of distinct social strata. And along with the preservation of the class structure went the preservation of the Burkean political notion of virtual representation, which claimed that "representation has nothing to do with obeying popular wishes, but means the enactment of the national good by a select elite."[28] Hence, the issue of the relationship of liberal education to society as a whole, and specifically to questions of leadership and political judgment within it, were not matters for debate. The ambiguities about liberal education that received attention were those concerning the content of the curriculum, and principally the place in it of the classics and the sciences. Furthermore, the debate became narrowly centered around the curricula of the ancient universities of Oxford and Cambridge—necessarily so, given their predominant role in deciding what was taught elsewhere.[29]

Whewell in *Of a Liberal Education in General* [30] presents what amounts to a political tract, aimed at persuading the University of Cambridge to recognize the existence of the physical sciences. To such an extent is it designed to placate the entrenched exponents of the grand old classical curriculum that it is difficult to know what Whewell did think about liberal education. Certainly he recognized the problem raised by the transformation of the liberal arts from a collection of skills to bodies of knowledge, and his exposition of the idea of inquiry could have served as an important contribution to the reformulation of the liberal curriculum. But, like most of his contemporaries, and those who were to follow later in the century, he was quite clear that discussion of liberal education was discussion of the education of the upper classes, and that the debate was only to a very marginal extent about the shaping of it to fit new conceptions of the sources of political influence and authority.

Twenty years later, Farrar, in his *Essays on a Liberal Education*,[31] devotes his own contribution to the question of whether boys in independent secondary schools should be required to write Greek and Latin verse, while his contemporary, Newman, prefigures Hirst's intellectualized version of liberal education. For Newman, the concept has become so closely tied to the idea of a university that it is expressed in terms of pure knowledge: "Its object is nothing more nor less than intellectual excellence . . . Knowledge is one thing, virtue another."[32] In spite of the wealth of writing to which it gave rise, the debate on liberal education in Victorian England was essentially sterile.[33] The social and institutional forces of the time prevented controversies about liberal education from being controversies about relationships of persons to societies, and directed them into discussion of what content best trained the mind for intellectual excellence, or, as Rothblatt has stated: "A change in education was made from social, or socio-moral ends to intellectual means not directly related to those ends."[34]

The effects of this emphasis on the intellectual content of liberal education, at the expense of its relation to the well-being of society, were enduring and plague discussion of liberal education in England to this day. Of the 19th-century writers Arnold alone (to whom we shall later return) retained a concern for the question of how to educate the whole person for political, social, and cultural participation in a complex and changing society. But his solution, too, rested on a view of society dominated by class distinctions, and on the affirmation that "the sound instruction of the people is an effect of the high culture of certain classes."[35]

But if Burke's justification of virtual representation in his *Address to the Electors of Bristol* can be taken as the seminal statement of the political context within which liberal education was debated in England, Jefferson's *Bill for the More General Diffusion of Knowledge* might serve as a contrasting text for the United States: "It becomes expedient for promoting the public happiness that those persons, whom nature hath endowed with genius and virtue, should be rendered by liberal education worthy to receive and be able to guard the sacred deposit of rights and liberties of their fellow citizens."[36] The spirit of Jefferson's words, more potent in their revolutionary implications than in their immediate intentions, was to be embraced by a society for which rights, liberties, and their relation to participatory politics were to be dominating concerns, and a society in which little impediment in the way of assumptions about class, hierarchy, or privilege was to hinder the exercise of such rights and liberties.

The result did not commend itself to European commentators. Tocqueville sums up their reservations about experiments in democracy:

> It must be acknowledged that in few of the civilized nations of our time have the higher sciences made less progress than in the United States; and in few

have great artists, distinguished poets, or celebrated writers been more rare. Many Europeans, struck by this fact, have looked upon it as a natural and inevitable result of equality; and they have thought that, if a democratic state of society and democratic institutions were ever to prevail over the whole earth, the human mind would gradually find its beacon lights grow dim, and men would relapse into a period of darkness.[37]

Though Tocqueville rejects the implications of the argument, he does not dispute the facts on which it is based. However, his analysis is evenhanded. "Whilst the social conditions and the institutions of democracy prepare (citizens) to seek the immediate and practical results of the sciences, permanent inequality of conditions leads them to confine themselves to the arrogant and sterile research of abstract truths."[38] Arnold was less charitable: "The countries which, like the United States, have created a considerable popular instruction, will long have to expiate the fault by their intellectual mediocrity, their vulgarity of manners, their superficial spirit, their lack of general intelligence."[39] Such a remark was entirely in line with his unease at the decline of the concept of virtual representation: "our whole scheme of government being representative, every one of our governors has all possible temptation, instead of setting up before the governed who elect him . . . a high standard of reason, to accommodate himself as much as possible to their natural taste for the bathos."[40]

Most European educators were baffled by the direction that American democracy took in the 19th century. Jeffersonian meritocracy they could grasp, even if they did not approve of it, but its Jacksonian derivative was beyond comprehension. In 1832, *Fraser's Magazine* in England warned Americans: "Against the single example of the United States we quote the whole history of democracy . . . we read one convincing tale, the despotism of the many occasioning the misery of all, terminated by the absolute power of the few."[41] Popular democracy, and its companion, the popular press, were widely scorned as pandering to low and ephemeral tastes. Farrar, in his discussion of "great books," rams home his argument that to read anything "written without a conscience or an aim is an inexcusable manslaughter upon time" by pointing to American newspapers and to Lowell's characterization of them as "the stagnant goose-ponds of village gossip."[42] On the other hand, attempts to develop institutions of higher education were written off as being directed toward skills of slavish utility, rather than self-justifying liberality of mind. Arnold comments that "the university of Mr. Ezra Cornell, a really noble monument of his munificence, yet seems to rest on a misconception of what culture truly is, and to be calculated to produce miners, or engineers, or architects, not sweetness and light."[43]

It is true that the new American universities, through the circumstances of their founding, were often concerned to justify themselves by the teaching of practical skills. This was a necessary stage in their development. It is also true that the older colleges such as Yale and Harvard were wedded to a view of the curriculum that gave a central place to the classics. But in both kinds of institution there were to be found educators who were assuming the great intellectual and practical burden of translating the conception of liberal education into a form appropriate to a popular democracy.[44] This was a more stimulating, productive, and demanding task than that engaged in by those English educators and writers who, convinced that liberal education was for the few, were exercising themselves on questions such as the place of Latin verse composition in the curriculum of the secondary school, or who were, in the manner of Arnold, trying to make old solutions fit new problems.

The struggle to develop new conceptions of liberal education suited to the American university has been charted by Charles Wegener. He identifies the pressures and ambitions that, in the late 19th century, shaped the progress of the new institutions of higher education. " 'Science' and 'democracy' are terms not inappropriate to point to the peculiar quality which the problem had assumed for those who labored in the American educational vineyard, though neither term would mean for them what it might suggest to us."[45] On the one hand, they took up with enthusiasm the directive idea of a university as a place devoted to the advancement of knowledge (an idea which, in England, had to be pursued with circumspection),[46] so that one strand in the argument about liberal education was concerned with "a reconstruction of institutionalized cognitive activities, creating a structure oriented toward discovery, growth, inquiry: 'research.' "[47] (A line of advance which Whewell might have pursued in more favorable circumstances.) On the other hand, they could not ignore all pervasive ideals of democracy that demanded that the intellectual and institutional apparatus so created was to be open to all, and dedicated to the benefit of all. Those who grappled with these ideas—White, Gilman, Eliot, Harper—were institution builders, not presiders over the hallowed rites and customs of foundations with an un-challenged claim to preeminence. They gave back to liberal education what in England it had lost—the language that connects thought and action. They created the tradition in which Schwab stands.

This tradition is not, however, represented by a unitary doctrine. Though ideas of science and democracy have guided the search, different educators and groups of educators have found different solutions to the questions raised by the enduring ambiguities of liberal education. Those who have tended to support the side of the ancients in the battle of the books have also been those who held the strongest views on the role of education as an instrument for perfectability. Liberal educators of this school, of whom R. M. Hutchins was the best known representative, took as their *locus classicus* Oakeshott's characterization of the great conversation:

> As civilized human beings, we are the inheritors neither of an inquiry about ourselves and the world, nor of an accumulating body of information, but of a conversation, begun in the primeval forests and extended and made more articulate in the course of centuries . . . Education, properly speaking, is an initiation into the skill and partnership of this conversation, in which we learn to recognize the voices, to distinguish the proper occasions of utterance, and in which we acquire the intellectual and moral habits appropriate to conversation.[48]

For Hutchins, the embodiment of the great conversation was great books (as opposed to the "stagnant goose-ponds of village gossip"). As a leading idea this had great proselytizing force and was raised to a visionary level never dreamed of by Farrar. Jefferson's dictum that the people themselves are the only "safe repository of the ultimate powers of society" and that we should "inform their discretion by education" is interpreted to mean that all should have available to them the education that Jefferson intended for the leaders of society: "Democracy requires liberal education for all. I believe this proposition to be true."[49]

Hutchins capitalizes on the fact that the proper exercise of power in a democracy depends on the wisdom of its citizens. Though, like Arnold, he espouses the side of the ancients in the battle of the books, unlike him he has seen the rise of the political institutions that can make Jacksonian democracy work. He no longer fears anarchy. He does, however, like the founders of the republic, fear faction, and the liberal education he advocates can be seen as a safeguard against the invitation to faction that undiluted democracy entails. His hope is that those who have been liberally educated will share a common tradition that has been presented to them in terms of the rational discovery of wisdom and will make democracy work through the fostering of community.[50] The weak point of this argument is that you need to have the community first in order to decide which are the great books. It is hard to see how the ambition of community is to be squared with the fact of pluralism. Hutchins' ideas seem open to the same fate as the melting pot ideology: when differences of interest turn out to be differences of passionately defended cultural identities, liberal education through reference to a supposed common intellectual and artistic heritage must be imposed, and hence become self-defeating. This is the problem noted by the Harvard Committee (1945) when they asked: "Are Jeffersonianism and Jacksonianism in fact complementary or do they struggle against each other?" and registered the ambiguity created for liberal education by subscription to the goal of equity as well as the goal of excellence. "The hope of the American school system, indeed of our society, is precisely that it can pursue two goals simultaneously: give scope to ability and raise the average."[51]

Once the argument for pursuing the highest form of culture is detached from the notion of class and applied across the whole population, then the practical definition of perfectability becomes a very strong one—so strong that the ambiguity of the dual goal of scope for ability and raising the average is effectively obscured.[52] The tradition that Schwab represents is less reluctant to face ambiguities of this sort. "[P]opular education has two quite different responsibilities. There is not only the responsibility for bringing all our population into the fold of literacy . . . If education is to continue to do for us what it has done in the past by way of improving the quality and quantity of self-determination, the modal level of education must itself be raised along the scale."[53] In other words, the goal of perfectability, which informs Schwab's conception of liberal education no less than that of Hutchins, is linked to a view of the democratic process in which forms of participation are immensely varied, rather than one that sees democracy as a finished structure guaranteeing automatically maximum participation for all. His conception combines strains of both idealism and realism in that, while it depends on a vision of what a democracy fully informed by liberal education would be like, it is also shaped by a recognition that democracy in practice often falls short of its lofty ambitions. Decisions are made on high and the rest of us are manipulated into agreement. "We will be flattered by being asked our opinion. We will be presented with carefully selected fragments of facts and arguments for our consideration . . . and as long as we are kept in the dark about the complexity of problems and the full scope of the process of decision making, we will have the illusion of full self-determination."[54]

But if Schwab tends to the side of the ancients in the matter of the relation of the arts and the sciences to politics, he seems to be a modern on the question of the content of the curriculum, and the part that science should play in it. He believes that knowledge of what he calls a "revisionary" character should have priority over knowledge expressed as a "rhetoric of conclusions," and that science should play a large part in a liberal curriculum because of its fitness for the fostering of "operative judgment."[55] But we have to be careful about the use of the terms *ancient* and *modern*. Schwab's approach to the problem of the knowledge most worth having can be seen as a restoration of the pre-Renaissance position when the disciplines were conceived not as established bodies of knowledge, but as arts and methods.[56] The phrase operative judgment is a key one. In contradistinction to many other contemporary writers on liberal education, Schwab is concerned not with the establishment of abstract principles on which the liberal curriculum should rest, but with what it means to develop the moral agent. In this he is reviving the kind of central purpose that the close study of Aristotelean ethics gave to the old scholastic curriculum.[57] So intricately interwoven was its structure that the undermining of Aristotle's *Physics* and

Metaphysics spelled its end[58] and (in England at least) a Baconian zeal was thenceforth applied to the design of curricula that led not to the perfection of moral agents, but to the profession of moral sciences.

Many writers on liberal education have been content either to follow this path and discuss the content of a liberal education in terms of abstract epistemological analyses (*vide* Hirst), or have reiterated a narrow view of the moral agent as a class-bound actor in a class-bound society. For Schwab, however, and some of his contemporaries at the University of Chicago, an inheritance of Germanic rather than English styles of scholarship, combined with a need to view educational problems in terms of the social and political conditions of a mature republican democracy, produced circumstances under which a brand of neo-Aristoteleanism became both possible and attractive. The exact nature of the scholarly traditions within which Schwab, McKeon, and others developed their ideas remains to be documented. The general point is amply sustained by Diehl: "Both the form and the content of modern American scholarship in the humanities owe their initial and principal debt to the great migration of American students to German universities throughout the nineteenth century . . . Virtually every one of the Americans who built the modern university system in the United States, and many of those who staffed the new institutions, studied in Germany."[59] The existence of such a legacy helped Schwab and others to swim against the tide of positivism and find intellectual stimulation in the works of continental philosophers such as Husserl and Heidegger long before these were discovered by new wave sociologists.[60]

Thus, Schwab's position amounts to far more than a particular set of solutions to the classical ambiguities about the means to a liberal education. He is concerned with the liberal curriculum as a practical endeavor, and shows how notions of practice and action can be used to explore the problems of conceiving and designing it. He is clear that he wants disciplines to be at the center of this liberal curriculum, but his discussion of their roles takes as its point of departure, not the character of a discipline as it functions to construe and explain the data that the world supplies, but the character of a discipline as it can be used by students to perfect themselves as social, political, moral, or intellectual agents.[61] To foster habits of inquiry and aid in the development of operative judgment, the disciplines are assigned roles which, while respecting them as self-contained arts and methods, are determined by the liberal goals of the curriculum as a whole.

His concern for the shaping of the student as an autonomous person also leads Schwab to a close analysis of teaching strategies. The germ of his approach is to be found in Whewell's *Of a Liberal Education in General*,[62] where he distinguishes between respectful teaching suited to permanent studies and critical teaching that should be used in connection with progressive studies. For Schwab, critical teaching is realized by discussion methods that, although not the only ones necessary to a liberal education, are particularly apt for it because "discussion is not merely a device . . . It is also the *experience* of moving toward and possessing understanding, and a liberal education is concerned with the arts and skills of understanding."[63] This central idea leads to an elaboration of teaching and the role of the teacher in terms of a cycle that includes both respect and criticism, and that is linked to a stage of germinal maturity in the student. "It is the germinal maturity in the young . . . which (the teacher) evokes and to which he ought to respond."[64]

The methodic arguments and procedures that Schwab applies to content selection and teaching strategies relate to the overall methodic approach to curriculum making that he exemplifies. In his view, liberal education is a process transacted by and for moral agents, not just a set of decisions, a stipulative definition, or a fully determined procedure. Just as its goals are seen in appetitive terms—knowledge, power, affection—rather than in such static categories as pure intellect or sweetness and light, so the means to a liberal education are construed as those processes by which planners engage with the problems of curriculum making, and teachers and students with its translation into activities.[65] These processes are the portions of the general category of operative judgment appropriate to the making of the liberal curriculum. Schwab closes the circle. It is through the exercise of the qualities produced by the liberal curriculum that the liberal curriculum is itself discovered.

Herein lies the strength of Schwab's vision. What he proposes is a way in which a liberal education can be truly free in that it is not an imposed formula, but the product of its own liberal aims. This he achieves not by putting forward pseudo-solutions to the ambiguities inherent in the liberal curriculum, or by pretending that such ambiguities do not exist, but by confronting them head on and subjecting them to rational deliberation aimed at finding accommodations that are not perfect, nor even necessarily the best, but those that would commend themselves to ethically and intellectually responsible people. His position stands not only as a clear and relevant statement on the question of liberal education in the late 20th century, but as one that bears the promise of pointing future deliberation in profitable directions. To borrow the words of the editors of Schwab's essays:

> The ideal of liberal education does linger. It might be that a conception of education that associates itself with conceptions of sociability, civility, and self can be restored. And if such restoration comes to pass, Schwab's essays and books will play an important part in the rediscovery of the meaning of these notions. He articulates a way of thinking which lets us see more clearly than does the way of any other contemporary thinker what thought about education *might* be and how it *might* be possible to give visions meaning. The

burden of his work is an invitation to the reader to participate in the search that he ventured.[66]

NOTES

1. Westbury, I., & Wilkof, N. J. (Eds.). (1978). *Science, curriculum and liberal education*. Chicago: University of Chicago Press.
2. Schwab, J. J. (1978). Science and civil discourse: The uses of diversity. In Westbury & Wilkof, *op. cit.*, p. 137.
3. Schwab, J. J. (1978). Eros and education: A discussion of one aspect of discussion. In Westbury & Wilkof, *op. cit.*, p. 125.
4. *Ibid.*, p. 106.
5. *Ibid.*, p. 109.
6. Science and civil discourse: The uses of diversity, *op. cit.*, p. 146. In this essay, Schwab dismisses the commonsense argument that, in view of the levels of ability that students currently exhibit, a program with such high ambitions would be a failure. " 'Common-sense' of the most rudimentary sort seems to tell us that students have all they can do to master the content of merely inculcative curricula. But the same apparently obvious facts and rudimentary common-sense spoke to the impossibility of widespread literacy when it was first suggested" (p. 147).
7. McKeon, Richard (1967). The battle of the books. In Wayne C. Booth (Ed.). *The knowledge most worth having*. Chicago: University of Chicago Press.
8. Rothblatt, Sheldon (1976). *Tradition and change in English liberal education: An essay in culture and history*. London: Faber & Faber.
9. McKeon, *op. cit.*, p. 174.
10. *Ibid.*, p. 183.
11. Rothblatt, *op. cit.*, p. 102.
12. *Ibid.*, p. 154.
13. *Ibid.*, pp. 100, 119.
14. McKeon, *op. cit.*, pp. 182, 183. The words quoted are those of the American Samuel Johnson (see Schneider, Herbert, & Schneider, Carol (Eds.). (1929). *Samuel Johnson, president of King's College, his career and writings*. New York: Columbia University Press). The distinction was a commonplace of the late medieval scholastic curriculum. It is interesting to see how neatly it blends with McKeon's own argument.
15. "Aristotle is almost entirely concerned to analyse the problems of the moral *agent*, while most contemporary moral philosophers seem to be primarily concerned to analyse the problems of the moral *judge* or critic" (Hampshire, Stuart (1949). Fallacies in moral philosophy. *Mind, 58*, p. 467).
16. *Op. cit.*, p. 176.
17. Hirst, P. H. (1965). Liberal education and the nature of knowledge. In R. D. Archambault (Ed.). *Philosophical analysis and education*. London: Routledge & Kegan Paul.
18. *Ibid.*, p. 113.
19. *Ibid.*, p. 116. Emphasis added.
20. *Ibid.*, p. 115.
21. *Ibid.*, p. 127.
22. "The heart of the problem of a general education is the continuance of the liberal and humane tradition . . . today, we are concerned with a general education—a liberal education—not for the relatively few, but for the multitude" (Harvard Committee Report

(1945). *General education in a free society.* Cambridge, MA: Harvard University Press, pp. viii, ix).

23. Hirst, *op. cit.*, p. 117.

24. Again, it is McKeon who encapsulates the distinction in a telling phrase, when he says of Aristotle's *Politics*, "Its purpose was practical, to lead men to perform good actions, not theoretic, to discover and demonstrate the final good" (*op. cit.*, p. 208). This conceptual separation of the practical and the theoretic is fundamental to Schwab's thinking on curriculum making.

25. Costello, William T. (1958). *The scholastic curriculum at early seventeenth-century Cambridge.* Cambridge, MA: Harvard University Press, p. 146.

26. See, for example, Knox, Samuel (1799). *An essay on the best system of liberal education adapted to the genius of the government of the United States.* Baltimore.

27. Rothblatt, *op. cit.*, p. 117.

28. Pitkin, H. F. (1967). *The concept of representation.* Berkeley, CA: University of California Press, p. 170.

29. "Education . . . in England is what the Universities choose to make it . . . This seems to me too great a power to be possessed by two corporations, however venerable and illustrious, especially since we know them to have grown up under very particular circumstances, and to be fortified by endowments against all modern influence, good or bad" (Farrar, F. W. (Ed.). (1867). *Essays on a liberal education.* London: Macmillan, p. 146).

30. Whewell, William (1845). *Of a liberal education in general, and with particular reference to the leading studies of the University of Cambridge.* London: Parker.

31. Farrar, *op. cit.*

32. Ker, I. T. (Ed.). (1976). *John Henry Newman: The idea of a university.* London: Oxford University Press, pp. 110, 111.

33. Even critics of the mainstream of discussion of liberal education accepted an elitist view of political leadership, and concentrated their strictures on the content of the liberal curriculum. An anonymous writer in the radical *Edinburgh Review* in 1868 stated: "The greatest danger to English institutions and to English society at the present time appears to us to consist in the fact that the education of the upper classes is not such as to qualify them to maintain the position they owe to their superior wealth or station" (Vol. 127, January–April, 1868, p. 165).

34. Rothblatt, *op. cit.*, p. 132.

35. See Dover Wilson, J. (Ed.). (1954). *Matthew Arnold, Culture and anarchy.* (1869). Reprint. Cambridge: Cambridge University Press, p. 18. Here Arnold is quoting, with approval, the words of Ernest Renan. His predilection for the phrase "sweetness and light" should not mislead us. Believing, as he did, that "without order there can be no society, and without society there can be no human perfection," he endorses the words of his famous father: "As for rioting, the old Roman way of dealing with *that* is always the right one: flog the rank and file, and fling the ring leaders from the Tarpeian Rock!" (Dover Wilson (1954). *Op. cit.*, p. 203–a passage that Arnold deleted from the 1875 edition). The phrase "sweetness and light" is, in fact, drawn from Swift's "Battle of the Books" and signifies Arnold's support for the ancients.

36. Boyd, Julian P., et al. (Eds.). (1950). *The papers of Thomas Jefferson.* Princeton: Princeton University Press, Vol. 2, p. 527.

37. Heffner, Richard D. (Ed.). (1956). *Alexis de Tocqueville, Democracy in America.* (1835). Reprint. New York: New American Library, p. 158.

38. *Ibid.*, p. 168.

39. Dover Wilson, *op. cit.*, p. 18. This also is a quote from Renan.

40. *Ibid.*, p. 114.

41. Simpson, William (1978). *Vision and reality: The evolution of American government*. London: Murray, p. 73.

42. Farrar, *op. cit.*, pp. 7, 9. Compare Arnold's cautionary reference to "America, that chosen home of newspapers and politics" (Dover Wilson, *op. cit.*, p. 19).

43. Dover Wilson, *op. cit.*, p. 22,

44. Rudolph, Frederick (1977). *Curriculum: A history of the American undergraduate course of study since 1636*. San Francisco: Jossey Bass, p. 99ff.

45. Wegener, Charles (1978). *Liberal education and the modern university*. Chicago: University of Chicago Press, p. 57.

46. Whewell, for example, although an advocate of inquiry and the progressive studies associated with it, had to insist that permanent studies "are the most important part of Education and must be mastered before the others are entered on" (Whewell, *op. cit.*, p. 21). Compare Farrar, *op. cit.*, p. 318.

47. Wegener, *op. cit.*, p. 57.

48. Oakeshott, Michael (1962). *Rationalism in politics and other essays*. London: Methuen, pp. 198, 199. The passage is quoted by Hutchins (Hutchins, Robert M. (1968). *The learning society*. London: Pall Mall, pp. 100, 101), and also by Hirst (*op. cit.*, p. 138).

49. Hutchins, Robert M. (1954). *Great books: The foundations of a liberal education*. New York, Simon & Schuster, pp. 7, 24.

50. See Hutchins (1954), *op. cit.*, pp. 62, 63. Hutchins persistently plays down the significance of individual differences. Compare "Politics . . . teaches us that we are remorselessly headed toward the unification of the world" (Hutchins, Robert M. (1953). *The conflict in education in a democratic society*. New York: Harper, p. 89). See also D'Urso, Salvatore (1978). The classical liberalism of Robert M. Hutchins. *Teachers College Record, 80,* 336–355.

51. Harvard Committee Report, *op. cit.*, p. 35. See also Bell, Daniel (1966). *The reforming of general education: The Columbia College experience*. New York: Columbia University Press. For the tension in American secondary education between equality and excellence, see Passow, A. Harry (1976). *Secondary education reform: Retrospect and prospect*. New York: Teachers College, Columbia University.

52. "If leisure and political power are a reason for liberal education, then everybody in America now has this reason" (Hutchins (1954), *op. cit.*, p. 47). Hutchins does not, however, advocate this for other, less developed societies except as an ultimate ideal.

53. Schwab. Science and civil discourse: the uses of diversity, *op. cit.*, p. 145.

54. *Ibid.*, p. 146.

55. *Ibid.*, p. 134.

56. McKeon, *op. cit.*, p. 175.

57. Costello, *op. cit.*, p. 64.

58. "The fault of scholasticism lay not in its building so towering a skyscraper, complete to the last bit of wiring and plumbing, but in its failure during the fifteenth, sixteenth, and early seventeenth centuries to produce teachers who could maintain the structure as a totality and forbear tinkering with the details" (Costello, *op. cit.*, p. 10).

59. Diehl, Carl (1978). *Americans and German scholarship 1770–1870*. New Haven, CT: Yale University Press, pp. 1, 148.

60. In spite of the casting of Aristotle on the side of the ancients in Swift's satire, McKeon claims that Aristotelean philosophy and criticism "as they emerge in . . . American education are clearly neoteric" (*op. cit.*, p. 191). For a recent attack on positivism by a Chicago scholar, see Booth, Wayne C. (1974). *Modern dogma and the rhetoric of assent*. Chicago: University of Chicago Press, and compare Schwab, J. J. (1969). *College curriculum and student protest*. Chicago: University of Chicago Press.

61. For a development of this point, see Fenstermacher, Gary D. (1980). The nature of science and its uses for education: Remarks on the philosophical import of Schwab's work. *Curriculum Inquiry, 10*, 191–197.

62. Whewell's ideas on teaching were connected with the existence at Cambridge of two distinct teaching systems: The college system and the professorial (university) system.

63. Eros and education: A discussion of one aspect of discussion, *op. cit.*. p. 105.

64. *Ibid.*, p. 110ff. This may be contrasted with the relative lack of comment on teaching among some exponents of the great conversation curriculum, and specifically with Hutchins characterization of childhood and youth as "these uninteresting and chaotic periods of life" (1954, *op. cit.*, p. 17).

65. *Ibid.*, p. 127.

66. Westbury, I., & Wilkof, N. J. (1978). Introduction. Westbury, I., & Wilkof, N. J. (Eds.), *op. cit.*, pp. 39, 40.

6

Does Schwab Improve on Tyler?

In the preceding chapters, I have reviewed an approach to curriculum that I have characterized through the use of terms such as deliberation, the method of the practical, and practical reasoning. I have claimed that it represents a distinctive way of conceptualizing and dealing with curriculum problems that differs on a fundamental level from other commonly promoted procedures for settling questions of what should be taught and learned. This claim has been disputed. Some commentators see a deliberative approach as simply a subvariant of a dominant perspective in curriculum theory, concerned with discussing and describing how curricular goals and objectives can be chosen and learning experiences devised to attain them. This was the line taken by Jackson in the introduction to his 1992 Handbook of curriculum research[1] *where, in a review of American curriculum theory over the previous 80 years, he presented the work of Bobbitt, Tyler, and Schwab as belonging in essentially the same tradition. I took up the challenge to make out a case for an alternative view in "Does Schwab improve on Tyler? A response to Jackson" which appeared in* Journal of Curriculum Studies, 25, 6, 1993, 499–510.*

The question, "Does Schwab improve on Tyler?" is Jackson's, not mine. My project here is not to show that Schwab is better than Tyler, but that he is different, and to try to explain how and why he is different.

The question, "Does Schwab improve on Tyler?" is posed by Philip Jackson in his introductory chapter to the *Handbook of Curriculum Research*, where he discusses how "university-based specialists [can] be of direct, practical help to classroom teachers and school administrators as the latter go about the day-to-day business of trying to improve the curriculum of schools"

(p. 21). It turns out that, for curriculum specialists, being helpful means, principally, advising on how curriculum decision making should be carried out, through acting as coordinators, developers, designers, or evaluators. Jackson examines the nature of this help-giving through a chronological account dealing mainly with the ideas of the American scholars Franklin Bobbitt, Ralph Tyler, and Joseph Schwab. What we have here is, essentially, a history of how curriculum specialists in the United States have thought about curriculum planning.[2]

Accounts that present a history of ideas can stress continuity or discontinuity, evolution or revolution. Discussion of ideas about cosmology, for example, can point to ways in which Newton built on the work of Copernicus, and Einstein, in turn, built on the work of Newton. On the other hand, it can equally well stress what was radically new about their thinking. Jackson chooses to emphasize evolution rather than revolution. In his story, Bobbitt, Tyler, and Schwab take their places as proponents of three versions of the dominant perspective at different stages of its development. The perspective in question is one which sees the task of curriculum as being to decide what goals or objectives the school should seek to attain and then to devise learning experiences that promise to achieve those goals and objectives. Tyler's answer to the question of how these tasks are to be conceived is seen as being more advanced than that offered by Bobbitt, "if only because . . . it seeks to be more comprehensive . . . and more refined" (p. 21). But does Schwab improve on Tyler? This question, which appears as a section heading in Jackson's chapter, does not receive a clear answer. On the whole, Schwab is depicted as drifting away from the standard set by Tyler; he is "further removed . . . from the day-to-day business of school affairs," his "piecemeal approach does not begin with an animating vision" (pp. 26–27), and his style of writing reveals "disturbing contradictions." In so far as he introduces new conceptions (e.g., through "his insistence that improvement be focused on local problems"), these reflect ideas that are already "immanent in the Tyler rationale" (pp. 30–31). But the important point to note is the way in which the question is framed. Jackson does not choose to ask whether Schwab is different from Tyler, but whether he "improves" on him, thus assuming that Schwab's view and Tyler's view are entirely compatible with one another. Of course, as he points out, there is one way in which the approaches under discussion are decidedly similar: they all construe the role of the curriculum specialist as being to advise practitioners. But is this an important truth, or merely a trivial one?

In favor of Jackson's view that Bobbitt, Tyler, and Schwab represent three versions of the dominant perspective, it could be argued that, where theories of social action are concerned, what is possible is constrained by the intrinsic and inevitable nature of the material to be acted on: that, just as classrooms in North America, Europe, or Australasia turn out to be similar-

looking places, so, what it is feasible to do by way of devising and implementing curricula turns out to be much the same the world over, and much
the same over time. This would be a valid point if Jackson chose to stress
only the practical aspects of the dominant perspective. However, although
its capacity to fit with the ways of working of teachers and administrators
is a central theme in his account, he also lays much emphasis on the
idealistic aspects of his three different versions of the model. Bobbitt, he
points out, speaks of a new vision, while Tyler's rationale depends on the
articulation of an educational and social philosophy. In this respect, Jackson
judges them to be superior to Schwab who, because of his "focus on the
concrete and the immediate . . . makes [his] curriculum planning groups
sound as though they would function more as troubleshooters than like
educationalists who were propelled by a vision of what the schools might
become" (p. 31). Thus, an important criterion for judging the relative worth
of the ideas of Bobbitt, Tyler, and Schwab is how far they are driven by a
vision of what might be. This suggests that real alternatives are indeed
possible, and, if that is the case, we are not then forced to assume that the
nature of planning theory aimed at helping teachers and administrators is
inevitably constrained to one basic model. So, rather than asking "does
Schwab improve on Tyler?", we might instead pose the question "how is
Schwab different from Tyler?"

But is this an important question to ask? I believe that it is of great
importance because we can turn to many serious critiques of the dominant
perspective, some of which suggest that its deficiencies are not to be remedied by extension, elaboration, or emendation of the Bobbitt–Tyler model.[3]
Jackson himself discusses these widespread dissatisfactions, and points,
without great conviction, to recent alternative proposals. What he does *not*
do because of the frame within which he chooses to present his history of
ideas, is to consider whether Schwab himself might not offer exactly the
kind of ideas that could answer some of the criticisms leveled at the established school of curriculum planning theory. He is unable to do this since,
if Schwab represents the dominant perspective, he cannot also be the means
of replacing it.

HOW CURRICULUM SPECIALISTS
HAVE THOUGHT ABOUT PLANNING:
AN ALTERNATIVE HISTORY

Writing a history of ideas is not simply a matter of telling a story. The
character of the story is determined by the application, conscious or otherwise, of some theory of the nature of the ideas under discussion. Jackson
stresses ways in which ideas are represented in action, and the action on

which he focuses is advice giving to classroom teachers and school administrators. Bobbitt, Tyler, and Schwab, he suggests, were all in the advice-giving business. They saw themselves as "trying to help groups of practitioners who want to improve the curriculum of their schools" (p. 32). In Jackson's story, the arrival on the scene of a new perspective has to await the emergence of specialists who move out of the traditional role of external expert and work inside the schools, or even with individual teachers, in a shared enterprise of curriculum improvement. "These two strategies," Jackson explains, "entail marked changes in the traditional relationship between the university-based specialist and the practitioner" (p. 33). His account does not envisage the arrival of new theoretical paradigms *within* the time-honored form of expert–teacher or expert–administrator relationships.

Personally, I do not find this criterion for writing a history of ideas at all satisfactory. The question of what Bobbitt, Tyler, or Schwab, or their new era successors did with school districts, schools, or teachers is elusive. In order to answer it in any real sense, we would need materials such as oral histories, case studies, or biographies (and availability of these might, I suspect, lead us to conclude that some specialists associated with the dominant perspective worked a good deal more closely with schools and teachers than those of the recent past who, for their own rhetorical purposes, have claimed kinship with practitioners). More secure as a basis for producing a history of ideas about curriculum planning are the published texts of the specialists in question, the contents of which can be set against some categorization of proposals for how social theory can be translated into social action.

An analysis of ways of linking thought and action is offered by McKeon.[4] He suggests three kinds of philosophies of the theory–practice connection: the dialectic, the problematic, and the logistic. He also points out that action does not need to be connected to theory; it can be organized in ways that derive future action from past action without the intervention of reasoning based on a priori abstractions. This he refers to as the *operational mode*. McKeon's classification provides an alternative basis on which a history of ideas about planning can be constructed. If we use this as an organizing principle, what answer do we get to the question of Schwab's relationship to Tyler? Do both belong within the same category, so that we can judge how far Schwab improves on, or falls short of Tyler? Or do Schwab's texts describe a theory of planning that is categorically different from that of Tyler, and should therefore be assessed as an alternative to it?

To take the case of Tyler first, we can confidently reject the idea that his conception of the theory–practice relationship is dialectical. *Dialecticism* rests on acceptance of interactions of a cyclical nature between theory and practice, involving thesis, antithesis, and synthesis. We find nothing like this in Tyler's writings. The *problematic* mode, on the other hand, conceives of theory and practice as separate, but presenting similar characters, since both involve the identification of problems, the search for data relating to problems, and the application of method to solve problems. Jackson himself rejects any suggestion that Tyler's approach is problem centered. In his discussion of the question "does Schwab improve on Tyler?", he implies that Tyler's notion of planning is superior because a "problem-centered, as opposed to a vision-centered conception of curriculum improvement . . . has nothing to set it in motion beyond the recognition of an immediate difficulty or the expectation that such difficulties are bound to occur" (p. 31). This leaves open the possibility that Tyler's conception is to be understood, within McKeon's schema, as either logistic or operational. The logistic mode works through a total separation of theory from practice. Theory is understood to consist of scientifically established knowledge, while practice requires the assertion of control over events that are too complex and unpredictable to be encompassed by the methods of science. Therefore, connection between the two has to be achieved through the development of theories of practice. The paradigm case is engineering. On the one hand we have mathematical, physical, and chemical knowledge, and on the other, materials and processes on which it is to be brought to bear. The predictable world of scientific theory is enabled to guide action on the uncertain material world through the application of the principles and methods of engineering, which are a collection of theories of practice.

Does this describe what Tyler is doing? Certainly, a case could be made out for it. Expressed in its simplest terms, the dominant perspective calls, as we have seen, for decisions on what goals or objectives the school should seek to attain, and then for the design of learning experiences that promise to achieve those goals and objectives. We might see the establishment of goals and objectives as the production of scientifically based knowledge about what should be done, which then has to be translated, through techniques that have the character of engineering, into actions (learning experiences), which promise (i.e., with uncertain probability) to bring about the outcomes that the methods of science have shown to be desirable. But, before assessing this proposition, we should note that our readiness to see Tyler's planning theory as logistic may owe much to the work of a number of more recent contributors to the field, such as Bloom and Pratt. Bloom, for example, offers a taxonomic approach to the statement of learning objectives, and an account of mastery learning that clearly aspire to scientific status, while Pratt draws on systems theory and explicitly describes curriculum planning as a form of engineering.[5] However, Tyler's text *Basic Principles of Curriculum and Instruction* precedes such overtly logistic accounts of planning theory by upwards of 15 years. We must leave on one side the use that later writers have made of his idea that the work of planning is to translate scientifically based knowledge into learning activities, and rely exclusively on his own text when we make our judgment about the character of Tyler's description of the knowledge source that should drive the planning process.[6]

WHAT SHOULD DRIVE CURRICULUM MAKING? TYLER'S ACCOUNT

What, according to Tyler, provides the knowledge base, external to the everyday concerns of schools and school systems, to drive curriculum planning? This knowledge, he says, should consist of educational objectives. But where do these objectives come from? They are provided by two sources, one of which is subdivided into two parts. The first source is studies of learners and studies of life outside the school, and the second is suggestions from experts who, for this purpose, are subject-matter specialists. The objectives that are generated in this way will, however, be too numerous and contradictory to be translated into practical activities, so they will first of all be filtered by screens consisting of philosophical and psychological principles. What are we to make of this? Is Tyler using a logistic or an operational approach to the linking of theory and practice? Objective knowledge is invoked through the conduct of studies. But these are not studies intended to produce disciplinary knowledge; they are studies that categorize and quantify existing practice and behavior. The source of suggestions is unclear. Subject matter specialists may base their recommendations on theoretical insights, or they may simply repeat prescriptions that reflect current practices. What is clear is that it is representatives of already established curriculum content areas who are to be consulted. The only way in which disciplinary, nonschool knowledge is manifestly involved is through the contribution it makes to the screening of objectives already generated from other sources.

From this account, it appears that Tyler is working in an operational rather than a logistic mode. Although disciplinary knowledge plays a part in the formulation of the theory, which is to drive the planning process, the principal source of ideas for curriculum activities is what is already being done in schools, or what is already happening in the outside world, which could provide objectives for the practice of schooling. This seems generally consistent with the tone of Tyler's book, which sets out to give advice on how to go about "viewing, analyzing, and interpreting the curriculum program of an educational institution."[7] Tyler is not concerned either to formulate a tight disciplinary base for the construction of a theory of practice, such as the logistic mode would demand, nor to scrutinize philosophically the nature of practice as would writers following a problematic perspective. He is truly an advice giver. He assumes that the people he is addressing are already familiar with the milieux within which their work must be done, and knowledgeable about methods and procedures. He does not risk dividing them into believers and nonbelievers by urging them to assent to any particular set of philosophical principles. An operational mode is comfortable one for those whose main concern is to help practitioners do better what they are already doing.

At this point, a difficulty has to be faced. If Tyler's approach to curriculum planning is operational, how does this square with Jackson's claim that his proposals are tinged with the idealism of social and educational philosophy? I think the answer lies in the scope that exists for confusion between idealism and modernism. At the time when Tyler wrote his book, modernism represented a social ideal. New methods and new ways of working were to be preferred. The old was thought of as lacking any sanction other than that of habit. The modern was based on research and on rationalizations of procedure. To talk of studies, objectives, and learning experiences was to be modern and, therefore, to be idealistic (and the same argument could be made about Bobbitt). True idealism, however, demands subscription to a morally or intellectually determined view of the world, which then becomes directive of actions taken within it, and excludes the possibility that these will result from operationally based forms of decision making.

WHAT SHOULD DRIVE CURRICULUM MAKING? SCHWAB'S ACCOUNT

Consideration of ideals in relation to the planning of curriculum provides a useful point of transition to the conception of the joining of theory to practice that Schwab represents. His method of uniting thought and action is inquiry-based, that is, focused on problem solving. Jackson considers that the focus on problems does not give Schwab's conception a fundamentally different character from that of Tyler's rationale. To start with problems is simply another way into the advice-giving process. But, he suggests, it does involve a retreat from ideals because in that case, curriculum improvement "has nothing to set it in motion beyond the recognition of an immediate difficulty or the expectation that such difficulties are bound to occur" (p. 31). This, to my mind, is an unwarranted assumption. Why should we suppose that if the problems of curriculum arise from "conditions that we *wish* were otherwise and we think . . . *can be made* to be otherwise,"[8] these conditions will inevitably relate to minor difficulties, so that "improvement will almost always be piecemeal?" No doubt, curriculum problems of a minor nature will need to be addressed, but I do not think Schwab intends that the full weight of large-scale deliberation should be brought to bear on them. Processes of deliberation generate principles and criteria for dealing with such operating problems. Provided that, in any given instance, we are alert to possible deficiencies, they can serve until situations arise where the conditions that we wish were otherwise clearly call for a fundamental reappraisal. When these conditions do occur, there is every likelihood that the problems to be faced will be major ones. While we would be right to believe that Schwab would prefer the difficulties that curriculum confronts to be of less than crisis proportions, we should note that the occasion of his advocacy of the problematic mode in his practical papers was his feeling that a crisis did indeed exist, and note also that, in support of this opinion, he cited "incoherence of the curriculum, failure and discontinuity in actual schooling."[9] It seems that this championship of the language of the practical was not in the interest of clearing up small problems. As Jackson points out in his chapter, "what Schwab does in his essays is to offer a stinging critique of the field of curriculum" (p. 28). This hardly sounds like a way of responding to a few minor and local difficulties.

But how is deliberation able to deal with problems of considerable magnitude if, as Jackson claims, it lacks an animating vision? Here we face an opposite paradox from the one we identified in the case of Tyler. Tyler is represented in Jackson's account as more idealistic than I believe him to be, but Schwab is depicted as lacking in idealism. In the case of Tyler, I have suggested that there may be a confusion of idealism with modernism. But what of Schwab's idealism? Why is this underestimated?

Schwab's place in Jackson's history of ideas rests on a reading of his four practical papers. But proper attention to his thought requires that these be seen within a wider context. At the very least, we need to take into account his essays on teaching and on liberal education. Preferably, we should also refer to his one book—*College Curriculum and Student Protest*—and to his essay "Education and the state: learning community."[10] Schwab was, par excellence, an essayist who, like many essayists, wrote from an established philosophical position that enabled him to treat a variety of topics in a consistent manner. But this position emerges with clarity only as we range over many examples of his work. Schwab himself was disingenuous in claiming, at the outset of "The practical 4" that "this paper stands on its own . . . by virtue of summaries, where necessary, of points made in earlier papers."[11] The already published comment of Westbury and Wilkof was more apposite: "There is in his writing a complex back-and-forth between the particular and the more general so that grasp of any one essay requires appreciation by the reader of other essays, and of problems already discussed and closed."[12] Examination of the wider context of the practical papers indicates a number of ways in which they must be seen as driven by an animating vision. In the first place, it appears that Schwab's adoption of a problematic mode for connecting theory and practice represents a moral as much as an intellectual choice. Far from promoting some kind of unambitious pragmatism, as Jackson suggests, Schwab, in advocating the method of the practical, endorses the moral principle that decisions about action should result from deliberation involving the widest possible representation of those who can contribute to understanding of the problem that action is to solve, and of those who will be affected by the consequences of that action. Politically he is choosing polity over "merely mechanical democracy, or worse still oligarchy or despotism."[13]

Second, and linked with this, Schwab has a vision of community. Education of the individual has meaning only in so far as it involves internalization, though practical experience, of community—understood to "consist of propensities toward action and feeling, and to be concerned with the relations of persons."[14] His proposals for how processes of curriculum planning should be carried forward through deliberative groups have to be seen as reflecting the complementary propensities to "purpose in common" and "honor difference" that lie at the heart of his conception of the ideal community.[15]

Third, and again consistently with his total philosophy, Schwab repeatedly defends a notion of liberal education that conceives its goals in appetitive terms—knowledge, power, affection—rather than in the static categories of measurable objectives. Liberal education, like curriculum planning, was, for Schwab, a process transacted by and for moral agents within the setting of a community whose values it reflected.[16] Commenting on these ideas Westbury and Wilkof concluded: "He articulates a way of thinking that lets us see more clearly than does the way of any other contemporary thinker what thought about education *might* be and how it *might* be possible to give visions meaning."[17] Consideration of the practical papers in isolation might provide no firm corrective to the view that curriculum planning, in Schwab's account, is driven, rather haphazardly, by the adventitious and often minor problems of schools and of educational jurisdictions. But, as we become familiar with the total scope of Schwab's texts, it is apparent that, while problems provide the occasion for the exercise of the method of the practical, the method itself represents a principled pursuit of ideals. Schwab's position is that ideals only become real in action. He rejects the Platonic notion that they exist, in some substantive sense, apart from events and actions. In the same way that the results of liberal education, as he construed it, only become visible when those who have experience of it are placed in the position of having to exercise operative judgment, so the forces that should drive curriculum only manifest themselves when there are real-world problems to be solved. Interpretation of Schwab's work as visionary in character sits much more comfortably with his occasionally passionate utterances, on which Jackson remarks, than does depiction of it as a piecemeal response to the concrete and the immediate.

CONCLUSION

To ask whether Schwab improves on Tyler makes sense within the history of ideas that Jackson presents. However, as I have attempted to show, there is an alternative history within which it does not make sense. Instead of seeing Tyler and Schwab as representing successive endeavors to develop the potential of the dominant model, we can view Schwab's problematic approach as an espousal of an alternative planning theory that sets out to remedy some of the deficiencies of operational accounts such as those offered by Bobbitt and Tyler. This is not the place for an extensive review of critiques of the dominant model. As Hlebowitsh[18] and others have pointed out, these have centered on two aspects of its nature: first, its unduly narrow focus on curriculum objectives, and, second, its subservience to existing frames of reference, and especially those defined by educational bureaucracies. These are the kinds of problems that are inherent in approaches to planning that are driven by operationalism. Its methods tend toward simplicity. In the absence of underlying theoretical commitments, against which practical prescriptions have to be checked, operational planners can appeal to the commonsense notion that complexity is inimical to effective action. Obviously, there are ways of achieving this simplicity that appeal even more to common sense than one that demands that action be based on objectives, but, as we have seen, Bobbitt and Tyler were committed to goals of modernism and wanted to find a methodology that was, at least to some extent, forward-looking. And when we come to the matter of the major sources of curriculum objectives, we find that these were, in Tyler's account, current practice and the opinions of subject matter experts. This being the case, it was very likely that curricula derived from these objectives would reflect values internal to the structures of education systems.

If we accept this argument, we must reject the construction put by Jackson on Schwab's remark that the conception of curricular method proposed in the first practical paper is immanent in the Tyler rationale.[19] Jackson takes this to mean that Schwab is putting himself within the same tradition as Bobbitt and Tyler. An alternative interpretation of Schwab's footnote to the first practical paper is that implementation of Tyler's rationale requires deliberation, but that Tyler does not raise deliberation as a method standing in need of analytical attention. In keeping with his operational stance, he assumes that skills of deliberation are routinely available and do not have to be talked about. Schwab's plea, in "The practical: A language for curriculum" is that this is exactly what *most* needs to be talked about. Tyler and Schwab, then, cannot be directly compared because they are setting out to do different things.

This might be seen as a merely intellectual point, but it leads to an important practical conclusion. If Schwab is not to be directly compared with Tyler, then, instead of dismissing him as someone who worked within the dominant perspective, but failed to advance it, we should examine how far elaboration of his alternative perspective can offer ways of avoiding the deficiencies that critics of the dominant perspective have targeted. Jackson himself provides us with incentives for extending and refining Schwab's work. In the case of Tyler, he suggests, not much remains to be done. *Basic Principles of Curriculum and Instruction* still stands as a comprehensive guide to the methods of the dominant perspective. In the case of Schwab, however, there are, he reminds us, evident shortcomings that need to be remedied. These can be seen as the converse of the kinds of criticisms that have been levelled at Tyler. While Tyler can, perhaps, be seen as over simple in his advocacy of the merits of educational objectives, Schwab's problematic mode tends to complexity and even obscurity. Although Tyler is, perhaps, too close to teachers and administrators, Schwab is remote and insufficiently comprehending of the conditions under which they have to work.

My reason for taking issue with Jackson's history of ideas about curriculum planning is that, while these criticisms of Schwab are well targeted, he misleads us by implying that the way to repair them is to refer back to the better version of the dominant perspective offered by Tyler. On the contrary, I believe that one way ahead for those who want to think about or act on these issues is to ask how the problematic approach advocated by Schwab can be developed as an *alternative* to the dominant perspective. First of all, it needs to be rescued from the obscurity in which he tended to cloak it, without sacrificing its complexities and ambiguities, which I see as realistic. Second, it needs to be awakened from its innocence of the nature of institutions, which I recognize to be profoundly unrealistic.

As an advice giver Schwab falls short, not because his advice is bad, but because it is not expressed in terms to which practical people readily respond. I have always found that teachers, who work closest to the business of curriculum, find the general thrust of Schwab's ideas quite realistic. Those who have daily experience of classrooms know that educating is a complicated and ambiguous activity. It is those who are more remote—principals and bureau people—who are more likely to respond to the apparent simplicity of the idea of placing heavy reliance on working with objectives. But, as Jackson point out, the language of the practical papers can be impenetrable to seekers after advice. Whether the answer is a Beginner's Guide to Schwab I doubt. More to the point, perhaps, is that those who have time to read widely in his works and think about them should communicate their understanding through workshops and discussions.

But if teachers are to be the litmus test of the worth of Schwab's problematic method, then we must also be attentive to their comment that, while his ideas are good, and he does understand teaching, he simply does not know how schools work. Of course, given the character of his career, it would be rather surprising if he did know how schools work. His primary experience in education was his engagement for over 50 years with the University of Chicago, while his involvement with public schooling was limited to his participation, as chairman of the committee on teacher preparation, in the Biological Sciences Curriculum Study.[20] But why should we assume that the problematic approach to curriculum planning is fatally flawed just because its most visible advocate had little experience of schools? Should we not rather strive to see how the method of the practical can be understood in ways that permit the nature of institutions and the institutional life to be comprehended within it? What this means, essentially, is unpacking the commonplace of the milieus which, in Schwab's practical papers, is called upon to do a huge amount of work, encompassing the classroom, the school, the community, the polity, and, ultimately, the world.

This is not the place to embark on the vast enterprise of conceptualization and elucidation that this would require. The main agenda is to find ways in which the quasiprivate character of the process of deliberation as depicted by Schwab can be made compatible with the clearly public framing of the work of schools. Some writers are optimistic that progress can be made along these lines. Westbury, for example, suggests that an authentically deliberative and problematic approach can be envisaged that embraces the work of centers and jurisdictions as well as the practical engagements with curriculum problems of schools and teachers. He concludes his discussion of a possible model for such a reconciliation with the observation that "the image of deliberation that follows from such a model is one which respects the character of *public* education: it gives form to the notions of the 'public', of public goods, and of authoritative public goals. It does not retreat into the small, self-contained worlds that are inherently 'private', individualistic, and even élitist. It shows a way in which the large world of the 'public' and the small world of face-to-face community can come together by way of a process of substantive interaction that is inherently deliberative."[21] As well as considering that deliberation has to take account of *different levels* where imperatives of practice or institution may be legitimately dominant, I believe that the character of curriculum deliberation should also be drawn so that arguments stemming from both practice and institution are confronted *at all levels*. This I have recently tried to do through reexamination of the curriculum commonplaces.[22]

Efforts to extend and refine ideas of inquiry and of the practical, such as those to which I have referred, are undertaken in the belief that Schwab's work is importantly different from that of Tyler, especially in his presentation of curriculum planning as a method that is continuously revised through its engagements with its subject matter. The essence of a problematic approach to planning and decision making is that what is thought and done reflects the best understanding that can be obtained, at any given moment, of a unique context. The final word is never said. This contrasts with the conception of a dominant perspective, which can be brought, through a process of refinement in its procedures, to a point where some more or less final statement can be made about how advice giving on curriculum matters should be conducted. It is easy to point to superficial similarities in the two positions; it is also the case, as I hope I have demonstrated, that at a more fundamental level, they are very different in character and spirit.

NOTES

1. Jackson, P. W. (Ed.). (1992). *Handbook of curriculum research*. New York: Macmillan.
2. It is a truncated account in that, following the convention of American curriculum history, it begins with Franklin Bobbitt, who was the leading proponent of scientific curriculum making in the early part of this century (most of his career was spent at the University of Chicago where he was Tyler's doctoral advisor. He is best known for his book *The Curriculum* (Boston: Houghton Mifflin, 1918)). In his final section, Jackson moves abroad to consider work done from the mid-1960s onward in the U.K. and Canada, but this is of only marginal relevance to the argument of the present chapter.
3. For a recent review, see Hlebowitsh, P. S. (1992). Amid behavioural and behaviouristic objectives: Reappraising appraisals of the Tyler rationale. *Journal of Curriculum Studies, 24*, 533–547. Hlebowitsh usefully draws attention to ways in which critiques of Tyler have been aimed at things that he never asserted. For example, he did not say that planning *must* begin from objectives. The argument of the present chapter rests on his claim that it *can* begin from objectives.
4. McKeon, Richard (1952). Philosophy and action. *Ethics, 62*, 79–100.
5. Pratt, D. (1980). *Curriculum design and development*. New York: Harcourt Brace, p. 9.
6. Hlebowitsh, *op. cit.*, p. 547.
7. Tyler, R. W. (1949). *Basic principles of curriculum and instruction*. Chicago: University of Chicago Press, p. 1.
8. Schwab, J. J. (1978). The practical: A language for curriculum. In I. Westbury & N. J. Wilkof (Eds.). *Science, curriculum and liberal education*. Chicago: University of Chicago Press, p. 289.
9. *Ibid.*, p. 287.
10. Schwab, J. J. (1969). *College curriculum and student protest*. Chicago: University of Chicago Press, and (1976) Education and the state: Learning community. In R. M. Hutchins & M. J. Adler (Eds.). *The great ideas today* (pp. 234–271). Chicago: Encyclopedia Britannica.
11. Schwab, J. J. (1983). The practical 4: Something for curriculum professors to do. *Curriculum Inquiry, 13*, p. 239.
12. Westbury, I., & Wilkof, N. J. (1978). Introduction. Westbury & Wilkof, *op. cit.*, p. 2.
13. Reid, William A. (1984). Curriculum, community, and liberal education: A response to 'The practical 4'. *Curriculum Inquiry, 14*, p. 109.
14. Schwab (1976), *op. cit.*, p. 236.
15. *Ibid.*, p. 246.
16. See, "Schwab's conception of liberal education" in this volume.
17. Westbury & Wilkof, *op. cit.*, p. 40.

18. *Op. cit.*
19. The practical: A language for curriculum, *op. cit.*, p. 320.
20. Westbury & Wilkof, *op. cit.*, pp. 1, 24.
21. Westbury, I. (1994). Deliberation and the improvement of schooling. In J. T. Dillon (Ed.). *Deliberation in education and society*. Norwood, NJ: Ablex, p. 63.
22. Reid, William A. (1994). *The pursuit of curriculum: Schooling and the public interest*. Norwood, NJ: Ablex.

PART

II

CURRICULUM AS INSTITUTION

Thus far, discussion of curriculum has been focused mainly upon its practical aspects. Curriculum is practical, in a philosophical sense, because it is about action, and choice of action, within the perspective of traditions of practice clustering around the activity of teaching. Teaching involves not only skill and knowledge but also assumption of the ethical responsibilities that go with care for the interests of clients, and adherence to professional standards of conduct. But though curriculum has need of teaching, teaching can survive without curriculum. Teaching has been carried on, throughout the ages, independently of schools and school systems, or colleges and systems of higher education. Curriculum, on the other hand, is not imaginable without an institutional apparatus. The key characteristics of curriculum—structure, sequence, and completion[1]—cannot exist outside an institutional framework: institutions structure learning in ways that reflect some wider reality. For example they operationalize some concept of general or liberal education; they determine generally applicable sequences of learning—perhaps that some topics in mathematics are more appropriately learned before others; and they define what counts as satisfactory completion of a learning program—criteria will be specified for promotion to a higher grade, or for the award of degrees or diplomas. Not only do institutions engage in structuring, determining, and defining, they also embody the means for ensuring that what happens under their auspices will generally reflect the structuring, determining, and defining that they have promulgated. However, realization of this depends on the cooperation of a teaching force.

Thus it appears that the two faces of curriculum—practice and institution—collaborate with one another. The institution provides a setting within which teaching can flourish, and the practices associated with teaching offer a means by which institutional goals can be achieved. Yet, from another point of view, institution and practice are in conflict: "institutions and practices characteristically form a single causal order in which the ideals and creativity of the practice are always vulnerable to the acquisitiveness of the institution, in which the cooperative care for common goods of the practice are always vulnerable to the competitiveness of the institution."[2] Thus, understanding of curriculum depends not only on appreciation of its two faces, but also on insight into the complex relationship between them that can be sometimes rewarding, sometimes fraught with difficulty.

The following chapters investigate the concept of institution in relation to curriculum. Chapter 7, *The Institutional Context of Curriculum Deliberation*, looks back 10 years to the publication of *Thinking about the Curriculum*, and examines ways in which that statement about curriculum had been neglectful of the idea of institution.

Chapter 8, *The Problem of Curriculum Change*, sets out a theory of the organizational aspects of institutions, intended to explore how curriculum deliberation, as a source of ideas for change, fits with nature of the context within which change is to take place.

The analysis of schooling and curriculum as organization is extended in chap. 9, *Curricular Topics as Institutional Categories*, to consider how institutions are embedded in communities that play a key role in shaping, and giving meaning to their activities.

To understand as fully as possible how curriculum change occurs, we need to move beyond theoretical formulations, to investigate how it has come about in specific historical circumstances. Chapter 10, *Curriculum Change and the Evolution of Educational Constituencies,* attempts to do this by tracing the historical evolution of the upper secondary school curriculum in England in the 19th century. Consideration of this example points to the necessity of accounting for the interconnection between classroom (or, in this instance, sometimes schoolroom) practice and the institutional images of education to which practice approximates. One possible link is provided by the idea of educational constituencies that foster images of curriculum and look for their reproduction in the schools; or that alternatively, are persuaded of the potential significance for them of inventions (such as classrooms) promoted by the schools.

On the Origins of the Institutional Categories of Schooling, chap. 11, returns in a more systematic way to the question of how and why educational categories become universal. Its thesis is that changes in the clientele for particular forms of schooling, and especially changes that incorporate new and less well-informed publics raise a demand for reassurance that the organization of schooling is a true reflection of a constituency's image of what should be happening. This reassurance is provided by visible implementation of the universal inventions that are thought to supply evidence of categorical conformity.

Finally, questions of how processes of deliberation should take account of the institutional aspects of curriculum provide the theme of chap. 12, *The Institutional Character of the Curriculum of Schooling*. For deliberation on the curriculum to be effective it has to be capable of building a fruitful alliance between, on the one hand, its own characteristic preoccupation with tradition, with ideals, and with exploration and, on the other, institutional tendencies to engage with forward planning, with practicalities, and with predictability.

NOTES

1. See, Reid, William A. (1994). *The pursuit of curriculum: Schooling and the public interest.* Norwood, NJ: Ablex, pp. 36, 103–106.
2. MacIntyre, A. (1981). *After virtue: A study in moral theory.* London: Duckworth, p. 181.

7

The Institutional Context
of Curriculum Deliberation

This chapter was given as an invited address to the Professors of Curriculum at the American Educational Research Association Annual Meeting in 1988, where I was asked to reflect on how my perception of curriculum questions had changed over the 10 years since the publication of Thinking about the curriculum. *It subsequently appeared in* Journal of Curriculum and Supervision, *4, 1, 3–16.*

In the course of the 1980s, fundamental changes occurred in the public perception of curriculum. As national budgetary policies tightened in both Europe and the United States, what was taught in schools came, as I had predicted in Thinking about the curriculum, *under close public and political scrutiny.[1] What I had failed to predict was the nature of the new arena that would emerge. In particular, it became obvious that previous confinement of curriculum theorizing to a small circle of professionals had led to an excessive emphasis on the technical aspects of devising learning programs, while questions about the institutional and political contexts within which such programs are planned and implemented had suffered neglect.*

I

The thoughts in this chapter were prompted by a reconsideration of my book *Thinking About the Curriculum*,[2] which was published in 1978. As I looked at it again, my feelings were both positive and negative: positive in that the book seemed more coherent than I had suspected in terms of the message it carried, but negative in that, from a vantage point 10 years later, the message appeared to be seriously incomplete. Before venturing on an analysis of the incompleteness, which is my present agenda, I'll first of all say something about what the text was attempting to do at the time of its composition.

Thinking About the Curriculum was an invitation to the field of curriculum studies to adopt a certain kind of identity, which I will expand on shortly, and to look at this identity in terms of a variety of facets of curriculum activity: research, planning, policymaking, and so on. I suppose the neatest way to sum it up is to say that it offered an exegesis of Schwab's pregnant remarks in "The practical: A language for curriculum"[3] that the field of curriculum was moribund, that what was needed was a redirection toward the practical, and that deliberation was the method of the practical. My puzzle, which I tried to answer in the book, was about what moving to the practical would mean in terms of the activities of the curriculum—that is, research, the subject of chapter 3, planning or decision making (chap. 4), and curriculum innovation (chap. 5). These, it is to be noted, are the traditional commonplaces of curriculum text writing (although with the omission of implementation) because I felt that respect for the idea of the practical meant it should not be separated from planning and evaluation since it too took its place as a view of planning, which saw it as the cyclical revision of proposals rather than as the production of finished blueprints.

But first I had to say why my puzzle was an important one because, if you think that the idea of the practical is significant, you should have practical reasons for believing that. My practical reason was that, in the late 1970s, I felt that education in general, and curriculum in particular, was beginning to assume a different place in the estimation of governments, nations, and publics. The first chapter of *Thinking About the Curriculum* began: "The 1970's are the decade of curriculum crisis: what could previously be left to the bureaucrats and the professionals is now a matter of acute public concern."[4] What was the nature of this crisis? From the vantage point of the 1980s we can, of course, see much more clearly what the issues were. At the time, attention was focused on the immediate problems for educators that arose from falling student enrollments, and a withdrawal of apparently impoverished governments from provision of the lavish resources that had characterized the earlier postwar period. Now, however, we are better placed to discern some of the deeper movements that lay behind the obvious operating problems of school systems, and we can appreciate in a more fundamental way why, in the 1970s, the work of education and curriculum ceased to be the prerogative of bureaucrats and professionals and moved into wider and different arenas of discussion and decision making. We can also appreciate why these discussions and decisions were specifically targeted on questions of curriculum.

Anyone whose education took place in the 1960s or earlier grew up with the idea that state education systems were fundamental and important expressions of national consciousness and national identity. In fully fledged form, they were still the carriers of the kind of mission given to the infant systems by U.S. state constitutions: to preserve democratic ideals and the revolutionary spirit. Because, by definition, schools and education systems were a public good, the policy imperative was essentially a simple one: how to make education available to more and more children for more and more years. The postwar national reports in the United Kingdom—Crowther, Robbins, and Newsom[5]—made much reference to enrollment but little to curriculum, while projects in the United States, such as Headstart, which were designed to check student drop out, asked few questions about what it was good to learn, focusing instead on ways and means of making existing curriculums more accessible.

Only a few years later, however, the first signs began to appear that the foundations of this system—its very status as a public good—were beginning to be questioned. Gallup polls in the United States showed declining confidence in the public schools. In the United Kingdom, the emerging voice of the New Right, through publications such as the "Black Papers,"[6] began to cast doubt on the desirability of funding schools that were not publicly accountable for the curriculums they taught. These deeper issues were being pushed to the fore by the transient phenomena of economic stringency and falling enrollments. If schooling was no longer one of the central means by which the modern state affirmed its character and ambitions to its own citizens, if it was now to be seen more as a delivery system for a product, then questions had to be asked about the nature of that product. This, of course, put the spotlight on curriculum and ensured that issues of what should be taught, how, and to whom could no longer be the sole preserve of teachers and administrators on the inside of schools and education.

As I said in 1978, "Crisis is creating a new arena for the resolution of curriculum problems. An arena which will offer new roles to public and to professionals alike. But to invite public discussion and debate is one thing. To see what kind of a debate is relevant to curriculum problems and to provide the situations and skills that enable it to be adequately conducted is another."[7] This was the practical context in which I was led to try to see what applications of the practical might mean for the activities of curriculum.

In pursuit of my goal, I wrote my essays and hoped that they added up to something. The critics were kind and came out with messages of wholeness rather than complaints about yet another collection of disparate papers.[8] If they were right, their verdict probably owes more to the solid groundwork of "A language for curriculum" and the other practical papers than it does to my own skills.[9] In those papers, Schwab truly provides a tool of great strength and wide utility for thinking about the problems of curriculum. In a great Chicago tradition, he recreates for curriculum the idea of a discipline as an art or method rather than a field of study or a body of knowledge, just as Wayne Booth did for literary criticism, Richard McKeon for philosophy, and R. S. Crane for the humanities generally.[10] The method is both widely applicable and integrating. Not only can it be applied to problems of planning and evaluating, teaching and assessing, and researching and policymaking, but it also shows how what we are led to do in those areas of curriculum activity can be part of a self-consistent project of educating. It does this because the choices Schwab made in arriving at his method were not simply intellectual choices but also moral ones. The practical is not a program for pragmatic or instrumental action; it is a program for principled action.

If we understand this, and if we accept the general philosophical character of the practical as something more than just the elevation of practice to the dignity of the core concern of curriculum, then the tool or method that Schwab provides is a dependable one for analyzing problems of curriculum in any context or at any level. Using it, we can conceptualize the debate about curriculum in terms of deliberative problem solving in the classroom, the principal's office, the local community, or the state legislature. What kind of character would these debates have? Again, I return to ideas expressed in the first chapter of *Thinking About the Curriculum*:

> They would equate practical problem solving with a process of learning.
> They would ground their discussion in a variety of knowledge-seeking procedures, not only those claiming to be scientific in nature.
> They would recognize that activities and situations have different meanings for different people. There is not simply one correct view of things.
> They would not assume that universally applicable, right solutions can be found.
> They would recognize that neither means nor ends can be used as fixed principles in the search for solutions.
> They would assume that the solution to practical problems comes only in action: They would not imagine that a blueprint or plan for action is all that is needed.[11]

Briefly, then, my argument was that fundamental changes in attitudes to schools and education was about to raise the need for new kinds of deliberation about curriculum, and that therefore the whole question of the nature of curriculum *discussion* had to be faced. The idea of the practical provided me with a program for analyzing discussion, or deliberation, and for identifying the issues that should be the concern of all the publics and professions actually and potentially involved in it.

II

Now, from our privileged position 10 years later, we can ask how accurate this appraisal of the position was and what in fact has happened to curriculum deliberation. First, I think we can agree that the diagnosis was correct. The curriculum has indeed moved away from being the exclusive concern of professionals on the inside and occupies the center stage of public policy. I can illustrate this with two quotations. The first is taken from Schools Council Working Paper 53, *The Whole Curriculum 13–16*, published in the United Kingdom in 1975:

> In the constitution of the Schools Council it is asserted that all its curriculum development work shall be governed by "the general principle that each school should have the fullest possible measure of responsibility for its own work, with its own curriculum and teaching methods based on the needs of its own pupils and evolved by its own staff" . . . We welcome . . . the decision taken by the Schools Council's Programme Committee . . . to develop programmes of curriculum development which address themselves to the problems of teaching and learning faced by practising teachers in their own classrooms and schools. We see this as representing a shift from curriculum development administered from the centre.[12]

The second quotation is taken from the Education Reform Bill brought before the U.K. Parliament in the fall of 1987: "In relation to any maintained school and any school year, it shall be the duty of the local education authority and the governing body to exercise their functions with a view to secure, and the duty of the head teacher to secure . . . that the National Curriculum as subsisting at the beginning of that year is implemented.[13] The contrast is dramatic: In 1975, a national body projected the curriculum as essentially a professional matter; 12 years later, the first chapter in a major piece of legislation is headed "Curriculum," and the effect of the legislation is to create and enforce a national curriculum.

In the United States, I see a story with some parallels, despite the federal government's lack of central powers over schools. The most talked-about report on education of the last few years was produced by a presidential commission and had for its title *A Nation at Risk*—not schools at risk, or children at risk, but a nation at risk. The nation was imperiled, claimed the report, by the failures of the professionals: "Secondary school curricula have been homogenized, diluted and diffused to the point that they no longer have a central purpose."[14] The remedy lay in emphasis on the new basics of English, mathematics, science, social studies, and computer science. (On this point the report is echoed in clause three of the United Kingdom Education Reform Bill, in which the core subjects are defined as mathematics, English, and science, while the other foundation subjects give priority to history, geography, and technology.) And, following *A Nation at Risk*, the curriculum has become a prime concern of state governors and legislatures.

But what of deliberation? The scope of debate on the curriculum has been vastly widened—surely a healthy development. But the new arenas into which discussion has moved—politics and business—have not shown themselves hospitable to the skills of deliberation. However, before I pursue that point, I should make an important distinction between the deliberation that goes on at the level of major national and state governmental administrations about the curriculum of the schools and the deliberation that goes on in the schools themselves and to some extent in local areas and school districts. My sense is that, at the school level, teachers and principals have become more skilled in and committed to curriculum deliberation than they were 10 years ago. (I say this mainly on the basis of my own experience of teaching graduate students in the United Kingdom and visiting schools there.) I do not attribute this to the appearance of *Thinking About the Curriculum*, though I think the book was, perhaps, symptomatic of a wider professionalism that was growing up among practitioners through the 1970s and 1980s. More of them were taking part in discussion of the curriculum, more were following courses in colleges and universities, and more were meeting curriculum problems in schools that outside agencies were doing little to solve. This would be an interesting line to pursue in relation to curriculum deliberation. However, my present concern is not with the place where deliberation is (or at least may be) doing well, but with the sphere in which its principles are little in evidence.

In policy arenas beyond the school, the entry on the scene of interests outside the professional world of education has not, as we might have hoped, signaled a more wide-ranging reflection on questions of what should be taught, but an intrusion into teaching and curriculum planning and policymaking of attitudes and approaches stressing top-down control and short-term goals. The situation in the United Kingdom echoes the remarks of an editorial writer in *Phi Delta Kappan* in 1986:

> The current situation is strangely familiar. Eighty years ago, during a period of feverish reform, the schools—short on resources as always—were called on to prove their efficiency to a society dominated by the interests of business. Today, too, the key words are *effective* and *efficient*. If you doubt that, read the recommendations of the National Governors' Association . . . Education has become politically important to the nation's governors—and that's good. It's what educators have long hoped for. Yet it also signals a reassertion of political control of the public schools—and that's ominous. . . . This time around, the education community is playing ball with the big boys of the political and business communities—and the big boys are making the rules.[15]

In the United Kingdom, as in the United States, the curriculum is coming increasingly under the influence of a business lobby, backed by politicians, which appears sadly ignorant of those recent best-sellers *In Search of Excellence* and *A Passion for Excellence*,[16] which argued that the most successful businesses were those that applied principles very like those urged by Schwab in his analysis of deliberation. The debate is not a process of mutual learning; it is not interested in knowledge; it does not take account of a multiplicity of views. It does believe in right answers, in ends as fixed principles, in blueprints as solutions to problems. Whatever success has been achieved, and I believe it is considerable, in raising the quality of deliberation in schools and among teachers, we must admit that educators have so far failed to address questions of the quality of curriculum deliberation involving wider communities. And here the deficiencies of *Thinking About the Curriculum* have to be faced. The diagnosis may have been right, the remedies may have right, but in some centrally important ways, the book failed to follow through the logic of its position.

III

The book's deficiencies stemmed, as I see it, from the familiar problem of putting new wine in old bottles, the problem Schwab discusses in "The 'impossible' role of the teacher in progressive education." There he points to the difficulty that Dewey faced in communicating his vision of education:

> Dewey seeks to persuade men to teach a mode of learning and knowledge which they themselves do not know and which they cannot grasp by their habitual ways of learning. It is the same problem of breaking the apparently unbreakable circle which Plato faces in *Meno* and Augustine in his treatise, *On the Teacher.*
>
> If the enterprise is to be successful, it is the new logic and not some radically mistaken version of it which must be tried. Yet this is the unlikeliest outcome ... For, if the new logic be described in its own terms, its hearers must struggle hard for understanding by whatever means they have. These means, however, are the old modes of understanding, stemming from the old logic.[17]

My exercise in communicating the nature and implications of the practical was hobbled by my inability to throw off the assumptions of the old logic. The problems I saw were the problems of an enterprise in the process of being ejected from its familiar and comfortable territory and sent to fend for itself in unknown regions. But the commonplaces of my curriculum text were little changed from the commonplaces of all such texts: curriculum planning, curriculum research, and curriculum innovation, understood in ways not very different from those hallowed by long usage. But, to adapt the metaphor of the editorial in *Phi Delta Kappan*, were these not the concerns of the little league? Where was the discussion of politics, of government, of interest groups, of national institutions—in short, of the field inhabited by the major league players? In a sense, government and the community are right to make greater and more specific demands on educators: we have suffered in the past from too much isolation in the comfortable, if demanding, world of schools and colleges. The intrusion of the outside world has found us unprepared. I am reminded of a phrase of Francis Cornford, written at the beginning of this century when the older English universities were truly ivory towers. "The Great World," he said, was "a distant and rather terrifying region, which it is very necessary to keep in touch with, though it must not be allowed on any account to touch you."[18] We have all, in one way or another, been touched by the Great World in recent years, and there is every sign that educators will continue to live in its shadow—or its spotlight. The choice of metaphor marks the pessimists and the optimists among us.

IV

I don't believe, however, that any of this negates the basic agenda of *Thinking About the Curriculum*. The possibilities that ideas of the practical and of deliberation have for giving direction and purpose to the activities of curriculum continue to demand our attention. But we must think with renewed vigor about how these ideas can be brought into contact with and made relevant to the new arena of public debate about what should be taught in schools. In *Thinking About the Curriculum*, I said that the conception of the practical introduced "a fresh and more appropriate climate of metaphor into curriculum theory and practice" by stressing key words like action, judgment, deliberation, appreciation, criticism, responsibility, argument, and justification.[19] But those are not the words we immediately think of when we see what has been done, in the United Kingdom at least, in national curriculum policymaking in recent years. Is it the case, as some have charged, that these ideas of deliberation and practical reasoning emerged in protected academic environments and are not adaptable to life in the Great World? Are such virtuous notions best kept within the communities that can nurture them, so that, as Dewey put it in an unusual outburst of eloquence, we can avoid "the pathos of unfulfilled expectation, the tragedy of defeated purpose and ideas, the catastrophes of accident?"[20] Indeed, this theme of virtue versus accident, or virtue versus corruption, is one that haunts Schwab's practical papers, though only seldom does it surface in an explicit way. We see it most clearly in the practical 4, in which teachers in their small communities are put forward as repositories of virtue and pitted against Moscow, which symbolizes the corrupting influence of centralism and bureaucracy in American life.[21]

I explored a similar theme myself in a recent paper on the language of reports on professional education.[22] In reading a number of documents—mainly in the area of medical education—I was struck by the frequent juxtaposition of virtuous language, embodying metaphors of caring and concern, with the language of power, status, and control that represents the other side of the coin. I tried to explain this by reference to MacIntyre's *After Virtue*, in which he analyzes the relationship of practice to institution:

> Practices must not be confused with institutions. Chess, physics and medicine are practices; chess clubs, laboratories, universities and hospitals are institutions. Institutions are characteristically and necessarily concerned with . . . external goods. They are involved in acquiring money and other material goods; they are structured in terms of power and status, and they distribute money, power and status as rewards. Nor could they do otherwise if they are to sustain not only themselves, but also the practices of which they are the bearers. For no practice can survive for any length of time unsustained by institutions.[23]

In this passage, MacIntyre draws our attention not only to the potential conflict between practice and institution, but also to their mutual dependence. Institutions are able to lay claim to society's resources on the promise that what they use those resources to support is good and worthwhile. Government, even of the most rigidly centralized and hierarchical kind, claims credit for its support of education, not on the basis that it exhibits and promotes centralism and hierarchy, but because it is a public good and fosters a virtuous population—even when good and virtue are narrowly construed. On the other hand, education as practice will survive only with the greatest difficulty if it is not in some sense institutionalized.

To bring the argument closer to the concerns of curriculum, deliberation about it—at any level—is only to the point if we accept the fact that results can flow from that deliberation through the involvement of institutions *as they exist* with their necessary commitment to styles of life other than those with which deliberation, as conventionally construed, might feel comfortable. I rely here on the definition of curriculum decision making put forward by Scheffler: "We consider decisions on educational content to be responsible or justifiable acts *with public significance.*"[24] We must think about curriculum, then, not simply as practice but as institutionalized practice. The rather inchoate commonplace of the milieus—the only commonplace that directly refers to the world beyond school and classroom—has to be given shape and sharpness.[25]

V

If we are to clarify our thoughts on these matters, we have a number of directions in which we can go. My own route has taken me along pathways of history and sociology, so those are the directions I will briefly consider.

I recognize that many other disciplines and fields of inquiry touching on public policymaking should also claim our attention.

Thinking About the Curriculum offered very little in the way of exploration of history, which at this distance I find strange, since history presents instructive examples of how the practice–institution relationship has been managed in the past.[26] It also shows us how the whole idea of curriculum was, from the outset, embedded in the development of institutions. Curriculum, in Europe, emerged as an organizing concept in the late 16th century. Prior to that, learning had taken place piecemeal, on an ad hoc basis. For example, students at medieval universities such as Paris or Bologna attended to whatever learning they pleased, came and went as they pleased, and received no final degree or testimonial. The context of education was "a loose-textured organizational form where student absenteeism or the fact that enrollment did not match attendance was not so much a failure (or breakdown) of organization as a perfectly efficient response to the demands that were placed upon it."[27] Use of the word curriculum signaled the arrival of a more closely knit structure of educational activities, and particularly of moves to make them sequential and capable of completion. Method was invoked to systematize teaching and learning and to clear up the apparently ragbag nature of medieval scholarship. All of this depended on a closer alliance between institution and the emerging practice of curriculum. Administration became an important part of university life, and students and teachers ceased to regulate their own affairs. The new statutes were no longer simply content to fix the general conditions of student life (prohibitions against playing noisy games, for example, or bringing women into college "unless they are so respectably escorted that the Prior of the house and the scholars are convinced that no evil suspicion can result"[28]). Now they went into details of everyday life, laying down a routine and a timetable of study. Henceforth the gap between student and teacher widened: a chain of command was established from principal or bursar to teacher and student.[29] The drive toward a modern conception of curriculum was encapsulated in the statement of Ramus in his *Dialectic* that "method is the disposition by which that enunciation is placed first which is first in the absolute order of knowledge, that next which is next, and so on."[30] And this had its counterpart in the rise of recognizably modern institutions, marshaling and distributing resources and built around structures of power, hierarchy, and control.

Here, then, is one thing to think about as we try to extend the utility of the idea of deliberation: that decisions on the curriculum as the outcome of responsible or justifiable acts with public significance are historically interwoven with the growth of public institutions; first with organized and regulated schools and colleges, and later with local and central governments and bureaucracies.

But within a strictly historical frame of reference, some of the significance of this interplay of curriculum and institution still eludes us. *Why* did the experience of school and college begin to assume such importance? *How* did widely shared meanings become attached to the study of classical texts, enrollment in secondary schooling, or the possession of degrees and diplomas? *What* has made educational practices definitive of national character? The genesis of this chapter was an invitation to reflect on something written 10 years ago. What was so special about the number 10? Objectively, nothing. A number is simply one in sequence, and the way it gets written is an accident of the code we happen to use. Yet we *do* think there is something special about 13, 21, and the Bicentennial. The comparison is not frivolous. Why, in England, is the age of 11 chosen to mark the transition from the primary to the secondary curriculum? There is no demonstrable logic to this, yet 11 has become an age invested with huge significance for all English children. Ariès in *Centuries of Childhood* presses the analysis much further.[31] All curriculums were, at one time, poorly associated with the age of the students enrolled in them. Even in the early 19th century in France and England, when a hierarchy of classes had been established in secondary schools, a student of 14 might be found in any class from the lowest to the highest. The immense significance of enrollment in age-related classes has to be seen as a kind of social accident. No doubt, with some exercise of ingenuity, we can suggest why some accidents are more likely to occur than others, but what is surer, and more practically important is that, once such things achieve social and cultural significance, they acquire a life of their own. They become institutionalized in a dual sense. They need institutions to preserve them, but they also *become* institutions in the more elusive sense of an idea that is integral to a culture and seen as significant by most of its members. Being in the third grade becomes an important defining characteristic of a person—as does being a third-grade teacher.

In *Thinking About the Curriculum* I quoted, approvingly, McKinney and Westbury's comment that the curriculum "is an idea that becomes a thing." The point of the remark was to stress one aspect of the relationship between curriculum and institution. As they put it: "Development and renewal are only meaningful notions in so far as they are embedded in structures."[32] Thus, deliberation, to be effective, must concern itself with the nature of those institutions within which renewal is aspired. However, I now think we should also consider the opposite proposition: a curriculum is a thing that becomes an idea. Once it has been institutionalized in the first sense, it also has to be institutionalized in the second sense. It must become culturally significant. Otherwise, external support will be lacking and it will fail. Many examples could be given. Following the Education Act of 1944, technical secondary schools were set up in England. Curriculums and examinations were devised and teachers trained. But the technical curriculum was never institutionalized in the public mind. The idea of the grammar school was too powerfully entrenched, and technical high schools disappeared. Today we see traditional ideas, institutionalized in society in this latter sense, still at work. Indeed, as curriculum debate extends beyond the sphere of the professionals, it becomes more open to the influence of basic and unexamined archetypes. The new Education Bill repeats, almost to the letter, the curriculum specified in the 1904 grant regulations for secondary schools, and the conclusions of the Committee of Ten live on the proposals of *A Nation at Risk*. But these are not matters to be dismissed as unworthy of the attention of better informed commentators; for we err if we see the curriculum too much as a thing or an object (which is the pitfall of the professional) and give too little consideration to the curriculum as idea, as symbol, as cultural institution. Meyer, in his discussion of the role of the teacher, illustrates the point I am trying to make:

> From a technical point of view . . . teachers are almost unrelievedly authoritarian: they talk all the time, dominate the agenda completely, and so on. Yet students rarely experience education in this way: they experience the larger invisible reality of education . . . because they are attending to [this] larger reality of "teacher" as an institutional category, students are often surprisingly inattentive to the particular characteristics of their individual teachers. . . . Perhaps effective teaching requires less the creating of a distinctive local world in the classroom than the activation of the larger institutional one: and perhaps this requires the partial concealment of the individual identity of the teacher behind the general role . . . It seems possible, even, that a teacher who blandly plays the conventional role . . . had found the most effective educational strategy.[33]

VI

These are my thoughts on the gaps that exist in our conception of the practical and my suggestions for places in which to find ideas to repair them. Basically, what is needed is a way of understanding institutions as the necessary context for curriculum deliberation and curriculum action—institutions as the partners of practice, institutions as the vehicles through which curriculums become real, and the curriculum itself as a social and cultural institution. Without such understanding, it will be hard for the study of the curriculum to establish its position as a relevant and integral part of the new, enlarged debate on schooling and education.

Schwab, as is well known, identified five crucial commonplaces that need to be represented in curriculum deliberation: teachers, learners, the milieus, subject matter, and curriculum making. A few years ago, we thought we knew what that meant. Now, as the milieus change, our understanding needs modification. I have, I think, in my discussion of neglect of ideas of institutions and institutional contexts, identified the kind of modification that has to be looked for. What I have not done, and what remains as work to be accomplished, is to show *how* such a modification could be brought about. Can we do it simply by opening up new lines of inquiry, by seeing the subject matter of curriculum as much broader than the professional techniques traditionally associated with curriculum making—planning, implementation, and evaluation? Or do we need to move out in some way from the restrictions imposed by the very definition of our work as professional? (It has been said that when an intellectual activity becomes a profession, its conception of the public interest is bound to become distorted.)[34] Or, finally, is it the case that we ourselves have to become political in a more overt and self-conscious way? The one constant in the present flux that is engulfing education as well as many other public endeavors is government itself. While other sectors of national life bear the burden of adjustment to change, government resists it. Government alone seems able to carry into the 21st century structures evolved to deal with the 19th. Should curriculum scholars abandon the limits imposed by scholarship and professionalism and join in a general movement to have the core assumptions of the apparatus of government itself subjected to greater scrutiny? There are, as yet, no answers to such questions. They are matters for other papers and other authors.

NOTES

1. Reid, William A. (1978). *Thinking about the curriculum: The nature and treatment of curriculum problems.* London: Routledge & Kegan Paul, pp. 1–2.
2. *Op. cit.*
3. Schwab, J. J. (1978). The practical: a language for curriculum. In I. Westbury & N. J. Wilkof (Eds.). *Science, curriculum, and liberal education* (pp. 287–321). Chicago: University of Chicago Press.
4. *Op. cit.*, p. 1.
5. Central Advisory Council for Education (1959). *15–18.* London: HMSO (Crowther Report); Committee on Higher Education (1963). *Higher education.* London: HMSO (Robbins Report); Central Advisory Council for Education (1963). *Half our future.* London: HMSO (Newsom Report).
6. Cox, C. B., & Dyson, A. E. (Eds.). (1969–1970). *Black papers 1–3.* London: Critical Quarterly Society; Cox, C. B., & Dyson, A. E. (Eds.). (1975). *Black paper, 1975: The fight for education.* London: Dent; Cox, C. B., & Dyson, A. E. (Eds.). (1977). *Black paper, 1977.* London: Temple Smith.
7. Reid (1978). *Op. cit.*, pp. 1–2.
8. See, for example, Handler, B. S. (1982). Coming of age in curriculum: Reflections on *Thinking about the curriculum. Journal of Curriculum Studies, 14,* 183–195; Eisner, Elliot W. (1981). A practical view of the theoretical in curriculum. *Curriculum Inquiry, 11,* 189–193; Connelly,

Michael F., & Clandinin, D. Jean (1980). Thoughts on *Thinking about the curriculum*. *Review of Education, 6,* 119–132.

9. Schwab, J. J. (1978). *Op. cit.*; Schwab, J. J. (1978). The practical: Arts of eclectic, and The practical: Translation into curriculum. In Westbury & Wilkof. *Op. cit*, 322–364 and 365–383; Schwab, J. J. (1983). The practical 4: Something for curriculum professors to do. *Curriculum Inquiry, 13,* 239–255.

10. Booth, Wayne C. (1979). *Critical understanding: The powers and limits of pluralism.* Chicago: University of Chicago Press; McKeon, Richard (1954). *Thought, action, and passion.* Chicago: University of Chicago Press; Crane, R. S. (1967). *The idea of the humanities and other essays critical and historical.* Chicago: University of Chicago Press.

11. Reid (1978). *Op. cit.,* p. 12.

12. Schools Council (1975). *Working Paper 53. The whole curriculum.* London: Evans/Methuen Educational, pp. 98–99.

13. House of Commons. *Education reform. A bill to amend the law relating to education.* London: HMSO, pp. 1, 4.

14. National Commission on Excellence in Education. *A nation at risk.* Reprinted in Gross, Beatrice, & Gross, Ronald (Eds.). (1985). *The great school debate: Which way for American education?* New York: Simon & Schuster, p. 34.

15. Cole, Robert W., Jr. (1986). A matter of balance. *Phi Delta Kappan, November,* p. 186.

16. Peters, Thomas J., & Waterman, Robert H. (1982). *In search of excellence: Lessons from America's best-run corporations.* New York: Harper & Row; Peters, Thomas J., & Austin, Nancy (1985). *A passion for excellence: The leadership difference.* London: Collins.

17. Schwab, J. J. (1978). The "impossible" role of the teacher in progressive education. In Westbury & Wilkof. *Op. cit.,* pp. 170–171.

18. Cornford, F. M. (1908). *Microcosmographia academica: Being a guide for the young academic politician.* Cambridge: Bowes & Bowes, p. 8.

19. *Op. cit.,* pp. 68–69.

20. Dewey, John (1929). *The quest for certainty.* New York: Capricorn Books, Chapter 1. Reprinted in McDermott, John J. (Ed.). (1981). *The philosophy of John Dewey.* Chicago: University of Chicago Press, p. 359.

21. Schwab (1983). *Op. cit.,* pp. 242–243.

22. Reid, William A. (1987). Institutions and practices: Professional education reports and the language of reform. *Educational Researcher, 16,* 10–15.

23. MacIntyre, A. (1981). *After virtue: A study in moral theory.* London: Duckworth, p. 181.

24. Scheffler, Israel (1973). Justifying curriculum decisions. *Reason and teaching.* Indianapolis: Bobbs-Merrill, p. 116.

25. See Reid, William A. (1994). *The pursuit of curriculum: Schooling and the public interest.* Norwood, NJ: Ablex, Chapter 9.

26. Reid, William A. (1986). Curriculum theory and curriculum change: What can we learn from history? *Journal of Curriculum Studies, 18,* 159–166.

27. Hamilton, David (1985). *On the origins of the educational terms class and curriculum.* Unpublished paper: University of Glasgow Department of Education, p. 5.

28. Ariès, Philippe (1973). *Centuries of childhood.* Harmondsworth: Penguin, p. 164.

29. *Ibid.,* pp. 165–166.

30. Quoted in Hamilton. *Op. cit.,* p. 18.

31. Ariès. *Op. cit.,* pp. 183–230.

32. McKinney, W. Lynn, & Westbury, Ian (1975). Stability and change: The public schools of Gary, Indiana, 1940–1970. In William A. Reid & Decker F. Walker (Eds.). *Case studies in*

curriculum change: Great Britain and the United States. London: Routledge & Kegan Paul, p. 50.

33. Meyer, John W. (1980). Levels of the education system and schooling effects. In C. E. Bidwell & D. M. Windham (Eds.), *The analysis of educational productivity*. Vol. 2. *Issues in macroanalysis*. Cambridge, MA: Ballinger, p. 42.

34. Lilla, Mark (1985). What is the civic interest? *The Public Interest*, Fall, p. 71.

CHAPTER

8

The Problem of
Curriculum Change

One idea to be contrasted with that of institution is practice. Another is organization. Institutions depend on organizational structures. But to use the word institution is to say that we have in mind some entity that embraces more than the kinds of notions that go with organization. Schools are organized in terms of grades, subject areas, semesters, classes, and so on, but these organizational features are given stability and significance by the fact that they are institutionalized in the minds of participants—teachers and students—and also in the minds of the public at large. An institution is an amalgam of organizational forms and of the generally shared ideas that they reflect and sustain. To the third grade, as organized within specific schools, districts, and states, corresponds a universal notion of third gradedness, which is a source of image, identity, and experience.

This chapter deals with the organizational aspects of the institution of curriculum, with occasional hints of how a merely organizational account may overlook some important elements that theory needs to take into consideration. It was written within the tradition of organizational analysis that begins with the problem of how intentions to change curricular aims and forms are mediated by the nature of organizations, and derives practical implications for curriculum planning and implementation. It was first published as chapter 5 in Thinking about the curriculum. *The question it set out to answer was, "What kind of a model of school as an organization might be compatible with a deliberative approach to curriculum planning?"*

Advocacy of practical reasoning as a means of solving curriculum problems implies acceptance of the proposition that changes in what is taught and how it is taught can be brought about in planned ways, or at least that this is to an important degree possible. It also implies that the nature of curriculum change is such that, of a variety of approaches to planned change that might be supported, this one is most likely to be successful in defining and realizing curricular purposes. Arguments of this type touch on an area of deep controversy with far-reaching implications for the theory and practice of curriculum. The two basic points at issue are: can change be in any fundamental sense planned, or is the evolution of the curriculum determined by forces that tend in a particular and irreversible direction? And must proposals for curriculum change be based on some set of values, or some ideological[1] position, or can they be, in some sense, value free? The approach through practical reasoning accepts that planning is possible, and that it must reflect ideological commitments. Two other, importantly different views of curriculum change are to be found in the literature of curriculum theory. For convenience of exposition, they are represented here in their extreme forms. The first claims that intentionality is indeed (or can be) the dominant factor in curriculum change, but assumes that a theory of practice can be nonideological. This is the position of writers of the school of Bobbitt and Tyler[2] who deploy a managerial perspective on curriculum theory. Management is, by definition, capable of being effective, but what management achieves is thought of as politically and ideologically neutral. The second view claims that any attempt to intervene in curriculum matters must be politically and ideologically motivated, but that the changes that actually take place are attributable more to sociocultural necessity than to the realization of freely chosen goals through managerial intervention. This view is implied in the statements of writers such as Young and Kallós.[3] When the argument is joined from the extreme positions, both sides are fairly invulnerable to the thrusts of the other, and the possibilities for achieving a synthesis are limited. The intentionalists cannot attack the inevitablists for being just as ideologically motivated as everyone else without admitting that they themselves are ideologically motivated, while the latter cannot mount substantial arguments against interventionism without admitting it may be effective—which they deny.[4] Of course, many theorists, while tending toward one view or the other, avoid the extreme and put forward ideas that are not obviously incompatible with either position. Sometimes, even, extremists of both types will find themselves on the same side, as, for example, in denunciations of the arguments of the proponents of deschooling, which suggests that their views may not be diametrically opposed after all.

Some theoretical deficiencies of the managerial approach have been succinctly documented by Kliebard[5] who points to its inability to give anything like an adequate account of where the objectives of the curriculum are derived from.

> The crucial first step in the Tyler rationale on which all else hinges is the statement of objectives. The objectives are to be drawn from three sources:

studies of the learner, studies of society, and suggestions from subject matter specialists. Data drawn from these sources are to be filtered through philosophical and psychological screens. Upon examination, the last of the three sources turns out to be no source at all but a means of achieving objectives drawn from the other two. Studies of the learner and of society depend so heavily for their standing as sources on the philosophical screen that it is actually the philosophical screen that determines the nature and scope of the objectives. To say that educational objectives are drawn from one's philosophy, in turn, is only to say that one must make choices about educational objectives in some way related to one's value structure. This is to say so little about the process of selecting objectives as to be virtually meaningless.[6]

But these are not deficiencies to be repaired by some reformulation of the theory that leaves its basic assumptions intact. Writers such as Inglis and Booth[7] have argued persuasively that the whole notion that policies with social consequences can be set up in some apolitical way is a dangerous nonsense. In the case of curriculum, we are talking about the distribution of advantage and disadvantage in society through the differential provision of opportunities to acquire knowledge or to acquire the status that goes with having been exposed to certain kinds of knowledge. There is no question of simply doing it more or less effectively. Effectiveness in such a situation only has a meaning when it relates to some set of recognized ideals or values.

On a practical level, the weaknesses of the traditional managerial approach are that the process it proposes is not one that curriculum designers find natural,[8] and that it has little to say about how a curriculum design should be implemented, so innovations that rely on this model may be ineffective in practice.[9] Nevertheless, the shortcomings of this branch of curriculum theory should not disguise the fact that its progenitors were inspired by an idea that was fundamentally right—that it is the business of curriculum theory to try to say something about how, practically, curriculum tasks such as design, implementation, and evaluation can and should be carried out.

Writers of the opposite persuasion tend to avoid the discussion of effective practices, and may go so far as to claim that nothing much can be said about curriculum change either. "Academic theorists, often in search of a spurious scientism, can be far more naive than teachers. They present curriculum as a reality to which the language of cause and effect, resistance and change, is appropriate, and we discover articles with absurd titles like 'How does the curriculum change?' "[10] Those who like to make such statements can always know that they are logically unassailable. Hume showed conclusively that, if we wish to push logic to its limits, the language of cause and effect cannot be applied to anything, whether it be the curriculum, the physical universe, or the writing of articles on the evils of using cause–effect language. Obstinately, however, people in their roles as academics, planners, and ordinary citizens have carried on using such language, first, be-cause most do not have access to any other language that could replace it, and second, because the asking of how and why questions, and the attempts to answer them, are useful ways of increasing our stock of perceptions, capabilities, and understandings. This is not to advocate simplistic analyses of curriculum change of the causes of the French Revolution type, but to accept a commitment to a view of human affairs that allows a place for choice and responsibility, and to a view of intellectual inquiry that, instead of placing limits on the permitted means for producing ideas and theories, stresses the critical evaluation of those ideas once they have been formu-lated. The fact that no conclusive arguments can be put forward for the operation of cause and effect does not logically entail the acceptance of determinism, neither is there any proven argument against determinism: whichever side of the controversy is espoused, it is on the basis of the acceptance of some worldview. What would be logically unacceptable would be to argue that the curriculum is capable of responding to the intentional interventions of planners of various kinds, whether classroom teachers or central administrators, and at the same time deny that such intervention reflected any kind of ideological or political stance. This is where the inevi-tablists are right: all attempted intervention is on the basis of value com-mitments, explicit or implicit. Their mistake is to suppose that a determi-nistic view of curriculum change can be presented as ideologically neutral. The starting point for the present inquiry is the belief that there are certain kinds of activity that one studies because of a commitment to a proposition that they are capable of producing worthwhile effects, and that planning curriculum change is an activity of this type. The practical, and undesirable result of a deterministic view of change is that decision makers must regard themselves as ineffectual, or, alternatively, as effective only in acting as agents for power groups. Either way, they are denied any sense that they might be able to act constructively or responsibly.

FUNCTIONAL AND CONFLICT THEORIES

To pursue an inquiry into curriculum change we do not need to debate lengthily about whether curriculum is or is not a reality (any more than the exponents of determinism need, for their purposes, to consider whether capitalism or socialism are realities). The focus of interest is on what is learned. The factors that promote the type of learning that takes place, or that lead to changes in types or patterns of learning, are allowed, initially, to be problematic. They may take the form of things that can be objectively studied and described—the architecture of schools, or the textbooks and teachers' guides that form the physical manifestations of a curriculum design—or they may be less tangible elements, such as the social relationships that exist between teachers and taught, or the implicit or explicit theories about the nature of children and learning that guide the activities of educators. The looseness of definition is deliberate. Several decades of experience of the managerial model should have resulted in at least one useful outcome: an appreciation of the danger of working with a tight definition of curriculum when our interest is not in making a theoretical point, but in providing grounds for the development of theories of effective practice to guide the conduct of curriculum tasks.

Most learning that can be associated with the nature of curriculum takes place in *open systems*. That is, parameters cannot be set and controlled so that learning outcomes are associated with selected stimuli. How a stimulus is applied is a matter of the beliefs and skills of the teacher, how children respond is a matter of the background and interests of the student. But, beyond this, the learning takes place in a situation that is not adapted to one-way stimulus–response processes: as well as being a place for learning, the classroom is a place where long-term interactive relationships have to be managed, and a place where the needs of individuals intersect with the organizational imperatives of institutions. Schools are not efficient delivery systems for a particular kind of goods, they are cultures promoted as an act of public policy in the belief that their existence will increase and enrich the stock of such goods in the community. Curriculum change is, therefore, a species of sociocultural change.[11] Adoption of this view leads us away from those types of inquiry (psychology, some types of history) that place the individual in the center of the stage, and toward those that stress the group, the culture, or the organization (anthropology, social psychology, organizational analysis, political theory). Theories of sociocultural change stemming from these traditions of thought can be divided into two broad categories: functional theories and conflict theories.

The basic position of the functionalist is well stated by Silverman:

> Functionalism begins with Hobbes' problem of order and proceeds to ask some important and interesting questions. "How is it" functionalists would ask, "that society manages to work and to survive continual changes of personnel? How do people with different genetic make-ups and personality types learn to co-exist with one another and even enter into more or less stable and predictable forms of relationship?" In answering these questions, functionalists take as their concern the relationship of the parts to the whole in order to show how what appear to be isolated, if not inexplicable, social phenomena may fulfil some wider purpose related to the stability of society. Thus, their perspective . . . generates a concern with the causes and consequences of social equilibrium; problems of change and conflict, while they are considered, are treated as subsidiary phenomena.[12]

Supporters of conflict theory would criticize this approach as allowing too little place for concepts such as power, and as preempting the question of what makes for change by seeing everything in terms of stability: since this situation exists, it exists necessarily and the task is to show why. Such a position, they would maintain, naturally reinforces dominant ideologies and particularly those that delay the realization of goals such as the reduction or removal of social class differences. Conflict theorists would prefer to regard what exists as the result of the exercise of power, and to see change as resulting from the shifting balances between groups in society that compete for the opportunity to exercise power. Since the examples to be given later in this chapter take a broadly functionalist view of what a theory of curriculum change might look like, it may be useful at this point to provide an instance of the kind of argument that a conflict perspective might produce, and to draw from it some conclusions about the relative advantages of the two kinds of approach, and about the extent to which they may be complementary or even compatible.

If we accept that sociocultural change results from the shifting distribution of power between competing groups in society, then the evolution of the curriculum of the English public school can be seen as a series of responses to the influence exerted by social classes maneuvering to try to exert control over it. (In England, "public school" denotes a high prestige private school, often with boarding facilities for all or most of its students.) First, in the early 19th century, the commercial upper middle classes laid claim to the services of the public school that, until then, had been the preserve of the landed aristocracy. But, in gaining acceptance, they imported into the schools a more utilitarian approach to the curriculum, backed up by an ethos that stressed protestant, capitalist values. The response of the schools was to offer not a completely new curriculum, but an alternative curriculum, and the system grew up of choice between classical, modern, or scientific studies that has molded the whole of the English secondary curriculum to the present day. Later, toward the end of the century, the public schools were conscious of the growing power of the lower classes whose ideologies could not be accommodated to theirs. By the time of the 1902 Education Act there was real anxiety among public school headmasters that their schools would shortly disappear. The conflict was not now about access to the schools, but about their right to exist at all, since they served to reinforce the dominance of the classes that already controlled the major power centers of society. The response of the schools this time was to play down their distinctiveness, to match their curricula more closely to those of the new secondary schools that were being set up under state control after the passing of the 1902 Act. At the same time, supporters of the public schools infiltrated the state system both as head teachers and as high-level administrators to make sure that the matching problem would not be made too great through adoption of radical proposals for the curricula of the new state schools. In more recent times, the public schools have gone further, and have taken the lead in curriculum development projects aimed at the secondary schools. In the 1960s they were pioneers in Nuffield Science schemes and new approaches to foreign language teaching, and were leaders in the General Studies movement.

The general drift of this kind of analysis shows up one important difference between it and functional analysis as a means of understanding curriculum change. Several different interpretations of the nature of curriculum knowledge can be fit to a functional theory, including one that would regard it as in some way objective,[13] but conflict theory seems to involve, necessarily, a relativist view of curriculum knowledge. Since the control of the curriculum is a political objective to be won, the knowledge that it represents is a good to be contested. The classroom is a battle ground in which conflicting stocks of knowledge confront one another. What the knowledge consists of is almost irrelevant. The point is that it should be valued by some and coveted or despised by others. It is an instrument of political domination, or revolutionary guerrilla warfare. If we think that knowledge can never under any circumstances be free from political implications, then the question of what should be taught becomes a matter of whose version of truth is politically dominant; since knowledge is a symbol or instrument of political supremacy, what we teach is a matter of fashion. To take the contrary view and assert that there *is* such a thing as objective knowledge is not to say that *all* knowledge, and especially curriculum knowledge, is objectively true or intrinsically worthwhile. We can still admit that some knowledge enters into the curriculum for political reasons, or that the choice of methods or materials can have a political bias, such as the use of middle-class story books in the teaching of reading to disadvantaged children. But acceptance of the possibility of objective knowledge provides a ground for building a tradition of critical argument about what should be in a curriculum that represents something more than just the maneuverings of power groups.

A second feature of conflict theory in its most extreme forms is that it allows little or no room for the exercise of judgment and responsibility in planning and policymaking. Social change, and therefore curriculum change, is depicted as something hinging on fundamental social conflicts over which we have only very marginal control, though we might be able to slow the process down or speed it up. This might be said to be true also of the extreme functionalist view: to account for a state of affairs in terms of massively interlocking component features of a society is to suggest that such systems are self-regulating and totally resistant to purposeful intervention. The difference is that functional theory does not claim that the equilibrium it describes is the only one that could exist, or that any given state of the system has a necessary antecedent or successor. If more than one state of a system is possible, it is equally possible that we could manage a transition from one to another and choose this other from a range of feasible states. In suggesting that this may be a difficult process, the functional theorist is reflecting the reality of actual experience of curriculum design. (One does not find writers complaining that curricula are difficult to plan and manage because they are so volatile: on the contrary, many books are written to show that curricula have a great tendency to move inexorably along established paths in spite of all the efforts of planners to deflect them.)[14] But this is not the same thing as saying that they never could be changed in consciously and rationally chosen ways,[15] and functionalist accounts can suggest methods by which change can be secured. Conflict theories, on the other hand, while they are concerned to highlight questions of change rather than documenting grounds for stability, tend not to point to ways in which responsible intervention can take place because it is a basic premise of such theories either that this kind of intervention is not possible, or that it has to be directed toward the achievement of goals that are known in advance of discussion or action. A conflict-centered account of change in the English public school does not suggest that options existed, or that at certain points a rational choice between options could have been exercised. In what ways is such an analysis helpful to anyone wanting to make and implement such choices? It documents a change process in such a way that a dramatic meaning is given to events in schools, and relationships between these and forces outside the school are suggested (a valuable and necessary exercise); but the documentation is of a process that is accepted as basically inevitable and the meanings arise from a presumed knowledge of future states of the school and the surrounding society.

The kinds of problems raised here about the practical utility and the explanatory power of functional and conflict theories arise only if these are presented as mutually exclusive and incompatible sources of knowledge. This is how they have, in fact, been put forward by some writers, but others have provided arguments for supposing that this need not and should not be the case.[16] Fallding expresses the point very strongly: "It has been very common . . . to oppose a Marxian-type 'conflict' sociology to a 'functionalist' sociology. But that is dealing in stereotypes in the most puerile way."[17] We need to see the two types of approach either as equally capable of providing useful insights or as capable of integration: though they seem incompatible, this need not be a reason for choosing one against the other: "we need for the explanation of sociological problems, both the equilibrium and the conflict models of society . . . [T]here is no intrinsic criterion for preferring the one to the other."[18] Those who are interested primarily in the practical advantages of understanding change processes will subscribe to whatever theories are available. But such a pragmatic approach may not be necessary. Fallding suggests that a broadly defined functionalism can accommodate change mechanisms that are conflict-related. A functionalist theory has somehow to account for the fact that what was stable at some time in the past has been replaced by a present stability of a different nature. This it does by recognising that if function is a viable concept, then the concept of dysfunction must also be accepted. Dysfunction will cause stress and pressure for change to establish a new functional equilibrium. There is no reason to suppose that conflict between social groups will not be an important factor in the creation and resolution of dysfunction.[19] In this way, discussion of aims and purposes can be imported into functionalist paradigms. Deliberation will be the means by which tensions are resolved through choice of a future system state that is attainable and that respects the aims and purposes of the participants. Functionalism can be seen as a capacious position, or a program of inquiry, rather than a strictly delineated conceptual position.[20]

The major charge that can be laid against functionalism is that it is too loosely formulated and therefore open to a wide variety of interpretations and to misuse in support of a priori positions. There is some justice in this criticism, but, as has been suggested earlier, the validity of inquiry is assured not by the refinement of conceptual tools, but by rigorous scrutiny of the ideas that these tools produce. And this will be a particularly telling point for those whose main concern is to gain understandings of social change that could have some practical utility. For, whatever theory of change we put forward, the account it gives will be partial and incomplete. Criteria have to be found for evaluating partial and incomplete theories. Among these might be questions such as: are the elements chosen in such a way that they reflect the results of empirical study? Do they have common sense as well as theoretical significance? Does the theory depict schools in terms of similarities with other organizations as well as in terms of uniqueness? Does the theory indicate how those interested in planned change could better understand their failures and successes?

To ask that empirical study should be reflected in a theory is not to ask that it should be empirically validated. It is impossible to prove or disprove social theory by the amassing of facts. Such theories remain, essentially, ways of seeing. But the scope for producing theoretical formulations is endless unless some empirical base is respected, and the multiplication of analytical proposals does not make for a coherent tradition of thought in a practical field. Practical concerns are also the reason for wanting theoretical elements to have commonsense significance. If they cannot be described in such a way that they can be recognized by teachers and administrators, then it is unlikely that they adequately reflect those aspects of schools and curricula that need to taken into account in the planning of change. But, at the same time, we should be suspicious of theories of the school and the curriculum that seem to bear no relation to theoretical formulations about other kinds of social institutions. A curriculum must in some ways be a unique phenomenon, but in others it must participate in the features of other comparable phenomena. A theory of curriculum change should be one of a family of change theories. Finally, it is a consequence of the interpretation of curriculum theory that is being adopted here that a theory of change should have implications for theories of effective practice.

A THEORY OF CURRICULUM CHANGE

The following discussion is not intended to present a final and conclusive theoretical account of curriculum change, but to put forward an example of functional analysis that tries to meet the criteria stated above. The starting point is evidence collected in elementary and secondary schools about how teachers see the forces that determine what is taught and how it is taught. This evidence is limited, in that it represents only one point of view, and also in that it is based on questionnaire surveys involving short response scales or yes–no answers. The data on the primary curriculum were provided by 120 teachers in 12 schools in the English West Midlands.[21] Their answers to a set of questions about constraints on the achievement of curricular aims were factored, resulting in the identification of three main dimensions relating to: (a) resources and facilities in the school; (b) children's attitudes, backgrounds, and experience; (c) aspects of relationships among teachers. Consideration of the defining variables of these factors suggested that they might represent some of the features of functional models of organizations that recognize three internal elements, usually described as technology, social systems, and theory (or aims), together with inputs and outputs. Factor (a) could be seen as reflecting technology, factor (b) inputs, and factor (c) the social system. No such theoretical framework had been considered in devising the questions, which had been suggested by teachers, but confirmation of its appropriateness came from analysis of two other item sets, relating to aims and influences. What was missing was any indication of an output factor to balance the input one, and any factor relating to theory—that is, to how the task of the school was conceptualized by the teachers. These were not found because none of the questions related to them. The omissions were repaired in a later survey of sixth form (11th and 12th grade) teachers.[22] Replies from 194 individuals in 31 schools yielded factors that confirmed the tentative model derived from the elementary school data, and enabled it to be elaborated and extended. This time, factors obtained from replies on both constraints and aims could be combined into a single theoretical formulation, which is shown in Fig. 8.1.

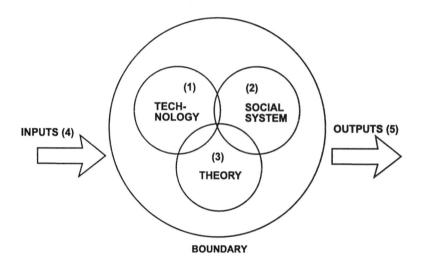

DEFINING VARIABLES

(1) Materials/equipment
(2) Communication/co-operation
(3) Curriculum content/evaluation
(4) Children's abilities/environments
(5) Demands of colleges/employers

FIG. 8.1. A functional model of the school.

Simply stated, the model represents the curriculum as, in some of its major aspects, the resultant of a balance that exists between three salient features of the school as an organization—technology, social system, and theory. This balance is affected by inputs to and outputs from the school, in the form of entering and leaving students, and social forces operating outside the school, either in the form of specific institutions, or the generally available stock of ideas, attitudes, and values. Whatever is outside the school is marked off from it by a boundary that in specific instances may be of greater or lesser strength. Technology here does not refer simply to actual equipment that may be used in teaching. Rather, it follows Perrow's definition of "a technique or complex of techniques employed to alter 'materials' (human or nonhuman, mental or physical) in an anticipated manner."[23] It is the means that an organization employs to get its work done. To an extent, the curriculum *is* the technology of the school—the means of achieving the task it sets out to do. But the technology is more than that. What is learned in school is also a resultant of the set of relationships that holds between teachers and teachers, students and students, and teachers and students, and of notions of the task of the school that may be only implicitly held and not deliberately expressed through the curriculum. It is through the social system that the technology of the organization is implemented; in the case of schools, principally by the teachers, administrators, and ancillary helpers. But sometimes students are held responsible for their own learning, or work collaboratively with teachers. They themselves then belong to that part of the social system that operates as a task group to implement the technology. Theory, like technology, is used in a somewhat technical sense to mean how the nature of the task is defined. In the case of schools, what do they exist for? What kinds of learning should they promote? How do children learn? What is counted as "achievement?" What constitutes appropriate behavior on the part of teachers and students? Sometimes, these questions may be formally posed and considered. But they do not have to be verbalized in order that a theory of the organization can exist. Whatever activities it engages in, these will betray the existence of implicitly held beliefs about teaching, learning, and the task of the school. Using a slightly different terminology, Perrow sums up these propositions as follows: "Organizations are influenced by three factors: the cultural system which sets legitimate goals, the technology which determines the means available for reaching these goals, and the social structure of the organization in which specific techniques are embedded in such a way as to permit goal achievement."[24] This may be compared to Sorokin's: "All empirically rooted socio-cultural phenomena are made up of three components: 1. meanings-values-norms; 2. physical and biological vehicles objectifying them; 3. mindful human beings (and groups) that create, operate and use them in the process of their interaction."[25]

Many writers argue that schools reflect society at large.[26] Broadly speaking, the analysis offered here supports this conclusion. Whatever technologies, relationships, or theories exist in schools are found there because they are drawn from a stock of models available in society. It does not follow, however, that in what the school does it must necessarily adopt whatever is currently the dominant model. It may use models that elsewhere are falling from favor, or it may incorporate ideas and behaviors that are characteristic of minority groups. The theoretical approach proposed here can help understanding of the circumstances under which one kind of adoption or another may occur, or be encouraged to occur.

The choices open to the school are practically limited by the propensity toward the establishment of internal equilibrium between technology, social system, and theory, and between the school and the surrounding environment. Change comes about mainly through the operation of external forces that tend to act differentially on the three components of the organization. Equilibrium may be restored through a return of the components affected to their former state. In that case, the change is only temporary. An example would be where an integrated curriculum replaces a subject-based curriculum, but solely on the basis of a change in technology, without compensating movements in social system or theory. For a while the curriculum is implemented, but only because teachers (and perhaps also students) are prepared to expend extra energy in overcoming the inertial effects of a social system and a theory that are incompatible with integration. Eventually, the inertial forces gain the upper hand and, though the semblance of the innovation may persist for a while, there is reversion to the roles and structures of subject teaching.[27] Very often, the return to a previous equilibrium follows on an attempt to change some part of the technology of the school,[28] since this is the organizational element most likely to be open to external pressure, and the one most likely to be targeted by innovators. Disused language laboratories, didactically taught discussion and discovery materials, unstreaming accompanied by rapid growth in remedial classes, are all results of initiatives that brought new technology to schools without effecting fundamental and lasting change in the curriculum.

Sometimes, however, the other elements move to adjust themselves to the one affected by an innovation. A new form of curriculum can then become institutionalized. This is most likely to happen when a change takes place in the theory of the school. There is then a commitment on the part of the task group to new goals and a willingness to explore and experiment with technology and social system in order to find ways of achieving them. Changing beliefs about the nature of young children and the nature of the learning process were accompanied in many elementary schools in the 1960s by the development of team teaching and open classroom techniques that allowed a new equilibrium to emerge so that innovation was effective.[29]

We can now postulate that the curriculum offered by the school will be to a great extent dependent on:

1. the stocks of knowledge, ideas, images, styles, and models available in its environment (for most schools, in society at large);
2. the nature of the input of students it receives;
3. the nature of the output of students (their destinations);
4. the influence channeled toward the school by other institutions;
5. the strength of the boundary around the school;
6. the need for congruence between technology, social system, and theory within the school;
7. the need for congruence between the activities of the school and the demands of outside forces.

Each of these factors will be briefly considered, and indications given of how they act to influence the kinds of curricula that schools offer.

FACTORS INFLUENCING THE FORM
OF THE CURRICULUM

A major limiting factor on the form of any particular curriculum is the variety of models available to influence it. Models relevant to the shaping of curricula are:

1. models of the nature of knowledge and knowing;
2. models of truth-seeking strategies within the subjects to be taught;
3. models of the nature of children;
4. models of desirable adult characteristics;
5. models of relationships between people and particularly between adults and children;
6. models of the role of the teacher and of effective teaching;
7. models of the curriculum itself.

Fundamental to any consideration of why curricula take the forms they do is the question, what ways of conceptualizing the nature of knowledge and the process of acquiring it exist in the surrounding society? And to what extent are these available for inclusion in the theory of the school? Schools do not necessarily have to wait until ideas about learning are generally accepted before adopting them, but there has to be some degree of acceptance before they can be successfully incorporated. Exactly how far ideas have to spread before they become influential upon schools will depend on the strength of the boundary between the school and the outside world, and on the school's relationship to institutions that generate and diffuse ideas on knowledge and learning. If a stage has not yet been reached when there are generally available technologies and forms of social system to support the theory, then disequilibrium and rejection may result. It is often the case that schools operate on a theory of knowledge that, though popularly held, is rejected by philosophers and psychologists. Teaching continues to be dominated in most schools by passive models of knowledge acquisition based on a naive theory of vision. According to this,

> the eye does not contribute anything to the object seen; it simply registers the object. Similarly, when understanding is treated as a kind of seeing, the mind simply registers the idea. . . . It follows from the supposed passivity of the eye that the object seen is wholly there, with all its *visual* properties, colour, shape, size. It exists prior to the act of seeing, and is unaffected by the act of seeing. . . . The vision-based theory of understanding states that direct inspection, or intuition, results in clear ideas. . . . Common-sense theories of understanding are still based on common-sense theories of seeing.[30]

The content of the curriculum will reflect the range of knowledge thought to be important and, in the case of academic subjects, the way they are conceived of and practised in industry, higher education, or learned societies. The biology curriculum in the 19th century had to be taxonomic in character because that was the state of the research paradigm on which it was modeled.[31] Chemistry, on the other hand, presented several different possibilities, but it was the one subscribed to by those high in the social structure of the discipline that became almost universally adopted.[32] The reform movements of the 1960s were concerned to persuade schools to respond to alternative models, either because they were clinging to a model that had gone out of date, or in order to promote acceptance of a variety of models capable of serving a wider range of purposes. Examples would be the introduction of new science curricula. The early Nuffield schemes in England were indicators to the schools that science's image of itself was changing, and that more emphasis should be placed on the innovative rather than the normative aspects of scientific activity. Later projects were more concerned with suggesting roles for school science other than that of inducting students into science as a professional career.[33]

Though the 19th century generally saw children as subordinate creatures, in need of moral correction and inspiration, and having to be disciplined on order to be taught, notions of the child as autonomous learner were not lacking. However, their entry into the language of educators was a very gradual process that can be charted through analysis of the language of official reports.[34] Similarly, there is, at any time, a variety of images of the desirable adults that children, as a result of education, should grow into, and of the relations that should exist between children and adults. The view that is projected in the schools may be one that relates to a particular section of society, if that is what the school serves, or it may be one that is widely accepted. A few schools deliberately set out to promote models that are not generally admired.[35] An example of shifts in the accepted models of behavior on the part of children and adults, and of relations between them, is documented by Mandel,[36] who discusses and compares two series of reading books for younger children, one the "Rollo" series, popular in the 19th century, and the other the 20th century "Dick and Jane" series:

> In the first group of books, the world is full of dangers and evil temptations, and the child himself is full of evil impulses that he must learn to control. In the second group, the world is full of good possibilities, and the child himself has only good impulses which should be given rein and encouragement. . . . With all the potential for badness outside and inside Rollo, it is natural that he should be given some sort of mechanism to protect himself from danger. From the first, Rollo is being taught a code of Christian virtues which he is to adopt in order to resist the evil around him. . . . The first step in inculcating such a set of rules for behavior is to impress the child with the wisdom and

sagacity of authority. Rollo himself must be taught to obey his parents un-questioningly.[37]

While Rollo is adopting precepts, Dick is adapting to social experience . . . Dick's world requires no constant watchfulness with confirmed inner virtues always on hand to protect him . . . his world is distinct from the world of adults. Indeed adults foster the autonomy of Dick and his group. Each individual finds self-confirmation and a source of meaning in social interaction with peers . . . The children spend their time having fun while playing with one another, while going to school, or while participating in humorous little incidents described as funny or silly.[38]

Mandel's discussion sums up well the curricular implications of the endorsement by the school of particular models of the child, the adult, and the relationships that should exist between them, and it is particularly useful in that it takes its example from what is apparently the learning of a value neutral skill—how to read.

Models of the role of the teacher and of effective teaching will be adopted to accord with images of adult and child, and of preferred styles of relationships. But they will also depend on the value placed by society on teaching, which in turn will affect the type of people who become teachers, and the experiences they are given to prepare them for the task. A view of good teaching will also reflect the state of knowledge about technologies for implementing theoretical conceptions of the purposes of the curriculum. If good teaching is extended to include planning as well as implementing the curriculum, then account must also be taken of what models are available for exemplifying a curriculum. In the last century, the curriculum could only be conceived as a schedule of content—facts to be learned or skills to be mastered, generally ranged under subject headings. Today we have discovered other possibilities: the curriculum can be seen in terms of aims and objectives, exploits or experiences, initiations or cultural confrontations. Also broader definitions have been accepted for what can legitimately be part of a curriculum. Not only can subjects appear in different forms, or be assimilated to one another in schemes of integration, but new areas of knowledge and experience, not before considered as material for a curriculum, can be imported—community service, Black studies, making TV programs, carrying out social and ecological surveys, to mention only some of the less extreme examples of innovation in curricular activities.

But, as has been pointed out, it is seldom the case that the choice of model is totally constrained by the absence of alternatives. One of the factors that plays a large part in deciding which set of models will, in practice, be adopted is the nature of the school's input and output of students. Who are they and where do they come from? Where will they go when they leave, and what expectations will be held of them by those who will continue their education, or give them employment? According to their family and community background, students will be more or less accepting of the school's valuation of what is suitable knowledge, more or less prepared to fit in with new definitions of proper social relationships, more or less ready to acquire new images of what they might become as adults. The extent to which the school accepts and encourages the inclinations of its entering students, or tries to change them, is largely a function of where they will go when they leave, and how far the environments they will enter are capable of influencing the school. If the success of a secondary school is judged by the number of students it sends to colleges and to prestigious occupations, then the demands of these institutions may outweigh the influence of the local community in determining where the school looks for appropriate models.

Moderating any interaction of pressures to adopt particular definitions of its task is the school's boundary—the psychological frontier that exists between members of the organization and their activities, and the outside world in the form of local and national communities, and of institutions capable of influencing what the school does. Generally speaking, schools have strong boundaries because inputs of resources into them are not directly linked to the sale of a product. The thought was well-expressed by Edward Thring over a century ago: "The old foundations [are] a great saving power in the land. Whatever their faults may be, they are generally free from meddling, free from the necessity of producing some show, something saleable. They are able to stand a storm without shrinking, and to face with calmness the morning letter-bag and the penny post."[39] The worthy ambition of many a school principal—"to face with calmness the morning letter-bag and the penny post"—is, as Thring perceptively observed, to be realized only if the school's output is not defined as saleable. The desire to avoid commitment to a saleable output is one reason why schools strive to identify themselves with scholarly traditions, and are reluctant to implement curricula that pursue overtly vocational objectives. However, schools are not always able to command this privileged position. At about the time that Thring was writing, English elementary schools were administered under a system of payment by results, which allowed them very little autonomy. But, as well as boundary control that regulates the imposition of specific performance demands on the school, there may be control over the selection of students and teachers. The English secondary school has always looked for opportunities to restrict student entry to those most likely to import ideas, behaviors, and aspirations consonant with the established theory of the institution.

Since the school functions as a single organization, and its ability to function depends on keeping dissonance and conflict within reasonable bounds, an overall determinant of the character of the curriculum is the way in which accommodation is achieved between technology, social system, and theory. This can be illustrated by examples. The English elementary school in the 19th century used a mass production technology, based on formal classrooms and recitation techniques, with little use of teaching aids. The social system was paternal and authoritarian. Children were expected to follow instructions and to be in all ways subordinate to and respectful of the wishes of teachers who themselves were products of authoritarian and rule-bound training colleges. The theory of the task was that the school should inculcate basic moral values, as propagated by the established church, and the basic skills of reading, writing, and simple calculation. The three elements of technology, social system, and theory were in harmony. It is difficult to see how a major shift could have taken place in any one of them without setting up an intolerable dissonance. Formal methods reflected the commonly held definition of the task and of the nature of children, while the established style of social relationships allowed that task to be carried out effectively. The modern elementary school presents a balance of a different kind. The technology is seen in much more interactive terms, with liberal use of teaching aids—not necessarily in the form of electronic gadgetry, more often in the shape of scissors, paste, and *papier mâché*. The social system tends to the maternal and the familial, while the theory construes children, at least some of the time, as active learners, and teaching as an engagement in a humanistic activity that attends to basic skill requirements, but also stresses, through concepts of growth, harmony, and discovery, the need to foster the developing social and intellectual capacities of the child. Here too, the technology, social system, and theory are consonant, but produce an arena for the enactment of curriculum that is supportive of quite different knowledge and values. Again, the whole would seem to be dependent on the harmony of the parts. Today's theory could not be implemented by the technology of the 19th century, nor could a 19th-century technology be sustained by today's social system.

ACCOUNTING FOR CURRICULUM CHANGE

This elaboration of the few simple propositions with which we started provides an account of the stabilizing tendencies which characterize the school as an organization, and tend to shape the form that the curriculum takes. But what account can it give of curriculum change? According to the view described above, change comes about mainly as a result of change in the factors in the environment of the school that control the internal balance between technology, social system, and theory. This does not provide an answer for the theorist who wants to know why any social change comes about because it pushes that fundamental question one stage further back without trying to solve it. But for those with a practical interest in curriculum change it offers ways of conceptualizing change that have some relevance to action. Schools are seen as reflections of particular sets of the stock of models of theorizing, doing, and relating that society possesses at any given time. The stock is continually changing. The range of models increases as new ones become popular and old ones are discarded.[40] Which set of models is relevant for any particular school depends on the character of its inputs and outputs, and the degree to which it can in other respects control its boundaries, so that it can respond selectively to the pressures of outside forces and institutions. These are matters that are, to a large extent, under administrative control. The question of curriculum change is centrally a question about change in the technology of the school, using that word in the broad sense that was indicated earlier. That is, it is mainly a process question. How does the school carry out its work? And why this way rather than that? But technology is inseparable from social system and theory. The answer to "why this way?" is partly "because that's how we see the task," and partly "because we get along together better that way." So changes in ways of seeing and way of getting along are linked with changes in the way the school gets its work done. An account of curriculum change in the English public school along these lines would point to different things than those highlighted by conflict theory: the change in the theory of the gentleman held in the upper reaches of society from a Christian to a more secular one, which is reflected in a more familial and less monastic social system in the school. The ways in which elected authorities have asserted more and more control over the school through legislation and imposition of financial regulation, and how the schools have resisted this erosion of their boundaries by devices, such as the development of the relationship with preparatory schools, to assure a homogeneous intake, and the sedulous fostering of a mythology of the school and its products: "When the editors [of the *Public Schools Yearbook* (1904)] spoke about 'public school spirit' and 'public school men' they enveloped the public schools in an air of mystery in order to distinguish them from state supported institutions and isolate them from criticism"[41]; and finally the changes in the university curriculum, which the schools have not been able to resist, and that have led to the development of strong commitments to science education.

IMPLICATIONS FOR PLANNING

Whether this kind of account is thought to be a more satisfactory one than one that places more emphasis on conflict all depends on the purposes of the theorizer. It is hard to see what practical consequences a conflict-based analysis can have for someone interested in planning a curriculum. It offers the choice of being on the side of social evolution, or against it. Either way, the planner can only try to speed up or slow down a process over which little or no control is possible. A functional perspective, on the other hand, does leave room for the planner, though it also, properly, demonstrates the magnitude of the task ahead. It does not suggest that the general course of events is predetermined, nor that, in the nature of things, a problem of technology/social system/theory dissonance can have only one solution. On the contrary, it argues against simple solutions that propose nothing more than a shift in technology, and points to many factors of which planning should take account, but that are often left on one side—the supply and training of teachers, the processes by which students move from grade to grade, or school to school, the destinations of students when they leave, the nature of the community within which the school is situated, controls over the admission of students, and so on. To recognize that the form of a curriculum is the result of shifting balances in complex systems, and to recognize also that many future states of the system are, at any time, possible is to deny isomorphism between managerial decisions and practical outcomes. It is not, however, to deny a role to purposeful management. In fact, once we accept that management is not simply the act of bringing about prespecified states of a system, or implementing predetermined objectives, its role is enhanced. It is no longer a technical affair of matching ends to means, but a creative process depending on wide-ranging consultation, on the interactive consideration of ends and means, and on the exercise of judgment over conflicts of interest. Its role is also enhanced in that we can no longer clearly distinguish between the managers and the managed. If management is not just a matter of technique, then it is not just a matter for the technical experts, but for all those who have knowledge of, and perspectives upon the system, and for all those who look to it to respond to their aims, wants, and desires. To construe schools in other ways, to see them as forming a rationally planned delivery system, is to move away rather than toward the realization of the purposes the curriculum is intended to secure.[42]

Good curriculum management, then, involves the clarification of purposes, the identification of possible system states that would contribute to the realization of these purposes, and decisions on how and where to operate on the factors controlling curriculum stability to try to bring about that state chosen as most suitable. Many curriculum changes have, in fact, been introduced in this indirect way, though seldom as part of a deliberate overall policy. Changes in the curriculum of the English elementary school were provoked by a program of designing buildings of a type that would encourage the development of social systems supportive of the theory and technology of open-class teaching. At the same time, the likelihood that the new technology would be implemented was increased by the move away from selection procedures at the point of student entry to the secondary school. It may be argued that if curriculum change were to be regularly planned in this all-embracing manner, it would require the creation of authorities with undesirably broad powers. But if these powers are used in the service of purposes widely and democratically deliberated upon, this would seem to be advantageous. It does not follow that because powers are wide, they have to be used for the furtherance of unique and all-embracing solutions. If we see the curriculum as determined by environments that are usually, in some sense, "local," rather than by national or global power struggles, then the management of the curriculum must be, to a large degree, local. It is surely better that powers should exist that can ensure the translation into action of purposeful curriculum decisions, rather than that authorities should have the ability to intervene in ways that upset the system without achieving any declared purpose. State legislation in the United States has been very effective in implementing accountability schemes, but this means of opening the boundary of the school has affected its technology in ways that conflict with theory and social system. There has been a consequent lowering of teacher morale and satisfaction, without any solid achievement of purpose to compensate for this. The objective of creating possibilities for more comprehensive approaches to the management of the curriculum would be that systems should be coaxed toward desired ends, not that attempts could be made to force them in particular directions.

Seeing schools as systems that tend toward equilibrium leads to an emphasis on gradualism in planning. The belief that change should be brought about rapidly, or in revolutionary ways, is rejected in favor of change strategies that allow that the interests of the community may best be served by moving in directions that are discovered, rather than predetermined, and by avoiding attempts to force the immediate realization of stated goals. The notion is one of working toward desirable states of affairs, rather than for the achievement of highly specific objectives.[43] Gradualists would, for example, have argued in the 1960s against the idea that all English secondary schools should, at some early and predetermined point in time, cease to control student entry through selection and become comprehensive. They would have pointed to the fact that different schools, in different parts of the country, were in varying degrees ready for such a change. In some cases, reorganization would strain the social system of the school by amalgamating buildings on widely separated sites, in others there would be dissonance with the values of the local community, in others technological problems in providing a curriculum because of lack of suitable models and suitable teachers. This is not a doctrinaire argument in favor of a system that tends to reinforce class inequalities, but in favor of seeing problem solution as something that, to be effective, must take account of local circumstances, and match expectations to the power of institutions to bring about change. Chosen purposes are not served by tactics that risk breakdowns leading to a hardening of opposition to innovation, nor by encouraging people to have unrealistic beliefs in the capacity of the schools to solve deep-seated social problems. A slower approach may work better: the time gained can be used to ask and to answer questions about the curriculum that must otherwise be glossed over. In the case of the comprehensive secondary school, how, in terms of actual encounters between teachers, children, and materials, are the new forms of organization to be used as arenas for the pursuit of new aims and new purposes? Merely to declare a school comprehensive, even to provide it with a nationally approved curriculum, is not enough.[44]

The argument about gradualism brings us full circle, for the question of whether we should incline to evolution or revolution relates closely to our theoretical views on whether, or to what extent, sociocultural change moves in an inevitable direction, and whether we prefer a functionalist or a conflict interpretation of how change comes about. The position put forward here is, first of all, that, although the distinction between function and conflict may in some ways be a spurious one, there is for practical purposes a real choice of perspective to be made, and one that we cannot avoid by adopting a managerial stance toward curriculum planning: and secondly that, although any view of curriculum change is necessarily partial and incomplete, a functional view is theoretically satisfactory and allows us possibilities for developing theories of good practice in the arena of curriculum planning. To hold the opposite view is to subscribe to a fundamentally pessimistic conception of the role of the planner, and to deny that curriculum theory can ever be anything other than a branch of social theory concerning itself with the connections between curricular forms and the patterns of conflict between power groups in society. Like arch conservatives, revolutionaries already know what the ends of action should be. Neither group is prepared to have their view of reality disconfirmed. Subscription to the idea of evolution implies an openness toward the directions that change might take, and a commitment to the discovery of desirable directions through processes of deliberation in which questions of public policy are decided in ways that respect the wishes of all those who will be affected by the answers that are given.

NOTES

1. "Ideology" here is intended to refer to any belief system, whether or not it is conventionally regarded as extreme. Compare Paulston, R. G. (1976). *Conflicting theories of social and educational change: A typological review.* Pittsburgh: University of Pittsburgh, University Center for International Studies, p. 3.
2. Bobbitt is taken as representative of the early curriculum management movement around 1920 (see Callahan, R. E. (1962). *Education and the cult of efficiency.* Chicago: University of

Chicago Press). Historically, Tyler links this phase of curriculum theorizing with the more recent objectives-centered phase associated with curriculum reform movements of the 1960s. See, for example, Taba, H. (1962). *Fundamentals of curriculum development: Theory and practice.* New York: Harcourt Brace, or Wheeler, D. K. (1967). *Curriculum process.* London: University of London Press.

3. Young, M. F. D. (1975). Curriculum change: Limits and possibilities. *Educational Studies, 1,* 129–138; Kallós, D., & Lundgren, U. P. (1976). *An enquiry concerning curriculum: Foundations for curriculum change.* University of Gothenburg: Pedagogiska Institutionen, mimeo.

4. Critics of interventionism may admit that policies can be effective in delaying the time when certain social groups acquire power over what is taught. Moves to improve the curriculum can always be represented as conspiratorial: "the collision between the rationally founded movement of educational technology and the social liberal ideology have [sic] emphasised the demand for measures whereby external control over the events in teaching are [sic] to be substituted by internal self-control. In practice this means a more subtle form of manipulation achieved via an increasingly invisible pedagogy" (Kallós & Lundgren. *Op. cit.,* p. 74). There are such things as conspiracies, but the demonstration of their existence should rest on empirical evidence, rather than on a priori ideological commitments. Educational events always can be interpreted as evidence of the maneuverings power groups, just as individual actions always can be seen in terms of a Freudian theory of motivations. This is made possible by adopting theories with such a wide range of convenience that anything can be made to fit them.

5. Kliebard, H. M. (1975). Reappraisal: The Tyler rationale. In William F. Pinar (Ed.). *Curriculum theorizing: The reconceptualists* (pp. 70–83). Berkeley, CA: McCutchan.

6. *Ibid.,* p. 80.

7. Inglis, F. (1974). Ideology and the curriculum: The value assumptions of system builders. *Journal of Curriculum Studies, 6,* 3–14; Booth, Wayne C. (1974). *Modern dogma and the rhetoric of assent.* Chicago: University of Chicago Press.

8. See, for example, Walker, Decker F. (1975). Curriculum development in an art project. In William A. Reid & Decker F. Walker (Eds.). *Case studies in curriculum change: Great Britain and the United States* (pp. 91–135). London: Routledge & Kegan Paul.

9. They may be effective in tightly controlled situations, where techniques such as programmed learning can be successfully employed. Most curricula have to be designed to function as part of an open system.

10. Young. *Op. cit.,* p. 130.

11. For a development of this viewpoint, see Sarason, S. B. (1971). *The culture of the school and the problem of change.* Boston, MA: Allyn & Bacon.

12. Silverman, D. (1970). *The theory of organisations.* London: Heinemann, p. 45.

13. For a discussion of the grounds for considering that knowledge can be construed in this way, see Popper, K. R. (1972). *Objective knowledge: An evolutionary approach.* Oxford: Oxford University Press.

14. Marxists might claim that this is true only of liberally inspired change that rejects revolution as a tool of innovation. But unless the revolution is to abolish schools (and most Marxists seem opposed to that), there is still a bureaucratic educational system to manage on the morrow of the revolution.

15. It is unfortunate that the word "rational" has been claimed by theorists who believe, implicitly or explicitly, that it is possible to match the future state of an education system to a predetermined plan. Rational action need not be so narrowly construed.

16. See, for example, Fallding, H. (1972). Only one sociology. *British Journal of Sociology, 23,* 93–101, and Dahrendorf, R. (1967). Out of Utopia. In N. J. Demerath & R. A. Peterson (Eds.). *System, change, and conflict* (pp. 465–480). New York: Free Press.

17. *Op. cit*, p. 94.

18. Dahrendorf, *op. cit.*, p. 480. Paulston (*op. cit.*, p. 39) says "I view the functional and conflict interpretations of total societies and of continuity and change in education . . . as dialectically related. Both views are necessary for adequate explanation of change and lack of change in social and educational phenomena and relationships."

19. "The key concept bridging the gap between statics and dynamics in functional theory is that of strain, tension, contradiction, or discrepancy between the component elements of social and cultural structure" (Merton, R. K. (1968). *Social theory and social structure*. 3rd. ed. New York: Free Press, p. 176).

20. The phrases are due to Fallding (*op. cit.*, p. 100) and Kaplan (in Demerath and Peterson, *op. cit.*, p. 428).

21. Reported in Taylor, P. H. et al. (1974a). *Purpose, power and constraint in the primary school curriculum*. London: Macmillan, pp. 31-37.

22. Reported in Taylor, P. H. et al. (1974b). *The English sixth form: A case study in curriculum research*. London: Routledge & Kegan Paul, pp. 99-100.

23. Perrow, C. (1965). Hospitals: Technology, structure, and goals. In J. G. March (Ed.). *Handbook of organizations*. Chicago: Rand McNally, p. 915.

24. *Ibid.*, p. 912.

25. Sorokin, P. A. (1938). *Social and cultural dynamics*. 4 vols. New York: American Book Company, vol. 4, p. 46.

26. See, for example, Jencks, C. et al. (1972). *Inequality*. New York: Basic Books.

27. For some examples, see Dickinson, N. B., The head teacher as innovator: A study of an English school district, and Hamilton, D., Handling innovation in the classroom: Two Scottish examples. In Reid and Walker. *Op. cit.*, pp. 136-178 and 179-207.

28. For a dramatic instance involving the whole technology of the school, see Smith, L. M., & Keith, P. M. (1971). *Anatomy of educational innovation*. New York: Wiley.

29. For a discussion of the extent to which the technology of the classroom is adaptable, see Westbury, I. (1973). Conventional classrooms, "open" classrooms and the technology of teaching. *Journal of Curriculum Studies*, 5, 99-121.

30. Schon, D. A. (1963). *The displacement of concepts*. London: Tavistock, pp. 173-174 and 176. Compare Popper's discussion of the "bucket" theory of knowledge (Popper, *op. cit.*, p. 341ff.).

31. Medawar points out that Victorian examination questions in zoology at University College, London, "called for nothing more than a voluble pouring forth of factual information," citing as an example: "By what special structures are bats enabled to fly through the air? And how do the galeopitheci, the pteromys, the petaurus, and the petauristae support themselves in that light element? Compare the structure of the wing of the bat with that of the bird, and with that of the extinct pterodactyl: and explain the structures by which the cobra expands its neck, and the saurian dragon flies through the atmosphere. This question, not the longest of the eight set in 1860, goes on for a further 16 lines (Medawar, P. B. (1967). *The art of the soluble*. London: Methuen, pp. 114-115).

32. See Layton, D. (1973). *Science for the people: The origins of the school science curriculum in England*. London: Allen & Unwin.

33. For a discussion, see Fensham, P. J. (1974). Science curricula and the organisation of secondary schooling. *Journal of Curriculum Studies*, 6, 61-72.

34. Cheverst, W. J. (1972). The role of the metaphor in educational thought: An essay in content analysis. *Journal of Curriculum Studies*, 4, 71-82.

35. Probably the best known example is Summerhill at Leiston in Essex, England, founded by A. S. Neill. For a general review of "progressive" schools that have deliberately set out to

go against majority views on how education should be conducted, see Skidelsky, R. (1969). *English progressive schools.* Harmondsworth: Penguin.

36. Mandel, R. (1964). Children's books: Mirrors of social development. *Elementary School Journal, 64,* 190–199.

37. *Ibid.,* p. 193.

38. *Ibid.,* pp. 197, 199.

39. Thring, Edward (1864). *Education and school.* Cambridge: Macmillan, p. 118.

40. The succession of models that inspired notions of "liberal" education in England is analyzed by Rothblatt (Rothblatt, S. (1976). *Tradition and change in English liberal education: An essay in history and culture.* London: Faber & Faber).

41. Rothblatt, S. (1968). *The revolution of the dons: Cambridge and society in Victorian England.* London: Faber & Faber, p. 53.

42. Compare the argument in Wise, A. E. (1977). Why educational policies often fail: The hyperrationalisation hypothesis. *Journal of Curriculum Studies, 9,* 43–57.

43. For an argument in favor of gradualism as a general approach to the planning of educational change, see Smith & Keith. *Op. cit.,* pp. 370–373.

44. Kallós and Lundgren show that even in the apparently thorough planning of comprehensive systems of education in Sweden, administrative arrangements were given more attention than the forms of the curriculum, which continued to embody many of the models derived from the old selective secondary school. This may have been due to conspiratorial action on the part of those who stood to preserve influence and power thereby: equally, it may have been due to lack of vision and knowledge on the part of planners who were committed to the goals of comprehensive education (Kallós, D. & Lundgren, U. P. (1977). Lessons from a comprehensive school system for curriculum theory and research. *Journal of Curriculum Studies, 9,* 3–20).

9

Curricular Topics as Institutional Categories

Pursuit of the idea of organization introduces us to some of the complexities with which an adequate theory of curriculum planning has to deal. But, to conceive of schooling and curriculum as systems still leaves out of account some of their essential features that have deep implications for how we should think about curriculum deliberation. Systems theory accommodates important ideas like conceptions of good teaching, public opinion, or images of the third grade student, but only on the basis of introducing them into change models as components, or inputs. What is still missing is a sense of what extra has to be added, so that our thinking can be informed by notions of institution as well as of organization—that is, by a feeling for schools and curriculum that apprehends them as living sociocultural phenomena with an existence in the collective mind, as well as in visible manifestations of practice and forms of organization.

This chapter, which draws on the work of John Meyer,[1] was a first attempt to repair this gap. It was given as a paper at the Sociology of Education Conference, St. Hilda's College, Oxford, in September,1982, and subsequently published as "Curricular topics as institutional categories: Implications for theory and research in the history and sociology of school subjects" in Goodson, Ivor F., and Ball, Stephen (Eds.), Defining the curriculum: Histories and ethnographies.[2]

This chapter assumes that the object of studying the history of school subjects, or of examining them from sociological perspectives, is to increase our understanding of how and why topics and activities acquire (or lose) educational significance. This view I contrast with one that would hold that work of this kind should be directed toward responding to historical or sociological rather than educational questions.

If it is an educational agenda that holds out attention—the aim to understand better the purposes and events of schooling, or the aspiration to manage and control schooling processes and outcomes—then the success of the endeavor depends on working with a conception of what education *is*. In other words, as a preliminary to asking the question, "what do subjects do?", we need to have some answer to the question, "what do schools do?"

WHAT DO SCHOOLS DO?

All educational research proceeds on some assumption, which may or may not be made explicit, about what it is that schools, and more particularly school systems, do. Sometimes the assumption is that they are self-organizing systems that transmit specific skills and knowledge. Other researchers see them as instruments of society at large that reproduce its social and economic structures.

This chapter explores a plausible alternative view that avoids simplistic assumptions about the self-directive nature of educational systems but, at the same time, allows that what actors within them do is the result of rational decision, rather than of forces over which they have little or no control. I find this alternative conception, which is expounded by Meyer,[3] plausible both in the sense that its predictions about the behavior of actors fit well with my own experience as student and teacher, and in the sense that it is consonant with many of the findings of recent research into the history and sociology of school subjects.

Meyer's ideas are a reaction against the commonly held assumption underlying much writing and research on the school curriculum that what is taught, and how it is taught, result essentially from decisions and initiatives taken within educational organizations. In his writings, external forces and structures emerge, not merely as sources of ideas, promptings, inducements, and constraints, but as definers and carriers of the categories of content, role, and activity to which the practice of schools must approximate in order to attract support and legitimation. The world external to the schools is thought of, not so much in terms of formal bodies and conventional groupings (trade unions, universities, parents, employers), as in terms of more loosely conceived publics or constituencies, for whom the elements of the curriculum have importance; for example, the public for whom history as a school subject is significant because its members provide resources to support it, or because they value it as something that enhances the social or intellectual standing of those who take courses in it. These interested publics that pay for and support education hand over its work to the professionals in only a limited and unexpected sense. For while it may appear that the professionals have power to determine what is taught (at school, district, or national level, depending on the country in question), their scope is limited by the fact that only those forms and activities that have significance for external publics can, in the long run, survive.

Such forms and activities Meyer terms *institutional categories*, where the word "institutional" connotes a cultural ideology, and is contrasted with "organizational," meaning enshrined within unique and tangible structures such as schools and classrooms. Institutional categories comprise schooling levels (such as elementary), school types (such as comprehensive), educational roles (such as college principal), and, importantly for our purpose, curricular topics (such as reading, the Reformation, or 10th grade mathematics). In each of these instances, the organizational form, as created and maintained by teachers and others, is parallelled by an institutional category that is significant for some wider public, or publics. When curricular practice strays too far and too visibly from the category as understood by interested publics, the result is loss of support, student alienation, and failure and collapse of efforts to sustain the legitimacy of the activity. The demise of William Tyndale School[4] provides a particular local example; the retreat from innovative mathematics programs in elementary schools a more general one. Innovation is not impossible—it may even be demanded; but innovation that is generated internally to the organization without much regard for wider publics is problematic. As Meyer puts it: "innovations sacrifice the categorical meaning of topics."[5]

The unexpected power that teachers retain is not to introduce, on their own initiative, new topical categories, but to represent the topics that are taught as properly belonging within the existing categories. Categorical meaning is either accorded or withheld; the professional art of the teacher lies in activating and maintaining the categorical status of what is taught. Teachers are most importantly not manipulators of realities, but purveyors of rhetorics, and professional ideologies are a means to the successful accomplishment of this role.

Thus far, the impression created is one of cynicism. In fact, once the initial step is taken of seeing the schooling system as being essentially concerned with offering membership in significant categories, that is, with status, rather than with the implanting of cognitive skills and knowledge, then the way is open to allow that educational actors behave with a good deal of genuine rationality in the resolution of real choices about what to teach, and what to study. Students, in Meyer's view, are centrally concerned with constructing educational careers connected to desired social and occupational statuses, while teachers (whom he considers "not much less sensible than young persons")[6] devote their efforts to ensuring that the categorical memberships on offer are, in the public eye, fully accredited and capable of conferring properly schooled labels.

TOPICS AND ACTIVITIES AS INSTITUTIONAL CATEGORIES

Thinking of school systems as organizations that are shaped from without (Meyer uses the metaphor of the exoskeleton to convey the essence of his idea) cautions us against analyzing them according to definitions and variables proposed by insiders. For this reason, it is appropriate to suspend, temporarily, use of the word "subject," in order to work instead with topics and activities. If the successful teaching of X, in the sense of its survival in school programs, is related to the rhetorical skills of those who teach and organize it, then the actual content of X, in topical terms, may be more problematic than we might at first suppose. Provided that no clues are given by changes in labeling, English literature may turn out to be topically quite close to sociology, or geography to statistics. However, we also need to import the idea of activity. School programs may become categorically legitimate as much through the promotion of certain kinds of activity, as through the inclusion of appropriate topics. Science in the English secondary school legitimates itself through laboratory work that is only loosely related to the demands of specific content (secondary modern schools in the 1950s and 1960s were frequently barred from claims to be teaching science because they had no laboratories). It is also the case that too much concentration on the idea of subject may lead researchers to neglect programs like art or physical education, which are essentially activity-based. The use of topic/activity avoids this problem, and enables us to ask questions about how topics/activities are marshaled into various curricular patterns and called subjects, or shared and exchanged between subjects. (From this point on, topic is understood to subsume activity.) It also directs attention to the critical role certain topics may play in the organization of school subjects. Calculus as a topic within mathematics, or classical texts in the teaching of languages would be examples.

A further point to be made is that the translation of a topic into schooled status may be a different matter than the translation of a subject. The constellations or sequencings of topics in school programs do not necessarily reflect those found in other contexts where subjects are taught or practiced. One of the problematic features of Modern Mathematics was its attempt to distort conventionally understood topic sequences so that college topics began to figure in elementary school programs (this disjunction between subjects and topics as content in schools and content in other places is generally ignored by philosophers of education seeking an episte-mological base for the school curriculum).

Of all the topics that might serve as the content of schooling, only a limited subset actually supplies the subject matter of the curriculum, and the subset of topics that achieves categorical status is even smaller. Over time, its composition changes. Old topics drop out of favor, and new ones are adopted within subject curricula, as teachers and administrators seek status for those claimed to be within their jurisdiction, disassociate them-selves from those that are losing esteem, and make bids for those that they think will enhance the prestige of their disciplines.

Four key and related characteristics of topics determine their attractive-ness: centrality, universality, sequential significance, and status relatedness. A *central* topic is one that is essential to categorical membership. For exam-ple, in English schools, enrollment in an A-level program has traditionally been a condition of membership in the categorical role of "sixth former" (11th/12th grader). Students have understood this, and have committed resources to mastering the A-level program competently enough to maintain themselves in good standing. On the other hand, in spite of the entreaties of educators, they have consistently failed to show commitment to general studies programs, which are not central to the claim of bona fide status as a sixth former. When publics recognize topics as critically related to mem-bership in significant role categories, these have centrality, and are ac-corded economic resources and the attention of politicians and planners.

Some topics that are central are also *universal*, such as mathematics. That is, there is agreement that enrollment in them is essential for all, or nearly all students, whatever the academic career they are embarked upon. How-ever, universality does not necessarily imply centrality. Physical education programs are practically everywhere universal, but hardly anywhere cen-tral. In countries such as England, where education systems direct resources toward 'abler' students, subjects tend to stress topics that permit them to be central without being universal, since this offers greater prestige. Foreign languages, even if universally taught at the outset of the secondary school, rapidly become a curricular option; mathematics is compelled to be univer-sal, but continues to stress high-status content; high-status subjects in de-cline, which try to rescue themselves by seeking universality, may fail dis-mally—Latin is an example.

Sequential significance characterizes topics that are prerequisites for fu-ture student progress. Reading is a simple case. Students who cannot read at a minimal level are debarred from higher status programs. Topics in science are sequential in a more complex way. Elaborate chains of topics can be created that mesh with choice points in student educational careers, and enable science content to become a significant marker of progress.

Some innovatory science programs have failed because they interfered with this process. The Schools Council Integrated Science Project, for example, rendered problematic the connections, previously well understood, by students, teachers, and publics, between O- and A-level programs.

Subjects that chain topics in sequences with career significance are frequently, though not always, strong on *status relatedness*. Enrollment in the A-level mathematics program becomes the mark of the outstanding student and is linked to entry to high-status university courses. On the other hand, progress through metalwork activities, where the curriculum moves from lower to higher level skills, does not confer status. In fact, metalwork teachers are often keen to exchange technical skill sequencing for the less clear progression of a curriculum based on design, with the idea that the importance of design in the modern world can enable them to teach topics with claims to universalism and centrality. This illustrates the point that status relatedness (which may or may not be linked to sequencing) works both ways; while some programs are associated with high-status futures, others lead to low status or stigmatized careers and occupations.

Centrality, universality, sequential significance, and status relatedness are sociohistorical, or ideological rather than educational, or epistemological facts. Much as teachers might like to believe that the categorical significance of a subject relates to its intrinsic character, curriculum history demonstrates that this is not the case. For many years, classics enjoyed all these marks of the successful school subject, and teachers maintained its supportive rhetorics with ease, even when there was evidence to show that actual levels of student achievement were quite low. Eventually, however, a shift in public appreciation of the category of Latin and Greek created an opposite situation. Now the work of rhetorically defending classics in the secondary curriculum is practically impossible in the face of scepticism on the part of students, parents, and employers.

But in the absence of such shifts in institutional categories, the work of establishing new topics is difficult. Where publics have been exposed to pervasive rhetorics of persuasion (computer studies), professional activity within the school system can result in innovation. Where this is not the case (integrated humanities programs), modifications in the topical content of curricula may prove to be of a temporary nature.

Since the attribution or nonattribution of topical status by publics is a social fact (though not necessarily in the sense that all publics are in agreement), school programs tend toward topical uniformity within politically united, or culturally homogeneous territories. This is true even where control over the content of the curriculum rests with local jurisdictions (the United States). It is still more the case where there is de jure central control (the United Kingdom). In Meyer's view, such administrative features of education systems have the effect of reinforcing an already strong tendency toward isomorphism between organizational practice and institutional categories.

TEACHERS AS MANAGERS OF TOPICAL CONTENT

Most teachers (and educational administrators) understand instinctively that the work of teaching consists importantly in promoting and exhibiting the isomorphism between practice and category. This helps explain the resistance of educational forms in the face of arguments for their reform on the part of educational theorists and teacher educators. Pedagogical forms (the recitation) persist because they are identified in the public mind with teaching, while other activities (class discussion, meditation) are not, unless they take place under special labels that limit their scope (debating society, yoga club). Even where proponents of pedagogical reform can convince professional colleagues of the value of their ideas, they still face the more essential and highly difficult task of converting outside publics.

There is also an understanding on the part of teachers that the categorical status of topics creates a special kind of logic that has to be observed in handling the rhetorics that surround them. An act of teaching, or the inclusion or exclusion of a topic, can never be judged on a scale of correctness. Event X is either a clear case of a categorically acceptable occurrence or it is not. There is no question of something being probably a remedial reading class, or possibly an instance of the teaching of calculus (though there is more scope for variation in practice in the former). This explains a special difficulty that new subjects have in becoming accepted as a legitimate part of high status curricula. Since they have not been previously taught, no one knows what a proper example of topic or teaching would look like. Yet the subject has to be totally acceptable or not accepted at all (there are few genuine examples of trials or feasibility studies relating to high-status content, even where this has been the declared strategy of curriculum projects).

Where subjects already have full acceptance, nothing must be allowed to jeopardize it, since the least departure from total affirmation of categorical legitimacy can result in a collapse of credibility. This is so even in the case of high-status schools. A 19th-century head of Eton College was quick to reject the suggestion of the Clarendon Commissioners that his pupils' knowledge should be tested by an examination with the comment that such "interference with authority and responsibility of the Head Master is calculated to produce serious evil."[7] Where the evidence cannot be withheld, Meyer notes, the damage may be contained by the adoption of a permanent posture of reform.

Since few subjects can claim all the possible marks of status, the judgment that teachers have to make is about when it is prudent to abandon one kind of legitimation for another (the case of metalwork versus design has already been noted). Perhaps the hardest judgment to make in recent years has been that between claims for universality and claims for status relatedness, since these are to a high degree mutually exclusive. The advent of the organizational change to comprehensive secondary education in England in the 1960s gave the impression that participation was to become a major system goal, and that subjects should embrace topics that enabled them to enroll the widest possible clientele. In the event, it seems that, though politically sanctioned, the changes that took place were more properly organizational than institutional. The norms imposed by university entrance requirements, and by General Certificate of Education (GCE) examining continued to set the parameters for educational categories that have proven remarkably resistant to attempts to democratize them (notably, the removal of the pass/fail boundary from examinations at 16+ has met with no response in terms of public categories; students, parents, and most teachers still talk of "passing GCSE" [General Certificate of Secondary Education]). Subjects such as science, which as few years ago were trying to develop topics accessible to a wide range of students, are now once again stressing high-status content and deemphasizing innovative teaching styles.

STUDENTS AS CONSUMERS OF TOPICAL CONTENT

Students, as rational consumers, are less concerned with knowing than with the status that comes from categorical membership, and the future promise that this implies. They are essentially engaged in building educational careers that have implications for future social and occupational careers. Like teachers, they judge the appropriateness of committing themselves to curricular topics in the light of estimations of centrality, universality, sequential significance, and status relatedness. Topics that rank high on these criteria will be accorded substantial levels of commitment; those that do not will attract lower levels of personal investment. In this way, students maximize the possibility that, for a given expenditure of effort, they can maintain their good standing as categorical members, and secure their chances of moving on to other desired categorical positions. The goal is success in the system, as opposed to success in learning (though the two are inevitably related). Hence, the kind of innovation that sacrifices the categorical meaning of topics will meet with low student commitment and will survive with difficulty, or not at all. This was the fate of many raising of the school leaving age (ROSLA) programs in England that emphasized relevance and life skills instead of academic properly schooled content. Students identify such curricula as connected with low-status futures, and find them meaningless in terms of their understanding of educationally significant categories.

Given that student commitment is closely related to the perceived significance of topics to an educational career, and that, as Meyer puts it, "programmatic membership is more certainly more vital than knowledge,"[8] it follows that students are likely to be only marginally concerned with attempted innovations in teaching and method that are ostensibly to their benefit. Subjects that reform their pedagogies cannot count on student support. Many studies show that one-way authoritarian teaching continues to predominate in schools. Yet it is also the case that students seldom experience it that way. This, Meyer suggests, is because "they are attending to the larger reality of 'teacher' as an institutional category" and are "surprisingly inattentive to the particular characteristics of their individual teachers."[9]

IMPLICATIONS FOR THEORY AND RESEARCH

If we regard the notion of institutional categories as providing a plausible key to the understanding of what schools do, what consequences follow for how we should study the evolution of those constellations of educational topics we call school subjects? Most broadly, we should be cautioned against attempting to interpret the history or sociology of subjects solely in terms of the accounts given by the actors most directly concerned—teachers and students. Especially, we should be on our guard against drawing our evidence about how subjects behave mainly from the activities and statements of teachers. What teachers can achieve may be importantly limited by what the understandings of outside publics impose in the way of parameters within which choices must be made. At least students provide us with a bridge between the school as organization and the external institutional categories. But preferably we should look for evidence also from the carriers of categorical ideologies—parents, employers, scholars, politicians, administrators, and others.

Further, we should be encouraged to consider that the fate of school subjects may be, to a large extent, in the hands of students as rational consumers, rather than be led to construe subjects as the means by which school systems and teachers produce effects in students. Understanding the evolution of the topics of the curriculum depends on a sophisticated knowledge of the behavior of students as clients of academic, disciplinary professionals. Subjects, and subject topics are the elements out of which students build careers, so that one central question to be asked about school subjects is, how are the topics they offer significant for student careers? And what effect do changes of topic have on this significance? That is, the histories of subjects need to contain also the histories of those for whom they have provided access to categorical membership.

Next, though the press to isomorphism between practice and category is strong, change does take place, and has to be accounted for. In the construction of such accounts, we need to focus on those features of the external, institutional world that cause categories to evolve, so that spaces for innovation are created. It is not to be denied that some of the initiative for this comes from educators and actors in school systems, but the primary changes that need to be described are those in the external category system, not those within organizational structures: Latin did not collapse because of failure on the part of teachers.

Finally, we have to take seriously the logic of categories, and accept that, within the terms of such a logic, successful rhetorics are realities. Though teachers and administrators have to be careful that disjunctions between practice and belief do not escalate to the point where credibility collapses, nonetheless it remains true that what is most important for the success of school subjects is not the delivery of goods that can be publicly evaluated, but the development and maintenance of legitimating rhetorics that provide automatic support for correctly labeled activity. The choice of appropriate labels, and the association of these in the public mind with plausible rhetorics of justification, can be seen as the core mission of those who work to advance or defend the subjects of the curriculum. The study of how they take such action will provide an essential key to the writing of subject histories. Here too, a condition of the conduct of research is that we focus not only on the professional actors themselves, but also on the evolution of institutional categories among external publics.

NOTES

1. Meyer, J. W. (1978). The structure of educational organizations. In J. W. Meyer et al. (Eds.). *Environments and organizations*. San Francisco: Jossey-Bass; Meyer, J. W. (1980). Levels of the education system and schooling effects. In C. E. Bidwell & D. M. Windham (Eds.). *The analysis of educational productivity. Vol. 2. Issues in Macroanalysis*. Cambridge, MA: Ballinger.
2. Reid, W. A. (1984). Curricular topics as institutional categories: Implications for theory and research in the history and sociology of school subjects. In I. F. Goodson & S. J. Ball (Eds.). *Defining the curriculum: Histories and ethnographies* (pp. 67–75). Lewes: Falmer Press.
3. See Note 1.
4. Inner London Education Authority (1976). *William Tyndale Infants and Junior School public inquiry*. London: ILEA.
5. Meyer (1980). *Op. cit.*, p. 54.
6. *Ibid.*, p. 47.
7. Reid, William A., & Filby, Jane (1982). *The sixth: An essay in education and democracy*. Lewes: Falmer Press, p. 217.
8. Meyer (1980). *Op. cit.*, p. 26.
9. *Ibid.*, p. 54.

CHAPTER

10

Curriculum Change and the
Evolution of Educational Constituencies

Thus far, my investigation into institutional aspects of curriculum has been theoretic. Although illustrative examples have been given, the main concern has been to construct an account of institutional behavior in terms of abstract categories. This chapter sets out to give more solidity to this account by examining a specific historical example of the institutionalization of curriculum change. In terms of making connections to the practical, this is a very appropriate project. Deliberation on the curriculum assumes that both perceptions of dissatisfaction, and proposals for how dissatisfactions might be mitigated, arise within an historical context, and that understanding of historical contexts must inform deliberative processes. The context chosen—the curriculum of the upper secondary school in 19th-century England—is one that I have striven to understand over a number of years, for the practical reason that the curriculum reform projects that I worked on in the 1970s were aimed at an institution—the English sixth form, which was, historically, shaped by 19th-century developments.[1]

"The evolution of educational constituencies" was written for inclusion in Goodson, Ivor F. (Ed.), Social histories of the secondary curriculum.[2]

The question I raise in this chapter is: how can the study of curriculum history help us understand (for practical as well as theoretical purposes) the nature of curriculum change? I answer the question in a way that is both general and particular: general, in that it suggests a broad framework for understanding curriculum change, and particular, in that the framework as presented is explored through consideration of a concrete case—the evolution of the curriculum of the English sixth form through the 19th century.

Two matters of explanation need to be settled first. These are: what meanings of curriculum, curriculum change, and curriculum history am I working with? And what do I see as the deficiencies of the available accounts of curriculum change that might be remedied by curriculum history?

I do not, in this instance, understand curriculum simply in terms of the subjects of which it is comprised, or of the contents of those subjects. Of more fundamental importance are questions of the aims associated with the teaching of particular subjects or content, and of the overall form and structure of the curriculum. In terms of texts read and constructions mastered, the classical curriculum of the 19th-century sixth form appeared to enjoy a long period of stability. But the aims of teaching shifted, with the appearance of a new middle-class clientele, from the finishing of the aristocrat to the induction of salaried administrators into careers. And the structure and ambiance of the students' curriculum experience underwent a radical change with the introduction of standard grammars, the growth of public examining, and the move from schoolroom to classroom. Stability of subject content tends to mask important shifts in the curricular meanings and significances that the transaction of that content has for teachers, students, and wider publics. Curriculum history is more than the tracking of new elements or techniques, and keeping a record of the loss of old ones: it is the recovery and explanation of how the curriculum comes to have new meaning, or the production of accounts of why, in some circumstances, meanings can remain stable for long periods. Such accounts may or may not center on changes in curriculum content as listed in lesson plans, syllabuses, and prospectuses.

The theories commonly invoked to explain curriculum change differ according to the emphasis they place on the role of external or internal forces. They also differ in the extent to which they represent change as resulting from purposive action, or from the effects of forces over which there can be little or no control. Externally driven change can be described within a frame of reference that stresses functionalist or determinist interpretations of social forces, or, alternatively, it can be seen as resulting from the mobilization of political and administrative resources targeted on policy goals. Equally, internally driven change can be represented as stemming from the actions of individuals who are actuated by societally determined self-interest, or as emanating from espousal on the part of key organizational figures of programs of educational reform. The most commonly encountered explanations of curriculum change are, on the one hand, those that emphasize external, determinist influences, and, on the other, those that give pride of place to the directive actions of policymakers internal to the educational system. Thus, to borrow their own language, revisionist historians of education in the United States explain change in the high school curriculum in terms of superstructural responses to dialectical evolution in the politicoeconomic infrastructure of American capitalism,[3] while historians of science education on both sides of the Atlantic have offered accounts of the reform movements of the 1960s that stress change as the result of conscious, goal-directed activity on the part of educators, for whom external events provided merely a rhetorical focus for action.[4]

Clearly, both perspectives have something to be said for them. Links between economic and political trends and the forms and structures of curriculum are too well documented for there to be much dispute about their importance. On the other hand, it is equally evident that some kinds of change, and some aspects of change are traceable to initiatives on the part of educators. The question is not whether one kind of account is right and the other wrong, but how these partial accounts, which grow from differing presuppositions, can be brought together within a common framework of understanding. One such attempt has been made by Westbury,[5] who conceptualizes the potential for curriculum change in terms of internal invention and external climates. Educators are productive of social and technical *inventions* (classrooms, for example), which have a potential for institutionalizing curriculum change. They also take over inventions supplied by the outside world (books, microcomputers). But the question of whether the potential of an invention is realized depends on the cultural climate external to the schools. Thus, in his study with McKinney of the Gary schools, Westbury points to the fact that the inventive resources for reforming the science curriculum were available there long before change in the external climate in the 1960s released the needed financial and ideological support for the introduction of a new curriculum. This formalization provides a useful basic ground for bringing together internal and external forces in a common perspective.

A tighter articulation of the internal and the external is offered by Goodson,[6] who sees educators as spontaneous actors, though constrained by aspects of the structure of schooling resulting from prior actions and policies that transcend the boundary of the school. On this view, educators pursue goals that they believe will lead to improvements in the quality of schooling (to use his example, the institution of an environmental studies curriculum in senior secondary classes in England), but in order to attain their goals are forced to adopt priorities that may be in conflict with their original intentions (for instance, to stress the abstract knowledge content of the environmental studies curriculum, when their educational purpose was to offer something more immediate and practical). This goal displacement results from features of the structure of the educational system brought about by past translations of ideologies into concrete form. In the case quoted, support for decontextualized learning had led to the promotion of structures supportive of it—channeling of resources through specialist academic departments within schools, the linking of teacher careers to departmental status, and the creation of an external examination system conferring legitimacy on certain kinds of subjects and contents. These are the realities that have to be confronted by educators who propose new subjects and new contents. Thus, Goodson represents the internal and the external as interpenetrating components in the change process. Educators have to play the game according to externally mandated rules that become internalized for schools and teachers because they are reflected in the shaping of the environment within which change has to be effected: on the other hand, schools and teachers are able to promote innovation and to work to change the ways in which environments encourage or restrain certain types of action.

Both Westbury and Goodson arrive at their formulation of the change problem through applying an historical perspective. McKinney and Westbury studied how the curriculum of the Gary schools evolved over a period of 30 years, while Goodson researched the evolution of curricula in geography, biology, and environmental studies in English schools over a similar time span. Westbury, working with data from a decentralized education system, emphasizes the fortuitous aspects of conjunctions between local curricular aspirations and the unlocking of federal and state resources that can make them productive of institutionalized change. Goodson, viewing action within a context that is much more closely integrated at the national level through centralized resource allocation, and a common system of public examining, highlights the interlocking of individual career with pervasive traditions that shape the terrain the innovator must traverse. There is certainly evidence here of the potential of historical work for assisting in the construction of change theories that can accommodate the internal and the external, directive action, and structural constraint in formulations of some subtlety and sophistication. But what more might history offer?

First of all, we might anticipate that history, which concerns itself with the particulars of places, people, and institutions, but over even longer time spans, might enable us to build up a view of curriculum change that sees the education system itself as variable in character. School systems, schools, and classrooms are sociocultural inventions (to borrow Westbury's terminology) that assume different meaning and significance according to the state of the community or society within which they operate. We would not expect that a fully elaborated change theory would propose that the same change mechanisms are salient in all times and in all places. This observation has practical as well as theoretical importance. Periods of sociopolitical stability alternate with periods of rapid evolution. If one reason for pondering on change theory is a wish to understand and manage curriculum change today, we should take account of the possibility that education systems in Western societies may be on the brink of a major adjustment in role and status. Weiler[7] documented the recent precipitate decline in confidence in education as a public institution; governments in the United Kingdom and North America are pursuing policies that tend to deemphasize the standing of public education as a uniform nationwide system importantly connected with consensually held values and priorities. If our attempts to guide curriculum change are posited on theories that assume the stability and permanence of national education systems as conventionally understood, we may be led to endorse irrelevant or misguided policies and proposals.

Secondly, we could expect that historical studies of the curriculum might enable us to move away from representations of external forces that show them on the one hand as monolithic, or on the other as capricious. Education systems are complicated and comprise a range of activities that respond to the wants and ambitions of a variety of social groups. It is unlikely that curriculum change in a rural secondary school, closely integrated with community interests, is to be explained in the same way as change in a suburban school with a cosmopolitan orientation and a heavy investment in college preparatory programs. This too may be a point with current significance. Modern society is tending to become more diversified in its groupings and interests; there is more emphasis on specialism of career and idiosyncrasy of lifestyle; curriculum change is drawn toward the particular need or demand rather than general or universal priorities (press on the part of authorities for uniform basic skills learning can be seen as a rearguard attempt to control what may still be controllable, rather than the signal of a new curricular uniformity).[8]

Change theories need, ideally, to be capable of being applied to a wide range of educational contexts, according to whether local or national interests are at issue, or whether the curriculum is under the control of private or public jurisdictions. What kind of conceptions might guide the historical studies that could be drawn on to build or elaborate such theories? No doubt a wide variety of these could be identified according to the orientation of the writer. This chapter draws attention to one conception that seems to provide a necessary link between curricular activity, enterprises of curriculum innovation, and sociocultural climates affecting the values and meanings attached to teaching and learning.

THE IDEA OF A CONSTITUENCY

The conception I wish to pursue is that of educational constituencies. The idea of the constituency that supports, or demands change in particular curricular arrangements was raised for me in the course of investigation into the evolution of the English sixth form in the 19th century.[9] The object of the study was a curricular category that persisted, in a recognizably continuous tradition, throughout the period in question, and experienced fundamental change, both in terms of content and of its significance for the students enrolled in it. At no point, however, was there any precise articulation between this evolution and initiatives on the part of central or local governments. In spite of this, the sixth form was, by the latter part of the century, clearly to be understood as a national institution. How, then, was its curricular evolution to be explained?

The fact that the sixth-form curriculum in the 19th century was a private and not a public affair (in spite of occasional attempts, as in the case of the Clarendon Commission, to bring public pressure to bear on its form and content) pointed to the need to import the notion of constituency as a means of explaining the nature of the changes it underwent. In the absence of visible legal frameworks that legitimate certain kinds of curricular arrangement, or that define whose view of appropriate arrangements shall prevail, the question of what gains support and why is clearly a question about the publics or constituencies that actually pay for education, and about their motives for doing it. This idea of the constituency that provides the link between what schools do and competing visions of what they might do is obscured for those whose studies of curriculum start with the assumption of a state education system, and with the concomitant assumption of the existence of a public that understands the idea of nationally significant categories of educational experience. Writers who are imbued with the modern notion of the universality of educational forms find it hard to construe national systems as an innovation that drove out a previous conception of education as private or domestic, and shaped to individual circumstances. But the study of history tells us that the linking of curricula to nationally understood statuses and careers was a 19th-century invention, which went along with the honing of devices to secure uniformity of practice (grant regulations, textbooks, examining) and the rise of conceptions of teacher professionalism. Prior to that, as Rothblatt reminds us, "A liberal education could be offered in boarding or grammar schools, or in Dissenting academies and private educational establishments, or it could be acquired by the wealthy on a grand tour of the continent. Locke thought a tutor would provide it, and while his influence lasted tutorial instruction was one major source of liberal instruction."[10] This historical shift from private to public conceptions of education has to be understood in terms of the willingness of individuals or small groups to prefer shared educational experience, provided through common forms and structures, to personal experience gained through idiosyncratic styles of learning. In other words, it is a matter of the emergence of educational constituencies consisting of people who believe that they have interests in common that can be served by certain kinds of more or less uniform curricula. The justifications for this choice are embodied in rhetorical language that connects the preferred forms of educational experience with praiseworthy statuses, careers, or lifestyles. To preserve and further their perceived common interest, constituency members are prepared to follow the imperatives of the rhetoric, and make available the resources of economic and ideological support needed to ensure preservation of symbolically important curricula. This process can take place with or without the involvement of local or national jurisdictions. The invocation of these may mark a step in the consolidation of constituencies that gain the backing of legal powers, though at the cost of freedom of maneuver.

The idea of constituency can provide a link that is at once stabilizing and flexible between the inventions and initiatives of educators and the restraint or impulse of outside forces. It helps us see how change, even quite rapid change, may be possible in circumstances where the structures of schooling seem to embody only obstacles to evolution, for the rhetorics of universalism may conceal the existence of variegated and unstable constituencies, offering points for experimentation, innovation, and the institutionalization of new curricula. On the other hand, a stable and ideologically unified constituency may be able to block the efforts of reformers, even when these are armed with legal powers and backed by the pronouncements of national reports. Key questions to be asked if constituencies are to be the object of historical study are: how do they come into being, how do they evolve, and how do they decline? How do they symbolize their perceived common interest, and what connections do they make between those symbols and the categories of educational experience? What marks of constituency membership are conferred by the experience of education? The connections to be studied between constituencies and curricula are connections that are rhetorically or symbolically made; they are about meaning and significance more than they are about knowledge and achievement. Thus the key curricular question becomes that of the experience of the student. Unfortunately, this is one that, though squarely in the province of historical investigation, is not readily amenable to research. Unless, like Costello, we are able to "pick over the contents of the . . . student's wastepaper basket,"[11] the mind of the learner is hard to penetrate, and has to be approached through second-hand testimony. Paradoxically, Costello's study was of the 17th-century student. With the spread of books and the ready availability of paper, the contents of the basket were less and less likely to be prized. For the 19th century they are rare, for the 20th, practically nonexistent.

THE SIXTH-FORM CONSTITUENCY

The sixth form had its origin in a small number of independent boarding schools. By the 18th century, these had become, sometimes despite the wishes of their founders, schools for the sons of aristocratic families where they might stay to the age of 18 or 19. They were not, however, at that stage, an essential part of the experience of being confirmed into aristocratic status. Upper-class boys, as well as girls, were, as we have seen, often tutored at home. Social customs such as making the grand tour were also sources of education. And, in so far as education depended on a knowledge of texts, it was not thought important that this should be acquired through the mediation of a teacher. The schools themselves followed no common patterns of education, though they agreed on taking the study of Latin and Greek as the main component of the curriculum. Each evolved its own unique forms of organization with idiosyncratic vocabularies to describe them. The boys inhabiting one end of the schoolroom at Westminster were known as the shell from its apsidal "conch-like shape"[12]—a name that subsequently spread to other schools. Winchester, at the time of the investigations of the Clarendon Commissioners in the 1860s, still preserved ancient "peculiarities in classical teaching" by the names of "pulpiteers," the "vulgus," and "standing up week."[13]The place of education was, everywhere, the large schoolroom in which all students were accommodated, and instruction proceeded, generally, through the giving of lessons to learn, which then had to be orally reproduced, though the content of instruction in terms of classical texts and grammars was a matter of local arrangement. "Each schoolmaster or teacher or tutor felt it incumbent upon himself to make his own selection of texts . . . This being the case, schoolmasters did not, on the whole, worry about continuity in studies from one place of education to another, either from the home to the school, from one school to another, or from school to university."[14] Where the students were divided into forms (a term originally referring to the benches on which they sat), this was done in a rough-and-ready manner for the convenience of teaching, and not with the idea of establishing a hierarchy of ability or a sequence of learning. The first form to establish an identity was the sixth. The idea of having six forms, with subdivisions where numbers demanded it, had spread from Winchester, which was a school of sufficient antiquity and reputation to be copied by other, equally venerable, establishments. The sixth was the highest form in that it contained the best (not necessarily the oldest) scholars, and was therefore fit to be taught by the headmaster who, in terms of status and learning, was in a different category from the assistant masters.

The sixth form at the end of the 18th century was a private institution that assumed a different character and significance in different places, and that was only marginally linked with the future status of its occupants. Membership in it was not essential either for entry to the universities of Oxford and Cambridge, or for membership in a social class (an idea that was, in any case, only just beginning to take shape). The nature of society was, however, changing. Industrialization, coupled with the demands for national coordination of resources made by the Napoleonic Wars, was beginning to shift the focus of interest and action for the upper echelons of society from the local to the national stage. Following the French Revolution, concern with confirming the unity of the elite that provided leadership in government and administration was heightened. There were, as Rothblatt points out, the beginnings of a shift of attention from civility and sociability to the Victorian virtues of duty and responsibility.[15] As the aristocracy became more aware of itself as a consensual interest group, and as the goals of action became more and more those associated with public arenas, it acquired a greater willingness to support organizations such as schools, which could claim to assist in the production of consensus, and of the virtues demanded of those with civic responsibility.

It was about this time that the word public began to be used in association with the long-established boarding schools to denote a general educational category, though "it was only in the period after 1840 that the phrase 'public school' came normally to mean a boarding school and the place to which well-to-do parents almost automatically sent their sons."[16] But around the turn of the century, the public school constituency was a small one, and a broad and uniform category was not what was wanted. Indeed, the preservation of the uniqueness of old established schools was more to the point. Small, discriminating constituencies want to be offered hand-crafted goods, not mass-produced articles. Their members are well informed, and well acquainted with one another. They can appreciate the finer points of choosing between variations on a quality product. Thus, although the categories of public school sixth form and public school sixth former were current, the question of curriculum change was one that could be answered only in terms of what individual schools and headmasters were doing to adapt to the evolution of society. Though the staple of the curriculum—Greek and Latin texts—remained, modifications began to be made in a variety of ways to the experience of being a sixth former. At Shrewsbury, Butler worked hard to raise academic standards in his sixth form—to such good effect that some of his students won university prizes that were then available for open competition. At Winchester, the notion was developed of the sixth as a source of example and authority for lower forms.

By 1830, a further evolution in the constituency was apparent. The increasing demands that were being placed on resources of government and administration outran the capability and willingness of the aristocracy to supply them. The new cadres of public servants had to come from another class that began to prepare itself for service in the public arena, for, as Bagehot noted, "the deference of the people to the spectacle of power can, in the modern state, only be secured by inconspicuous collaboration of the middle class."[17] Consensus of interest between middle class and aristocracy was to be the goal, and the schools were to be an important means of achieving this. The Clarendon Commissioners, in 1864, were repeating what was, by then, a piece of conventional wisdom when they said in their Report: "all the boys should, in their general education, pursue the same studies in kind, though not in degree, on the grounds . . . that . . . education . . . should generate as much sympathy as possible between the leaders of different departments, and also between the leaders and their followers."[18] This precept was put into practice not only in the Clarendon schools, but more importantly in the new schools founded in the 1840s and 1850s on the pattern of these, to extend public school and sixth form education to an enlarged constituency.

The middle class was an invention of the early 19th century, and soon rhetorical connections began to be made between it and categories of schooling; promoters of educational reform spoke of middle-class schools, and even middle-class examinations. But the newly self-conscious class did not see it as in its interest to foster categories of education that were significantly different in meaning from those patronized by the aristocracy. Nor, on the other side of the picture, was there any reason why the upper class should depart from the consensual ideology that enabled it easily to absorb new elements. The extension of the sixth-form constituency came about through the transplanting of the category to new schools where, in spite of curricular differences, such as the addition of modern subjects (history, foreign languages), categorical meaning was preserved. Thus, a first step was taken toward transforming the private institution of the sixth form into a category with some of the characteristics of a national institution. That is, one that can be seen as linked to a constituency that is defined, not by race, creed, class, or locality, but by commitment to a rhetoric connecting particular forms of educational experience with nationaly significant roles and statuses. Salient features of the rhetoric that joined middle class and aristocracy in a shared consciousness of affinity with nationally defined responsibility and privilege, were an emphasis on christianity, which did not exclude any particular sect; on loyalty and devotion to duty; on the value of solidarity and consensus. The old and the new public schools, through curriculum change, were able to reflect just such a rhetoric.

The needed change had to bring about an identity of interest between organization (the school, or schools) and institution (the educational category as understood by the constituency). Such adjustments come about through movement, initiative, and accommodation on both sides. In the case under discussion, the middle class was seeking an identity that was, as yet, not clear. Nor was it yet obvious what part education should play in the shaping of that identity, or whether that education should be supplied by existing schools, by new schools, by private initiative, or by government intervention (Matthew Arnold argued strongly for the latter). Identity crystallized as educators proffered models of practice, and practice evolved according to the response of the publics it was aimed at. Schools and constituency collaborated in the development of the informing rhetoric—in this instance, centered on concepts of manliness, gentlemanly conduct, and intellectual excellence. The process was aided by important mediators who produced the books, stories, and sermons that served as texts for the shaping and preservation of the categorical rhetoric. Much of this writing, in the 1850s, clustered around Arnold's Rugby, which embodied some of the most significant inventions, and notably the projection to a more morally conceived status of sixth forms as sources of authority in their schools. Ahead of his time, Arnold was also a promoter of the classroom against the schoolroom, something noted by historians, but not by propagandists, and, retrospectively, was credited by Thomas Hughes and others with the invention of organized games as part of the school curriculum—something for which he was not responsible. Such is the fate of those who are raised to be important legitimators of practice. The rhetoric, once established, became the means of shaping and stabilizing what schools did. Inventions contributed to a curricular orthodoxy, and could be changed only to the extent that the orthodoxy was not interfered with. On the other hand, deviant, inefficient, or ignorant practice could exist provided that it could be represented as in tune with the rhetoric. This was especially true for schools with powerful reputations. At a time when much was made of intellectual excellence it could be said that "hardly any amount of ignorance prevents a boy's coming to Eton."[19]

Thus, change in the curriculum of the sixth form over the period 1830–1860 is thought of as, on the one hand, the trying out of inventions and, on the other, the development of a national middle-class constituency allied to, and in some ways identified with the already existing aristocratic constituency. It also has to be thought of in terms of the construction of rhetorics connecting curriculum to constituency, and providing a means whereby each can assume a coherent identity. The significant inventions were: the association of membership in the sixth form with the exercise of moral authority, the development of a mimetic tradition of sixth-form teaching, and the fusing of religious and classical elements of the curriculum into an undogmatic christian humanism. The exercise of moral authority, as fostered by Arnold in the Rugby sixth, began the process of marking off the curricular experience of sixth formers from that of other students, thus enabling the act of becoming a sixth former to assume the quality of a rite of passage. Now it could be a means not simply of confirming students in the social standing of their families, but of marking a movement to a new status. This possibility was reinforced by the particular emphasis given to the role of the headmaster in sixth-form teaching. The mimetic theory of education holds that what the teacher most significantly provides is not knowledge, or skilled instruction, but example. To become educated is to imitate and internalize the manners, tastes, enthusiasms, and preferences of the teacher. In the public schools, access to the role model of the head, who was on a different plane from other teachers, was restricted to members of the sixth form. The pivotal importance of the head also contributed to the transformation of the sixth from a school-based institution to one that transcended these bounds to become a national one. Uniformity of theory and practice grew up through personal contact among a small number of men who, in any case, shared the common educational background of Oxford or Cambridge (to quote a small, but significant example of this, Kennedy of Shrewsbury produced his Latin Primer when, in the 1830s, "the public school headmasters decided on the desirability of a common textbook").[20] Finally, the merging of classical and religious themes in the curriculum to make the former "the complement of Christianity in its application to the culture of the human being"[21] enabled non-Anglicans to share in the experience of being a sixth former, while, at the same time, the moral aspects of that experience continued to be buttressed by religious principle.

Research has shown that schools such as Rugby appealed to a new middle-class clientele, and did not merely extend the provision for those already catered for by public schools with longer established reputations, such Eton and Winchester. They provided what the newly evolving constituency needed: a means of conceiving of itself as a nationally significant group, sharing symbols and interests with the ruling elite, and fit to embark on careers in the public service. They fostered a rhetoric centering on the reviving notion of chivalry,[22] which could provide both educational aims plausibly connected to curriculum content, and standards of honor and loyalty by which the new constituency could recognize itself. The idea of a chivalric order offered a basis for the creation of a new group that was cohesive, yet made up of people from different social origins. On the one hand, this was a model for the status passage experience of becoming a sixth former; on the other, it was a rationale for the life and careers of constituency members.

THE SIXTH FORM AS A NATIONAL EDUCATIONAL CATEGORY

Recognition on the part of government that sixth-form education had assumed national significance was accorded incidentally as a consequence of its perception that the education offered by the major public schools had become a national issue. This was marked by the setting up, in 1861, of the Clarendon Commission to inquire into the Revenues and Management of Certain Colleges and Schools. There was apparently much to criticize, in the view of some, in the way the schools were organized, and in the teaching they provided, and a good deal of the evidence the Commissioners heard was to their detriment. Charles Neate, Fellow of Oriel College, Oxford, testified that the classical languages, the heart of the curriculum, "are now so ill taught, or at least so little known by the great majority of those who are supposed to have learnt them, that half the time now bestowed upon their acquisition would be a great deal too much to give for the result obtained."[23] But the Commission did not, on that account, conclude that the schools were unsuccessful. While admitting some shortcomings, they instead drew attention to the fact that they "have been the chief nurseries of our statesmen; in them, and in schools modelled after them, men of all the various classes that make up English society, destined for every profession and career have been brought up on the footing of social equality, and have contracted the most enduring friendships, and some of the ruling habits of their lives; and they [sc. the schools] have had perhaps the largest share in moulding the character of an English Gentleman."[24]

The language used here by the Commissioners shows a fine appreciation of the fact that what matters to a supportive constituency is not the learning of curriculum, but the experience of it (learning might, in some circumstances, be at issue, but not inevitably). The description given of the virtues of the schools records the change that had taken place over the previous half century—in spite of the persistence of Greek and Latin texts as its staple content. Learning is now public, not private, national, not local. The curriculum has become a symbol of common experience looking forward to public service careers, emphasizing group solidarity, and lending significance to belief and action through the rhetoric surrounding the concept of the gentleman.[25] The fact that the Clarendon Commission was set up at all is evidence of the connection that had been made between the character and ability of the governing classes and the nature of the education they had received—a connection that would not have been at all obvious 50 years earlier.

The Clarendon Report provides a marker of the successful fusion of upper- and upper-middle-class elements through schooling. But already events were moving on. As the demand for induction into gentlemanly roles through education expanded, and the constituency grew, the problem of the connection between the legitimating rhetoric and the forms of the curriculum took on new dimensions. Firstly, the need arose for tangible proofs of the quality of teaching. The comment that boys left Rugby with "stagnant and ill-formed minds" could be shrugged off, because Rugby was Rugby.[26] But, as the Rugby sixth form, which had been copied in the newer public schools, spread even further afield after 1860 to the reviving endowed grammar schools,[27] the boundary between curriculum experience, which was categorically acceptable and that which was not had to be clearly marked, or the whole notion of the expanded constituency would collapse. The inventions that could fulfill this need were those tending toward uniformity and predictability of curriculum. But secondly there was a need for curriculum variation. The teaching of classics demanded either the conjunction of highly qualified teachers and highly committed students, or, as at Eton, a centuries-old reputation that allowed poor performance to pass unremarked. For the newer schools, especially the grammar schools, this posed a problem. On the other hand, there was a positive demand from those who would take up lower status careers for more utilitarian studies: English, history, modern languages, as well as mathematics, which was already taught in the universities and some public schools.

The invention that did most to promote uniformity of curriculum, while tolerating or even encouraging some variety of content was the public examination. Beginning in the 1850s, entry to the army and the home and overseas civil service moved toward selection by examination for which the schools prepared sixth-form students. At the same time, demand on the part of schools for evidence that their teaching programs were categorically acceptable resulted in the offering of public examinations by the College of Preceptors and the Local Examinations Syndicates of the universities of Oxford and Cambridge. These examinations were seen just as much as tests of the schools as of students. For example, when the Secretary of the College of Preceptors was interviewed by the Taunton Commissioners, and asked whether the effect of the examinations had been to improve middle-class education, he replied that "a school examined by us for the first time . . . is generally speaking very unsuccessful in the examinations . . . but they persevere . . . and you see a gradual improvement, until at last some of these schools distinguish themselves even above others."[28] All this took place without any intervention on the part of central authorities, providing a good illustration of the fact that the institutionalization of national categories is not to be confused with the centralization of educational policymaking. The growth of examining on a national level paved the way for success in sixth form studies to be tied to uniform tests of achievement, clarified in the mind of a broader constituency the conception of sixth-form work, and enabled the places where that conception was implemented to be identified (so that, to this day, arguments about where real sixth-form work is done are conducted by pamphleteers who base their conclusions on the statistical manipulation of examination results).

Even more important for the sixth forms of the late 19th century were the entrance examinations set by the universities of Oxford and Cambridge. These tightened and formalized the link that had long existed between sixth form and university and fostered a pattern of curriculum that has persisted ever since. As Annan explains, "[T]he Oxford and Cambridge scholarships were far more influential than the reformers ever dreamed. They transformed the pattern of national secondary education. If anyone asks why it is that children specialize at such an early age at school . . . and why so many arts graduates are innumerate, the answer is simple. The Oxford and Cambridge scholarships were the blue riband of sixth form education."[29] The specialization that was thus permitted and encouraged enabled commonality to be combined with variety. While students following other studies could share in the experience of the sixth, the true scholars and leaders could continue to pursue the classics.

Examining was not the only invention that enabled sixth-form experience to assume a more standardized character. This trend was also greatly assisted by the move away from the system of having everyone taught in the big schoolroom, and toward the consistent use of separate classrooms. Those of us who have always thought of classrooms as the conventional arena for the transaction of a curriculum might wonder why, once the idea and possibility of classrooms existed, their virtues were not immediately perceived. The reason lies exactly in the area that we are exploring. The supportive rhetoric of the schoolroom meshed with the career anticipation of the constituency—as long as this was broadly aristocratic. This is quite clear from the Clarendon Report, which came down against any rapid extension of the classroom system, precisely because of the understanding it held of the constituency of the nine schools: "It may admit of doubt whether . . . schools are not moving faster than the world, for which they are a preparation, has followed or will be able to follow them. It is necessary at the Bar, and in other careers in life, and in the Houses of Parliament, that much mental work should be done of all kinds, amidst many outward causes of distraction."[30] The schoolroom lived because it was an invention that had meaning beyond the immediate tasks of the accomplishment of teaching. But its days were numbered. Classrooms came with their own wider meanings, centering around collectivist sentiments of sympathy and emulation, which were to be unlocked by the new teacher professionalism that class teaching made possible.[31] These meanings made more appeal to the new majority bound for lesser administrative posts than those of the schoolroom, which were suited to a minority of leaders. Not surprisingly, the more aristocratic schools clung longest to the old traditions. But, by 1885, even at Winchester the "once thronged room was derelict." And when, in the 1890s, the headmaster summoned his sixth form to meet him there he "was shocked to find that it was no longer known where to sit or what to do in School."[32]

The uniformity brought by classrooms and examining counteracted the other imperative of the enlargement of the constituency—that the content of learning become more diversified. To begin with, the introduction of new subjects created difficulties. Butler of Harrow reported that "[a]t a large school, where tradition and emulation act so powerfully, boys are not likely to work vigorously at any subject in which the majority of their companions are not keenly interested . . . If exempted from . . . regular work, or from any part of it, they are likely to become listless and idle."[33] The experience of being a sixth former depended on doing what was seen as regular work, a point made even more forcibly by Westcott of Harrow: "A boy may rise most rapidly into the upper sixth form without being at any time distinguished for scholarship, by the help of modern languages and mathematics . . . [I]t happens continually that a boy reaches the upper sixth who is a very bad scholar."[34]

Or, cast in a logical form, only scholars should be sixth formers, one can only become a scholar by studying classics, therefore only classicists can be sixth formers. That the contest between those who took this view (and supported the old constituency) and those who urged the introduction of new subjects (and therefore supported the new) was resolved in favor of the latter was due to the opportunities offered by examinations and by class teaching for holding together diverse interests in a common framework. These were the inventions that permitted the realization of the aim for middle-class education expressed by a head of one of the new public schools, Bradley of Marlborough: "[It] should be at one *general*, i.e., like the education of other classes, and *special*; and special in two senses, first, as putting forward certain subjects more prominently than they are brought forward in ordinary education; secondly, as trying to form tastes which will in some degree counteract the hardening and deadening influences of engrossing occupations, which are not in themselves of an elevating or refining nature."[35] The evolving curriculum framework allowed the definition of sixth-form status to be not scholarship, as conventionally defined, but specialization, whether in classics, modern studies, or, later, the sciences. In this way, experience could be shared, but at the same time varied, and the broader constituency could embrace a range of interests and aspirations.

These new contents and frameworks for the curriculum brought with them a new justificatory rhetoric. For the most part, the vocabulary was the same as that which had supported Arnold's new model sixth, but the signification of the words had been modified. "Manliness," which had been linked to the idea of christian moral responsibility, was gradually transmuted into the manliness of the games field—"honour, loyalty, skill at games, and a certain stoical acceptance of pain."[36] The militant christianity of Empire replaced the earlier concern with personal rectitude and avoidance of sin. Control over others, associated with captaincy and prefectship, was more emphasized than responsibility exercised on a personal level. If the curriculum in its overall form was more uniform and predictable, so were personal conduct and relationships, down to niceties of dress, posture, and demeanor. And when the time came for the national institution of the sixth to be incorporated into a centrally controlled system of education after the passing of the Education Act of 1902, it was this powerful rhetoric, meshed with the curricular forms to which it gave meaning, that ensured that many issues of policy that might have seemed open to debate were not, in fact, so open. Should upper secondary education be on the pattern of the curriculum of the higher grade school, or of the independent public school? Should the curriculum provide choices between specialisms, or a general range of studies for all on the model of the French Baccalauréat or the German Abitur? Should secondary education rest on the foundation of the elementary school, or should it represent a different but parallel educational experience? All of these seemed to be contentious issues. They were not. The constituency understood what sixth-form education was, and acted in accordance with that understanding, with important consequences for the whole future development of English secondary education.

CONCLUSION

This brief study of the evolution of the sixth-form curriculum in the 19th century suggests the importance of the notion of constituency in explaining change. Left to itself the educational community had transformed an idiosyncratic, aristocratic form of curriculum into a national institution, capable of holding together a diverse population of mainly middle-class students, and initiating them into a kind of freemasonry where they could share common values with the governing class, and move into the cadres of public servants and administrators needed to run a complex industrial society and an overseas empire. Both the content and the significance of the curriculum had changed. How is this change to be accounted for? Directive initiatives on the part of public authorities are part of the story, but cannot stand on their own as explanations. If we look at the national level, while it is true that government concern with secondary and sixth-form education grew over the period under review, control was minimal and exercised indirectly through the restructuring of private funding by the Charity Commissioners, the channeling of small amounts of public funding through the Science and Art Department, and the publication of reports of Royal Commissions. Government action was sometimes of considerable significance, as for example in the introduction of science teaching into sixth forms, but it does not assume major importance in an account of curriculum change. At the local or private level, the inventions of headmasters, textbook writers, and examining boards are factors that play a critical role in any account of curriculum innovation. But, without the backing of central authorities, what was it that enabled them to be significant? The case of the classroom is instructive. It was not a superior technical device that drove out the inferior. As the Clarendon Commissioners noted: "All the teaching of all the classes at

Winchester School has for centuries been conducted in one room" and "there has been a considerable amount of efficient teaching."[37] The contest was between technical systems that grew from and supported different accounts of desirable educational experience. We have to inquire into the reasons why one form of experience was favored at Rugby, and another at Winchester.

If, on the other hand, we look to explanations that stress the primacy of social and economic forces, perhaps pointing to the development of class conflicts, as the effects of industrialization moved the basis of power from land and consols to the management of risk capital, we again have to face the problem of making connections between such forces and the reformist inventions of public school headmasters. Butler, Arnold, Thring, Kennedy, and Farrar set out to devise and promote forms of teaching and learning connected to the realization of well-articulated social and cultural aims. Were the Rugby prefects, the Winchester classrooms, or the Uppingham playing fields called into being by determinist forces rather than by conscious agents? If we dismiss internal, directive explanations altogether, curriculum change has to be represented as meaningless, whereas the most significant thing that emerges from the study of 19th-century educators is the extent to which they concerned themselves with meaning, and the connection of meaning with forms of schooling and with personal and professional careers.[38]

Obviously, the importance of the constituency as bearer of meanings that mediate between reformist invention and the broader forces of social and economic evolution is thrust to the fore when the instance under discussion relates to a form of education that can be seen as private. But what about the case where public authorities have assumed control of education and the system is national, not just in the sense that the sixth form in the 19th century became a national institution, but in the sense that policy and administration are provided through central government agencies?

The contention of this paper is that, while the intervention of central authorities certainly acts to modify the ways in which constituencies relate to curricular forms, it is not necessarily the case that such intervention detracts from the importance of constituencies as critical integrating agencies in the explanation of change. The idea of constituency could, for example, extend and enrich understandings of modern examples of curriculum change provided by Goodson.[39] The meanings carried and responded to by educational constituencies can provide an important key to his discussion of the encounter between reformist aspirations and the organizational structures that hinder or subvert them. Secondary schooling has been shaped in ways that favor certain kinds of hierarchical arrangements and promote certain kinds of career patterns because the policies that brought this about—allocation of funding, definitions of qualification—have been the expressions of meanings attached by constituencies to the educational categories they support. For example, support for subject specialism was not simply something that weighed in the scale when decisions about resource allocation were being made: it formed part of a coherent rhetoric connecting forms of education with constituency beliefs about how people should relate to society and build careers within it. Goodson's story is different from the story of the sixth form in the 19th century because his protagonists can use central authorities as a resource when constituency interests are challenged: a resurrected notion of regular subjects, which alone confer sixth-form status, could be promoted with the active support of schools council subject committees with jurisdiction over the sanctioning of A-level syllabuses.

The modern picture is also complicated in that, once education is legally promoted and controlled, constituencies can act through local and national political systems, as well as in direct concert with schools. For example, an account of how and why the curriculum changes associated with the introduction of comprehensive schools in England in the 1960s and 1970s came about would have to work with a rather elaborate conception of the nature of the constituencies of secondary education, and the scope for action open to them. It seems likely, however, that studies focused on the notion of constituency would shed more light on the complex development of the comprehensive secondary curriculum than studies of administrative action, or of the inventions of educators, pursued in isolation.

The richness of historical inquiry will no doubt lead us to other ideas that can provide a connective tissue between partial and sometimes conflicting accounts of how the curriculum changes, but the notion of constituency seems to be an example of the kind of conception that helps us understand the process of curriculum change under a great variety of conditions, and to evaluate, for any given occasion, the relative importance of other, and perhaps more obvious, sources of explanation.

NOTES

1. See Reid, William A., & Filby, Jane (1982). *The sixth: An essay in education and democracy.* Lewes: Falmer Press.
2. Reid, William A. (1985). Curriculum change and the evolution of educational constituencies: The English sixth form in the nineteenth century. In I. F. Goodson (Ed.). *Social histories of the secondary curriculum: Subjects for study* (pp. 289–311). Lewes: Falmer Press.
3. See, for example, Katz, M. B. (1971). *Class, bureaucracy and schools: The illusion of educational change in America.* New York: Praeger; Bowles, S., & Gintis, H. (1976). *Schooling in capitalist America.* New York: Basic Books.
4. Waring, M. (1979). *Social pressures and curriculum innovation.* London: Methuen. See also the accounts of the introduction of new science courses in Heath, R. W. (Ed.). (1964). *New curricula.* New York: Harper & Row.

5. McKinney, W. L., & Westbury, I. (1975). Stability and change: The public schools of Gary, Indiana, 1940-1970. In William A. Reid & Decker F. Walker (Eds.). *Case studies in curriculum change: Great Britain and the United States* (pp. 1–53). London: Routledge & Kegan Paul. Westbury, I. (1982). *"Invention" of curricula: Some notes directed at opening a theme for discussion.* Paper presented to the conference on the History and Sociology of School Subjects, St. Hilda's College, Oxford.

6. Goodson, I. (1983). *School subjects and curriculum change.* London: Croom Helm.

7. Weiler, H. (1983). Education, public confidence, and the legitimacy of the modern state: Is there a "crisis" somewhere? *Journal of Curriculum Studies, 15,* 125–142.

8. *Ibid.,* p. 140.

9. Reid & Filby. *Op. cit.,* chapters 1–5.

10. Rothblatt, S. (1976). *Tradition and change in English liberal education: An essay in history and culture.* London: Faber & Faber.

11. Costello, W. T. (1958). *The scholastic curriculum at early seventeenth-century Cambridge.* Cambridge, MA: Harvard University Press.

12. *Shorter Oxford English Dictionary,* vol. 2, p. 1971.

13. Report of H. M. Commissioners appointed to inquire into the revenues and management of certain colleges and schools, etc. (Clarendon; 1864).

14. Rothblatt. *Op. cit.,* pp. 45–46.

15. *Ibid.,* pp. 102, 154.

16. Seaborne, M. (1971). *The English school: Its architecture and organization, 1370-1870.* London: Routledge & Kegan Paul, pp. 79, 246.

17. Bowles, J. (1954). *Politics and opinion in the nineteenth century.* London: Cape, p. 259.

18. Report. *Op. cit,* vol. 2, p. 68.

19. *Ibid.,* vol. 2, p. 127 (Evidence of William Johnson [Cory]).

20. Oldham, J. B. (1952). *A history of Shrewsbury School, 1552-1952.* Oxford: Blackwell.

21. Report. *Op. cit,* vol. 2, p. 43 (letter from W. E. Gladstone).

22. Girouard, M. (1981). *The return to Camelot: Chivalry and the English gentleman.* New Haven, CT: Yale University Press.

23. Report. *Op. cit,* vol. 2, p. 49.

24. *Ibid.,* vol. 1, p. 56.

25. Although Eton held on to the older tradition, resisting, in the person of its head, Dr. Balsdon, Lord Clarendon's suggestion that it should "render obligatory a thing (French) which they thought ought to be part of an English gentleman's education" (*Ibid.,* vol. 1, p. 85).

26. *Ibid.,* vol. 2, p. 314.

27. These were often old foundations like the public boarding schools, but had remained as day schools, serving a local clientele. Many, in the early 19th century, had seen their supply of students dry up almost completely.

28. Report of the Schools Inquiry Commission (Taunton). (1868). Vol. 4, pp. 5–6.

29. Annan, Noel (1981). A spontaneous liberality. *The Times Literary Supplement,* July 31, p. 862.

30. Report. *Op. cit.,* vol. 1, p. 287.

31. Hamilton, D. (1980). Adam Smith and the moral economy of the classroom system. *Journal of Curriculum Studies, 12,* 281–298.

32. Firth, J. d'E. (1949). *Winchester College.* London: Winchester Publications, p. 155. Sociotechnical inventions, once abandoned, are lost forever, despite the heavy meanings they may once have carried.

33. Report (1864). *Op. cit,* vol. 1, p. 218.

34. *Ibid.,* vol. 1, p. 217.

35. Report (1868). *Op. cit.,* vol. 4, p. 419.

36. Worsley, T. C. (1940). *Barbarians and Philistines: Democracy and the public schools.* London: Robert Hale, p. 98.

37. Report (1864). *Op. cit*, vol. 2, p. 287.

38. Westbury's notion of "invention" gains power as an explanatory concept if we extend the scope of the word beyond the cataloging of technical attributes (seating in a classroom, allocation of space) to include the *meanings* an invention might be able to bear for those who encounter it (sympathy, emulation, hierarchy). Inventions are adopted into systems not by virtue of their technical efficiency, but because of their consonance with meanings that constituencies project onto the forms of schooling.

39. *Op. cit.*

11

On the Origins of the Institutional Categories of Schooling

The historically based analysis of the role in curriculum change of institutional categories is extended through some differently targeted arguments. This chapter, which uses evidence from a similar, though more extended period of history, is more concerned with linguistic factors—how things are named—and with the physical structures through which categorical ideas are molded and expressed. My project is to see how our perception of familiar things—for much of our thinking about curriculum is shaped by the familiar—can be made more complex and objective through confrontation with the strangeness of long-lost curricular forms.

This chapter was first published in Journal of Curriculum Studies, *22, 3, 1990, 203–216, under the title "Strange curricula: Origins and development of the institutional categories of schooling."*

From Ash-Wednesday, unto the said Thursday, all the Commencers . . . are to come to the Schools upon every Monday, Tuesday, Wednesday, Thursday & Friday, at one of the Clock in the afternoon, & to bring thither with them every one a Sophister . . . the said Commencers are there to be ready to define 2 or 3 theses, which they shall themselves make choice of, & deliver unto those Bachelors of Arts, not of the same College, who shall think fit to come thither to reply upon them. (University of Cambridge, *Statutes of Elizabeth I*).[1]

Quotations such as the above have more than curiosity value: They provide us with an opportunity for improving our understanding of curriculum through the removal of taken-for-granted assumptions. The lore of schooling and our familiarity with the world of the classroom can divert our attention from important questions we might be asking about the present functions of curricula, and how new functions might be envisaged. One way to raise such questions is to turn away for a while from what is normal, and look instead at things and places that strike us as strange. History offers us one medium for achieving this shift of vision.[2] The quotation at the beginning of this chapter refers to a method of instruction that was familiar to university students and teachers in the Elizabethan University of Cambridge: so familiar that conveyance of its meaning does not require explanatory phrases: the reiteration of key categories will suffice—"Sophister," "Commencer," "Theses"—and documentation need only be concerned with administrative arrangements relating to those categories—"From Ash-Wednesday," "at one of the Clock in the afternoon."

I use the word "category" here in the technical sense proposed by Meyer,[3] who considers that much thought about schooling, and therefore curriculum, is misguided in that we are overfascinated by modern administrative and political rationalizations of the work of education. The centrality that, since the mid-19th century in Europe and North America, has been given to the idea of national education systems has led us to base our understanding of how and why schooling is delivered on administratively centered accounts, which stress internal organization and decision making, that is, under one aspect, the planning and creation of the categories—subjects of the curriculum, for example—that figure in official descriptions of educational practice. These Meyer calls "organizational categories." Neglected, but much more important, he suggests, are the "institutional categories," which are the socially or culturally held conceptions of wider publics concerning significant features of schooling and curriculum. In the long run, or even the medium run, it is the extent of conformity to institutional categories that determines whether curricular evolution can come about, not the efficiency or directive power of the education system itself.

A small example will serve to illustrate this point. In the mid-1970s the Schools Council and the Department of Education and Science agreed that the public examination then taken by students in England and Wales at age 16 should cease to have its results reported on a pass/fail basis. Grades would be given, and it would be up to users of examination results to decide what these grades meant for their purposes. The general public—even most teachers—never accepted this: they continued to talk about "passing" and "failing," linking pass and fail to the grade scheme in the way it always had been. The examination, as an institutional category, was inextricably intertwined with the concept of success and failure, and administrative changes in the organizational category could not alter this larger reality.[4]

The curricular categories that occur in the Elizabethan Statutes of the University of Cambridge are organizational. Quite a lot of people would also have had an institutional understanding of them, but these would almost all have been insiders in some sense, and the categorical understanding would have been unique to Cambridge—there was only one other university to be considered (if we exclude Scotland) and that had its own subtly different way of organizing things.[5] So what has to happen in order that categories can exist that are predominantly institutional, in the sense that they are culturally held and transcend any particular organizational location? How can we have a conception of the testing of 16-year-olds that is not tied to any individual place where courses are followed or examinations taken? Such is our familiarity with modern thinking and practice that it may not occur to us that such questions even arise. Looking at strange curricula can show us that these are indeed real questions with practical relevance.

In pursuing the puzzle of the origins and development of the institutional categories of curriculum and schooling, I shall look at three subquestions. First, the issue of how ideas move from having a particular reference to a universal one, since it is only possible to talk about institutional categories under conditions where ideas that can form the basis of such categories are capable of bearing a universal meaning. I will examine the process by which curriculum became a universal idea of this kind, and look at some of the consequences of this shift. Secondly, I shall look at ways in which the reflection of universally held ideas in particular organizational settings is recognized, and shall claim that this is mediated through the installation of appropriate inventions. My example will be the classroom. Finally, I shall consider how the combination of universally held ideas and categorically appropriate inventions results in the creation of dominant institutional categories, which then exert a powerful influence over what can, or cannot be done by curriculum planners.

To conclude this introduction, I offer another instance of a strange curriculum, this time from our side of the watershed of the English Renaissance, and therefore somewhat more connected with modern understandings of schooling. We will be referring to it in later sections of this chapter:

Afternoon school [at Winchester] lasted from two till six; in the vast schoolroom, lighted at that time only by candles in the sconces; the boys sitting at their "scobs" or movable desks, while the commoners were accommodated also at friendly scobs, or sat at two long "commoner tables." Against the walls were the "Tabula Legum," or rules of the school, and the curious "Aut disce" tablet offering a three fold alternative of study, with a mitre as its reward; timely withdrawal to wield the lawyer's pen or the soldier's sword; [or] the "sors tertia" of the rods, which stood throughout the school time in a compartment of the Headmaster's seat, and were used when school ended. Order was preserved by two prefects, the "Ostarius" or doorkeeper, and the "Bible-Clerk," exempted from lessons for police work, and armed each with his ground ash.[6]

UNIVERSAL CATEGORIES: CURRICULUM

There are certain terms in both our everyday and our theoretical discourse that we take to relate to concrete particulars. Thus, to take a curricular example, if we talk about the McGuffey *Readers*, we understand that the matter at issue is a particular set of books that were used in particular schools in a particular epoch with particular students. We know that they could not have been part of a curriculum before their publication date, and we would not expect to find them in schools today. If we use a term like this, that we take to be particular, outside its historical context, we are aware of the incongruity. Thus, Malcolm Seaborne in *The English School: Its Architecture and Organization 1370–1870* refers to the orthographical desk, which was an aid to spelling and made its appearance in schools in the early 19th century.[7] In explaining what it was, he uses the word "teaching machine," but puts it in quotation marks to show that his usage is anachronistic. Whatever claims the orthographical desk might have had to be a teaching machine, it could *not* have been one, since the conception "teaching machine" did not exist in the early 19th century. Seaborne, however, is a careful historian. It would not be surprising to find other writers talking about orthographical desks as teaching machines without discomfort, that is, treating the idea of teaching machine as universal, rather than particular.

Some terms, however, in spite of their particularist connotations, have achieved universal status, even in the discourse of serious historians. One of these is curriculum. As Hamilton points out, historians of higher education often refer to the curriculum of the medieval university, whereby "they unwittingly impose the language of the present onto the schooling of the past."[8] Typically, students at medieval universities, such as Paris or Bologna, attended to whatever learning they pleased, as made available by various masters, came and went as they liked, and received no final degree or testimonial. It was, as Hamilton says, "a loose-textured organizational form," where student absenteeism or the fact that enrollment did not match attendance "was not so much a failure (or breakdown) of . . . organization as a perfectly efficient response to the demands that were placed upon it."[9] No one in that situation would have described what they were doing as "following a curriculum," yet so capacious has the term now become that it can be used retrospectively to refer to educational activities that predated the technical use of the word: activities showing all those characteristics of looseness and serendipity that the arrival on the scene of the concept of curriculum was to mark as outdated.

For curriculum signaled, through its entry into the vocabulary of education around the end of the 16th century,[10] the arrival of a more closely knit organization of educational activities, and particularly the fact that they had come to be conceived of as *sequential* and capable of *completion*. Significantly, the first references to curriculum occur in relation to the granting of degrees or testimonials. It was found, for example, at the University of Leiden in 1582 in the phrase "having completed the curriculum of his studies."[11] A necessary condition of curriculum moving from its previous connotation of simply an *elapse* of time ("curriculum horae" was as likely to be found as "curriculum studiorum"[12]), was that the time taken over studies began to have some enduring significance, such as marking a point of completion at which the award of a qualification was merited or permissible. This notion of completion was connected with the greater levels of organization of studies that came about as a result of growing student numbers and the efforts of Renaissance scholars to systematize teaching and learning through applications of method, a notion particularly associated with the name of Peter Ramus. The 1569 edition of his *Dialectic* offers this explanation, "method is the disposition by which that enunciation is placed first which is first in the absolute order of knowledge, that next which is next, and so on: and thus there is an unbroken progression."[13] Progression is the counterpart of completion, and makes possible the idea of curriculum as an educational category. Thus, curriculum was, like the orthographical desk and the McGuffey *Readers*, launched upon the world at a particular time and place in history, and was associated with tendencies in learning and in the wider society that were peculiar to that time and place.

Where pedagogy was concerned, we should note, for example, that the move away from loosely connected studies and toward curriculum went along with a shift from the first-hand study of texts to the use of textbooks, which became available with the invention of printing. Indeed, a condition of curriculum making was the provision of printed books that enabled the unbroken progression of learning to be uniformly paced and monitored ("turn to page 10, line 1" would have been a strange instruction to possessors of books written in different hands). A concomitant implication was that students no longer necessarily had access, even via lectures, to the original texts of authors, since these were now mediated by textbook writers who created forms of school knowledge qualitatively different from the authorially based arts and disciplines that had been at the heart of medieval learning. And, on an even wider stage, claims have been made that the rise of curriculum was intimately linked with the growth of administrative bureaucracy stimulated in Europe by the development of the nation state.

Thus, study of history suggests that, for some purposes, we should regard curriculum as a particular term, in the same way that Seaborne took teaching machine to be a particular term. But, in modern usage, curriculum has attained an exclusively universal connotation, and we happily apply it to all kinds of educational activities in many different times and places. Like all such terms, it has become decontextualized and prone to be regarded as definable rather than problematic (we note the frequency with which writers of curriculum textbooks insist on offering stipulative definitions of what curriculum is). Curriculum as a definable universal has become an assumption of the field.

Is this merely an academic point, or does it have practical or theoretic significance? First of all, from a practical point of view, if we assume the curriculum to be universal, we run into problems of international communication and research. Though curriculum is treated as universal, actual discourse about it is, inevitably, particularistic and has, as reference points, "specific actions within specific contexts."[14] In the case of the United States, for example, "the localized and decentralized structure of the school curriculum puts a premium on the communication of ideas and technical solutions from centers to peripheries—and there are many centers and many peripheries." Thus, "it is service-delivery rather than service-planning which offers the most visible and characteristic forms of real world thought about the curriculum."[15] Very different is the style of curriculum discourse, and therefore the implicit significance of the word curriculum, which prevails in countries such as Sweden, or the United Kingdom, where decision making is much more centrally politicized. Mistakes and misconceptions can, and frequently do arise as nations strive to study and learn from each other's conduct of education systems because of misplaced assumptions about the universal nature of the term curriculum.

But even if we confine our considerations of curriculum to one location, we still risk adopting a myopic stance in our attempts to understand it if we regard it as an unproblematic category. Terms that are not really universal, though they are treated as such, become assimilated to the concrete circumstances in which they are used, and we tend to see these circumstances—of style, control, and delivery—as having a much higher degree of centrality than a more flexible view might indicate is appropriate or necessary. An instance of this want of flexibility is the current neglect, in studies of the effectiveness of the curriculum, of certain kinds of outcome that are not felt to be part of this implicit definition of the universal curriculum. As Doyle points out, classroom methods that are apparently ineffective under a definition that assumes effects to be immediate may, under less restrictive assumptions, turn out to be quite defensible:

> The teacher . . . emphasized problem-solving and reasoning skills in units on the metric system and laboratory measurement and on scientific research methods. The students completed only fourteen tasks (low for the sample of teachers we have observed), and 80% of the total class time was devoted to only six tasks. Moreover, engagement was not always high, productivity was sometimes low, and work was not always conducted efficiently. Yet, the logical progression or semantic thread of the content was quite explicit and clear, and students were pushed to deal with some fundamental issues in science. In addition, many novel tasks were used in which students were required to discern relationships, assemble information and solve problems.[16]

INVENTIONS: THE CLASSROOM

In presenting his example, Doyle wants to make a somewhat different point
than the one I have drawn from it. His focus is on the proposition that the
form of the curriculum is essentially determined by the pedagogic arrangements through which it is embodied. The conclusion he arrives at is "that
certain types of task are *suitable* for classrooms, that is, they fit the constraints of teacher and student work systems in these environments."[17] But
we can go further than this by enlisting the aid of history in attacking our
problem. Just as we associate the idea of curriculum structure with certain
taken-for-granted circumstances related to social and political beliefs and
traditions, so one of the salient aspects of the curriculum process—the
classroom—is conceptually linked with specific sets of sociotechnical arrangements through which its pedagogic work is conventionally accomplished. This time, the strangeness comes about through the perception of
these arrangements as historically created, and the leading idea is that of
"invention."[18]

As we look into history, we realize that, in spite of the way that current
conceptions of curriculum are dominated by the apparatus of the classroom,
teaching and learning went on before such a notion existed. The story of
how classrooms evolved is somewhat different according to where one
looks. I take my example from the English "public" schools of the 19th
century.[19] Unlike curriculum, the work of schooling can be readily exemplified through images, and many images exist of teaching and learning in
English public schools before the advent of the classrooms. They typically
show educational activity going on in a single large room accommodating
up to about 200 students. The Winchester schoolroom of the 1680s, referred
to in my earlier quotation, is a case in point. A picture shows a high
room—probably about 30 feet to the ornate frieze that surrounds it—with
dark paneling reaching about a third of the way up the walls, and large
windows admitting ample light, without giving a view of the outside world.
The scene is dominated by the famous "Aut disce" tablet on the end wall.
Book boxes stand open along the sides of the room, while the well-lit center
is taken up with desks and tables. Few students are present, but other
pictures of similar schools show students and teachers standing, or seated
at tables and desks (those of the teachers often more like thrones, with
elaborate canopies) in what to us is a random or even disorderly way. It is
not clear whether there are several lessons in progress, or perhaps none,
for Ramist ideas were slow to penetrate these schools, and much of what
we are looking at still reflects the loose-textured organizational form to
which Hamilton referred in his discussion of medieval universities. Hardly
any of the attributes of the conventional classroom are present. Simultane-
ous instruction is not in evidence, nor a clear focus on the teacher. What

we are looking at here is a *schoolroom*, which tells us nothing more than that it is the place where members of a school meet. In fact, it was often referred to simply as "the school." This to us looks ambiguous, as we assume structurally marked differentiation of space within a school. However, structure can be as much within people's heads as in architecture. School was certainly divided into "forms"—though membership in these was not closely age-related (and so it would be anachronistic to refer to them as grades). Often too, academic ranking within forms was signaled in some way. But most of this escapes us as we look into schoolrooms with modern eyes. The fact is that, despite our extensive experience of teacher and student roles, if we were to step into the world shown in the Winchester picture, we simply would not know how to act as either student or teacher: the technology of the schoolroom, so well known to the participants, is hidden from us, so that we wonder how anyone could tolerate such strange arrangements.

One important reason why they were not just tolerated but even welcomed, is that educational settings are more than areas for the deployment of technologies of teaching and learning, more even than functional constellations of sociocultural relationships: they are cultural microcosms that derive meaning from the macrocosmic institutions of the world of adult endeavor. This is how the Clarendon Commissioners saw the situation. In 1864, they were called upon to pass judgment on whether the public schools should move toward a system of classroom, as opposed to schoolroom organization, and defended their coolness toward classrooms in their *Report*: "It may admit of doubt whether . . . schools are not moving faster than the world, for which they are a preparation, has followed or will be able to follow them. It is necessary at the Bar, and in other careers in life, and in the Houses of Parliament, that much mental work should be done of all kinds, amidst many outward causes of distraction."[20] The schoolroom was still alive in the English public schools of the 1860s because it was a form of organization that had meaning beyond the immediate tasks of the accomplishment of teaching and learning. But its days were numbered. Classrooms arrived on the scene with their own macrocosmic resonances centering around collectivist sentiments of sympathy and emulation that were to be unlocked by the new teacher professionalism.[21] These had a stronger appeal for the new majority bound for lesser administrative posts in government and commerce. Not surprisingly, it was the more aristocratic schools that clung longest to the old traditions. But by 1885 even at Winchester the "once thronged room" was deserted. And when, in the 1890s, the Headmaster summoned his sixth form to meet him there, he was "shocked to find that it was no longer known where to sit or what to do in School."[22]

The strangeness of the schoolroom and the familiarity of the classroom both relate to their success as *inventions*. An invention is a new solution to a problem, but to be successful it has to be more than technically feasible.

It has to fit with theories of practice, and with social relations and conventions. More than this, if it an educational invention, it has to mesh with the meanings that the world outside schools projects on it. Discarded inventions, such as schoolrooms, puzzle us, while living ones, such as classrooms, dull our imagination with their excessive familiarity. Yet they too are inventions of their times, with a beginning and, we can confidently predict, an end. Though the classroom places constraints on the delivery of curriculum, we need not view these constraints as fixed for ever. Just as history can remove from our thinking the limiting assumption of curricular universality, so it can also remove the assumption of the immortality of inventions.

INSTITUTIONAL CATEGORIES:
THE UNIVERSALIZATION OF INVENTION

The final stage of my present project is to draw together the ideas of universal and invention into a third notion: that of the institutional category.

Looking at the strange curricula of previous epochs forces us to confront the question of how they acquired more than parochial significance, when national and local governments were not involved in the provision of education, and there was no apparatus of qualification or statutory enrollment to secure the legitimacy of schooling. As long as we are dealing with the loose-textured fabric of medieval education there is little problem. Learning was ad hoc and on demand: it did not stand in need of legitimation. To put the matter very simply, no one was concerned in any practical sense with questions such as, "What is a real education?" or "What is a real school?" Education was something you picked up as you went along. It came in disconnected bits. A school was sui generis. There was seldom any need to compare one with another. But, beginning in the 18th century, issues of the reality and authenticity of types of teaching and learning came to assume practical importance. There is visible evidence of this in, for example, the architectural styles adopted in the building of English secondary schools. Before the 18th century, school buildings reflected the vernacular traditions of the area in which they were constructed. A Cotswold school was a Cotswold building; a Yorkshire school a Yorkshire building. Some clues to their function may be externally present, but often we have to be told "This is a school." By the middle of the 19th century, the reverse is true. We know from their Elizabethan Gothic design that Liverpool Collegiate and Cheltenham College are secondary schools, but we would not be able to place them geographically.[23]

In the mid-19th century, the English public schools began to exhibit not only architectural uniformity, but also uniformity in organization and curriculum. To take a minor, but significant example of this, Kennedy of Shrewsbury produced his *Latin Primer* when, in the 1830s, "the public school head-masters decided on the desirability of a common textbook."[24] Once such a book was universally available, there was an answer to the question "How do we know we are doing proper Latin?"—"Because we are following *Kennedy's Primer*." Previously, a variety of texts had been used, some printed by the schools themselves. And uniformity spread even to details of dress and manner. As sequences of photographs of school cricket or football teams show, the casual poses (sometimes with pets) of the 1860s gradually give way to more and more regimentation until, by the end of the century, players appeared in identical kit and carefully ordered rows, all facing the camera.[25] Through widespread adoption of inventions (the textbook, games played according to agreed rules, classrooms) what had been particular became universal. By such means, ideas like public school assumed the status of institutional categories. Their conscious molding of internal organizational categories around the approved inventions won for the schools authenticity in the eyes of their public.

This movement from the particular to the universal through shows of categorical conformity, based on the implementation of standard inventions, can be represented diagrammatically (see Fig. 11.1). We begin at the bottom with a situation such as obtained in public schools in the early 19th century, where organization was specific to a particular establishment: Winchester College was a unique school, with its own way of doing things, and not especially to be compared with any other school. It had its own terminology (e.g., Ostarius), which might or might not be to some extent shared with, or familiar to other schools. In subsequent decades, through social and technological developments (some very simple and obvious: Tom Brown arrived at Rugby in a stagecoach, but left in a train[26]), the clientele for these

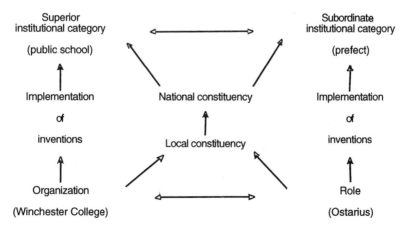

FIG. 11.1. The evolution of educational constituencies.

schools became national and general, rather than local and particular.[27] It was larger and more mobile, but grew to include people with little knowledge of the schools. Comparison within a secure framework became an important issue, and there was a shift of emphasis from what was unique to what was common and therefore comparable. "Ostarius" becomes assimilated to the subordinate universal category "prefect"; Winchester joins the superior category of "public school," within which "prefect" finds its meaning.

The essential mediating factor in this process was the constituency of people who supported the schools as users of their services in one way or another. They became the bearers of the educational categories in their institutional aspect, making connections between category and invention, and exercising judgment over questions of which inventions should be indicative of categorical membership, and whether the implementation of inventions was genuine enough to sustain claims of categorical conformity.

Then, in a further development, the clientele became larger than the old schools could cope with and new ones were set up. This created a broader and more powerful impulse toward conformity. The older schools had been able to adopt a somewhat relaxed attitude toward orthodoxy. While other headmasters rushed to copy Arnold's combination of the office with that of chaplain, the head of Eton declined to do so on the grounds that boys were so easily impressed with anything said from a pulpit that he should not presume to extend his authority in that way. And, as we have seen, Winchester felt comfortable with its schoolroom until the 1880s. But newcomers had to be more careful, and the categorical inventions were respected in excruciating detail. To be quite sure of its status, Marlborough, a new foundation of the 1860s, had before the turn of the century already acquired a school ghost. This we learn from one of several popular boys magazines which, as well as features on real schools, also ran fictional accounts of school life, dealing in categories so familiar to those who had never been near a public school that they needed no more explanation than did sophisters or commencers to bachelors of arts in 16th-century Cambridge.[28]

CONCLUSION

The importance of this relationship between universal categories, implemented inventions, and educational constituencies tends to get lost as we look at modern educational systems that are legally sanctioned. Yet much that is puzzling in the present-day curriculum may become explicable, and even predictable, if we ask the same kinds of questions about current arrangements that we are driven to ask as we look into the strange schools of the past. We can see, for example, why innovative programs in the humanities have often failed, while, in a very short time, programs based on learning about or working with computers have become securely established. Media coverage of computers, and ideas associated with computers, ensures their acceptance as part of the "real" world that needs to be reflected in the microcosm of the school, while evidence that the work of the schools conforms to the universal category is readily available in the highly visible invention of the computer laboratory. "Humanities," on the other hand, is an organizational category that is only dimly connected to the institutional categories held by constituencies, who are more familiar with "English" or "History," and it has no readily recognizable invention to support it. Similarly, one can see why worries are expressed at grade inflation, since this strikes at one of the most important universals holding together constituency support for American high schools. And one has to wonder what light the analyses offered by this chapter might shed on the arrival of a national curriculum in England and Wales. How and why has categorical support for the schools become so weakened that legal intervention of this kind becomes possible or necessary?

Many questions of this sort, which we might not ask at all, or might not ask in quite the same way, are raised for us if we confront the strange curricula of the past with curiosity, and with respect for those who taught them and followed them. For strange curricula were also, in their time, rational and appropriate. Such curiosity and respect also offer us tools for developing answers to our questions that are interestingly different from those we might arrive at if we had to depend solely on the confused alliance between a universal conception of curriculum and a preoccupation with the accidents of present-day practice that tends to dominate so much of our current thinking and writing.

NOTES

1. Quoted in Costello, W. T. (1958). *The scholastic curriculum at early seventeenth-century Cambridge*. Cambridge, MA: Harvard University Press, p. 15.
2. Other possibilities are comparative studies or futures studies. History offers the advantage when the questions being asked require examination of developmental sequences.
3. Meyer, J. W. (1980). Levels of the education system and schooling effects. In C. E. Bidwell & D. M. Windham (Eds.). *The analysis of educational productivity. Vol. 2, Issues in macroanalysis*. Cambridge, MA: Ballinger.
4. As I suggest later on, recent political initiatives on the curriculum in England and Wales make interesting material for the kind of analysis proposed in this chapter. The general tendency of these initiatives has been to move organizational categories closer to institutional ones. The structure of the new national curriculum reflects rather faithfully the institutional categories that have shaped public thinking on the secondary curriculum at least since the drawing up of the Board of Education Grant Regulations of 1904.
5. Educational organizations that prefer to preserve an image of uniqueness have many little strategies for avoiding submersion in universal categories. Detail becomes important:

Oxford and Cambridge propel punts from different ends and have different styles of carrying umbrellas.

6. Gosden, P. H. J. H. (1969). *How they were taught: An anthology of contemporary accounts of teaching and learning, 1750-1900.* Oxford: Basil Blackwell, p. 80.

7. Seaborne, M. (1971). *The English School: Its architecture and organization 1370-1870.* London: Routledge & Kegan Paul, p. 144.

8. Hamilton, D. (1989). *Towards a theory of schooling.* London: Falmer Press, p. 35.

9. Hamilton, D. (1985). *On the origins of the educational terms class and curriculum.* Unpublished paper: University of Glasgow Department of Education, p. 5.

10. Inquiries into the use of the word curriculum need to adopt a more sophisticated approach to the study of language. It is clear, as I point out in the text, that some early occurrences of the word simply refer to elapse of time. The important question is not about the use of the word but about the intended meaning, and for that a considerable sensitivity to context is required. Nevertheless, in spite of my doubts about the data, I am sure that studies such as that of Hamilton (1985, 1989) are basically right in their conclusions.

11. Hamilton (1989). *Op. cit.,* p. 45.

12. "Curriculum horae" might be rendered as "the passage of an hour," while "curriculum studiorum" signifies "course of (his) studies." The later idea is an extension of the former and the movement from the one to the other involves no sharp discontinuity of meaning.

13. Hamilton (1989). *Op. cit.,* p. 46.

14. Westbury, I. (1985). *Curriculum research and curriculum theory in international perspective.* Unpublished paper: College of Education, University of Illinois at Urbana-Champaign.

15. *Ibid.,* p. 9.

16. Doyle, W. (1986). Content representation in teachers' definitions of academic work. *Journal of Curriculum Studies, 18,* p. 378.

17. *Ibid.,* p. 377.

18. Westbury, I. (1984). *Invention of curricula.* Paper presented at the Annual Meeting of the American Educational Research Association, New Orleans, LA.

19. In English education, public school refers to a high status private school. Most such schools provide boarding accommodation for the majority of their students.

20. Report of HM Commissioners appointed to inquire into the revenues and management of certain colleges and schools, etc. (Clarendon). (1864), vol. 1, p. 287.

21. Hamilton, D. (1980). Adam Smith and the moral economy of the classroom system. *Journal of Curriculum Studies, 12,* 281-298.

22. Firth, J. d'E. (1949). *Winchester College.* London: Winchester Publications, p. 155.

23. For illustrations, see Seaborne. *Op. cit.* Whereas, for example, Sir William Craven's School, Burnsall, Yorkshire (c. 1605) and Clipston School, Northamptonshire (1667) faithfully reflect their local architectural traditions (Plates 42 and 62), Liverpool Collegiate Institute (1843) and Cheltenham College (1843-1850) share the same Elizabethan Gothic styling (Plates 204 and 205). It might be argued that changes in building style simply reflected the need to design on a larger scale as school populations grew. But there are many counter instances. In Wolverley (Worcestershire), for example, the small room of the grammar school, which never held more than about a dozen pupils, was fronted by a large and structurally irrelevant neo-Gothic porch (Seaborne. *Op. cit.,* p. 194).

24. Oldham, J. B. (1952). *A history of Shrewsbury School.* Oxford: Basil Blackwell.

25. For illustrations, see Mangan, J. A. (1981). *Athleticism in the Victorian and Edwardian public school.* Cambridge: Cambridge University Press, and compare, for example, the Harrow cricket team of 1863 (Plate 15) with that of 1912 (Plate 18).

26. Hughes, Thomas (1857). *Tom Brown's schooldays.* London: Macmillan & Co.

27. To say simply that the constituency moved from being local and specific to national and general is to cover up a good deal of complexity, which there is no space to examine here. In one sense, the clientele of the old schools was already national, in that some of them drew students from the whole country, but it was also, in a sense, local, in that families might preserve an automatic allegiance to one school. In other cases, schools that had been endowed with a local population in mind might, with doubtful legality, be opened up to a national clientele of those able to pay fees.
28. Reid, William A., & Filby, Jane (1982). *The sixth: An essay in education and democracy*. Lewes: Falmer Press, pp. 78–80.

12

The Institutional Character of the Curriculum of Schooling

Our extended excursion into the organizational and institutional aspects of schooling brings us back to the practical question of how an historically grounded understanding of curriculum can be translated into proposals for action. Part 1 of this book concluded with a deliberatively based vision of some of the ends in view that should animate the making of curriculum. Such visions are long-established commonplaces of the deliberative tradition. What the tradition has lacked has been an adequate account of how visions can be accommodated to reality.

First of all, it has been seen as retreating into "the small, self-contained worlds that are inherently 'private,' individualistic, and even elitist."[1] Secondly, and connected with this perception, it has been criticized as lacking respect for the public character of education systems.[2] Exactly why deliberative theory should be singled out as displaying an ivory tower image is a little mysterious. It could be pointed out that many advocates of systematic, managerial approaches to curriculum design have woven their theories in isolation from the hurly-burly of real schools and real students. Perhaps the problem for deliberative theory is its tendency to use terminology that has an old-fashioned, common sense ring to it, so that its scholarly pronouncements seem more transparent and open to criticism than those emanating from purveyors of technological models of schooling. But lack of discussion of how practical deliberation can engage with the realities of public institutions is indeed something that needs to be remedied. Perhaps the problem here is that, in recent years, such agendas have not been raised for deliberation because it has not been invited into public areas—has indeed lost its hold in public arenas of government and administration where it once held sway.[3] But if it is to become a model for policymaking on a larger scale than that of the small business, or the university department, questions of

how its inherent concern with public goods can be translated into action for
the securing of such public goods need to be faced and answered.
    This chapter attempts to make a beginning on defining the questions that
need to be asked, and seeing where answers might be sought. It was first
published as a section of Curriculum planning as deliberation, *Rapport*
No. 11, Institute for Educational Research, University of Oslo, 1994.

THE IDEA OF CURRICULUM

Understanding of how deliberation on the curriculum can be brought to
bear on an institutionalized system of public schooling depends first of all
on an appreciation of the historical nature of curriculum as an institution
operating in relationship to other institutionalized activities. How has the
idea of curriculum, with which we must currently deal, arisen? Under what
circumstances was curriculum institutionalized? How should we conceive
of the nature of schooling in its organizational and institutional aspects?
Unless deliberation is informed by insights into these kinds of questions, it
will be severely limited in its ability to promote the public good through
processes of planning and policymaking.

    Some writers have seized on the relationship of curriculum to currus,
and on that word's commonest meaning, and claimed that its original significance came from the metaphor of the "race." We run races over (or
through) various courses and, at the end, prizes are awarded. The truth is
more mundane. The diminutive form of currus came into common usage to
denote passage of time, so that, along with phrases such as curriculum
horae—the passage of an hour—there also occurred, and quite naturally
occurred, curriculum studiorum—the time taken up by studies. As the notion
of simple passage of time in relation to learning was gradually transformed
into one that saw time as structured to contain a sequence that could be
completed, curriculum acquired institutional significance. The transformation began in the European universities in the late 16th century. Before then,
knowledge was offered and acquired as and when the opportunity presented
itself. There was no fixed notion of what should be studied, by whom, at
what age, in what order, or with what result. The possibility for movement
toward the modern notion of curriculum depended on the conjunction of a
number of social, cultural, and technical factors. The countries of Europe
were abandoning feudalism in favor of more centralized forms of government. National cultures were challenging the dominance of classical language and thought. Commerce and industry were being organized on a
grander scale. These trends all depended on the development of styles of
discourse and behavior that were public and literate, rather than private
and oral. The idea of curriculum was an outgrowth of this process, and also

became a vehicle for it. Such a development came about through technical innovation in the form of printed texts, which made possible the specification of uniform course content, and through sociocultural innovation leading to the creation of bureaucracies. The growth of printing led to the development of standardized courses of study centered on the use of textbooks that presented learning as a sequence: simultaneously, the elaboration of procedures for detailed record keeping paved the way for the idea that students could complete the curriculum of their studies and receive degrees and diplomas, which were increasingly valued in societies where objective measures of status were becoming important. Thus, those features of curriculum that are most likely to divide theorists into opposing camps—regulation, uniformity, hierarchy—were there from the start and necessarily so, since these were the features that gave curriculum its identity as something different from teaching and learning, and that launched it as institutionalized practice. What was striking was what was different: predictability where there had been idiosyncrasy, the idea of curriculum as a common experience, the need for the student to deal with public as well as private aspects of learning. But a great deal remained unchanged, or changed only very slowly. If the idea of curriculum as a public institution was, by the beginning of the 19th century, well established in schools as well as universities, its practical realization retained much of the nature of the older traditions. Learning continued to be directed to heterogeneous groups of students, to use literate resources, such as the textbook, in a thoroughly oral manner, and to preserve medieval habits of confrontation and agonism[4] in teaching.

But the central ideas of curriculum were clear enough: these were the concepts of structure, sequence, and completion. Without structure, sequence, and completion, we can have learning, we can have teaching, we can have education, but we cannot have curriculum. And structure, sequence, and completion are all universal notions that require the intervention of organizations and institutions to establish and maintain them in the public domain.

The next important development in the idea of curriculum took place through the 19th century. Again it resulted from a combination of social evolution and technical inventiveness. The 19th century in Europe and America was the era of the growth of nation states that claimed for themselves a place on the world's stage. Centralization and control went hand in hand with international rivalry and communication, made possible by inventions such as the steamship, railways, and the telegraph. Nationalism marched along with the launching of new institutions and the transformation of old ones. The 19th century saw an unparalleled burgeoning of institutional activity: post offices, public libraries, department stores, government ministries, and national banks are just some of the institutions that were essentially 19th-century inventions. Though curriculum was not a 19th-century invention, its coupling to national education systems was. The development of the nation state crucially depended for its success on the creation of symbolic institutions. If we look, for example, at the annual reports of the U.S. Commissioner of Education in the late 19th century, we see that not only was there a concern with the setting up of domestic schooling systems, but also intense interest in what was happening elsewhere in the world. The reports are filled with accounts of the organization of schooling, not only in the countries of Europe, but also South America, the Middle East, and Australasia. Schooling systems were flag carriers for the developing nations of the 19th century, just as national airlines are flag carriers for developing countries today.

The principal technical inventions that made this possible were classrooms and systems of grading and certification. These provided the means by which education systems could be rationalized and made comparable across cultures. Thus the orderly nature of the curriculum was matched to the orderly, hierarchical forms of schooling. Curriculum structure was mirrored by tracking and promotion systems, curriculum sequence by progressions of age-related grades and classes, and curriculum completion by standardized certification procedures. And all of this was backed by the highest political authority. The fully articulated curriculum matched the forms and structures of actual organizations, such as schools, to abstract, but widely shared and understood institutional categories, consisting of curricular topics, roles, and statuses.

And, once again, what was central to the evolution of curriculum at this point—grading, classrooms, nationalism—are issues that today cause deep controversy over how we should view the curriculum. Grading seems to elevate the national interest above the individual interest; classrooms are apt to be seen as coercive and alienating arenas, which promote failure at least as much as they deliver success; nationalism is associated with support for governmental attitudes to peace and the environment that seem shortsighted, or even immoral. It may be that the harnessing of curriculum to goals of nationhood that took place a hundred or so years ago was something that left serious problems for curriculum as practice, yet it is part of the reality of its history. It seems that institutions bear for a very long time the marks of the period of their founding. National schooling systems are no exception to this rule.

But what of more recent history? We might anticipate that the latest technological advances in communication and control systems, together with social evolution in the contradictory directions of greater individual freedom of choice and access to information, on the one hand, and greater subordination of choice to homogenizing multinational corporations on the other, will lead to further change in the institutional character of curriculum.

We should suspect that this will indeed be the case. The fact that governments in the United States and the United Kingdom can find no better means of responding to failing confidence in schools and curriculum than by reasserting policies articulated close to 100 years ago is seen by some as a signal of the end of the historical development of curriculum. But this does not necessarily follow: curriculum may still have some capacity for evolution as an institution, though, if it does fall as institution, it falls as practice as well. If history urges anything, it is that, rather than denying, or rejecting the institutional role of curriculum in national schooling systems, we should be looking for new ways of interpreting it. If we are not happy with it, it is because the work of the 19th-century founders was too well done. Curriculum has difficulty in finding a truly contemporary role. But if we want it to find that role, we cannot do it simply by reflecting on curriculum as practice. We have to conceive of it as an historically determined institutionalized practice.

CURRICULUM AS AN INSTITUTIONAL CATEGORY

But what is the core of this institutionalized practice? Today, students in many different places, constituting many different instances of curricular experience, can all feel that they are undergoing a common, progressive, goal-oriented experience. In the United States, for example, the feeling of commonality can come from enrollment in programs such as sixth-grade social studies, advanced placement French, or freshman algebra, all providing, whatever their actual location, a universal reference point in the career of the student. This is made possible through a social process described as the creation of institutional categories. These are divisions of the world that exist in people's minds, independently of any physical manifestations that are associated with them. They are not quite universal and eternal, but they tend toward universality and timelessness.

Curriculum, in modern societies, has become an institutional category. It can be promoted, denigrated, written about, or made into an election issue. Governments can preside over a national curriculum, as in the United Kingdom or Sweden, just as well as they can preside over a national debt, or a national health service. What these things have in common is, first of all, that, whereas they are somewhat abstract in character, their continued existence depends on corresponding organizational categories—schools, national banks, hospitals—in a way that the existence of greater abstractions, such as education, prosperity, or health, does not, and, secondly, that they can be seen as the possession of a community. A national curriculum defines sequences of structured, completable subject matter in terms of the interests and traditions of the nation that specifies it (a sure way to know when a national border has been crossed is to check out the content of the geography curriculum).

The overarching institutional category of curriculum contains a wide range of subcategories referring to content belonging to subject or topics of significance, or to content belonging to subdivisions of the student population, classified by age, grade, ability, or destination: the reading curriculum, the junior high school curriculum, the college preparatory curriculum, and so on. Associated with these are categories that belong more properly to schooling than to curriculum: elementary school teacher, high school principal, 12th-grade student. All of these institutional categories, which represent universal ideas, shape, and are in turn shaped, by the corresponding organizational categories that are their practical embodiment: what happens in classes labeled 12th grade is influenced by what the universal institutional category of 12th grade is understood to demand; conversely, that understanding is itself influenced by what happens in many thousands of individual 12th-grade classes.

What has been described is the institutional mechanism by which students, teachers, and administrators are engaged by and in the institution of curriculum. Policy and planning must address this aspect of the nature of curriculum, conjointly with its other, and in some ways contrasting aspect, stemming from its character as practice.

DELIBERATION AND INSTITUTIONS

Administrative and pragmatic perspectives on curriculum planning take no account of history. They propose, in one way or another, to deal with existing states of affairs, as though the processes through which these states of affairs came about is of little significance—for example, through treating curriculum as a matter of deciding on outputs and proposing inputs designed to deliver them. Deliberation, however, is naturally equipped to respect origins as well as present circumstances—indeed, it has difficulty in conceiving of present circumstances apart from origins. Practical inquiry does not see itself as delivering final answers to questions because practical problems always arise out of unique circumstances, and these circumstances are historically determined. Moreover, the judgment brought to bear on efforts to resolve practical problems is the judgment of individuals acting on the basis of experience, rather than as practitioners of sciences and procedures (though these individuals may be well versed in science and procedure); therefore this judgment, which constitutes the agency through which decisions are made, stems from the histories of practices, traditions, and personal careers that these individuals themselves represent.

Curriculum deliberation, which is itself an institutionally embedded practice, sees that successful curricula cannot emerge simply from consideration of inputs to, and outputs from a system: the question is always about how engagements with curriculum as institution can be engendered, and how the varied interests that affect that engagement can be reconciled. In answering that question, it does not seek to find some least common denominator that can account, in some way, for all the interests that are implicated, but strives to discover a *public interest*, centered on the maintenance and improvement of institutions, for purposes of sustaining effective practice, which can *stand* for all of them.

DISCOVERY OF THE PUBLIC INTEREST

Jurisdictions differ from groups consisting of collaborating individuals in their possession of institutions that embody and preserve traditions of collective action, intended to secure the generally agreed-on values of a society, with respect to some identified purpose. Curriculum, and schooling with which it is intimately related, are both institutions. The reason for the existence of institutions is that modern, large-scale jurisdictions find it necessary to organize and systematize the operations of practices. Practices are activities, such as teaching, healing, ministering, and governing that, undertaken on a basis of ethical responsibility, supply nonmaterial needs that individuals are not able to satisfy for themselves (curriculum planning itself is here regarded as a practice, as are also other activities necessarily associated with curriculum, such as teaching). The relationship between institutions and practices is constantly evolving and can never be assumed to have reached a situation of final stability. Therefore, it is necessary that planning processes, such as those directed to the improvement of curricula, should take account of critiques that raise fundamental questions about the nature of this relationship.

Institutions have both abstract and concrete aspects. Schooling is an abstraction related to the larger idea of education, which is the preferred term when the institution is depicted as not only abstract, but ideal. Schools and schooling systems are the concrete, or organizational representations of the institution. Curriculum is an institution subsidiary to schooling and schools, which also exists both as an institutional ideal (what is proposed, or aimed at) and as an organizational reality (what is actually done in school classrooms and associated settings).

Institutions, then, exist first of all as collections of commonly held ideals, and, secondly, as organizational forms intended to translate those ideals into activities. Within any given jurisdiction (usually equated with a state or country), there are commonly held notions about the purposes curriculum should serve, and there are also commonly held notions about how those purposes should be realized through organizational categories—ministries, school boards, schools, and so on.

Institutions have to serve and reflect a wide spectrum of interests. But their successful existence depends on their capacity for doing this in a unified way. The essence of public institutions lies in their claim to universality within jurisdictions. This is most obviously the case where legal institutions are concerned. It is not acceptable that the processes of law should depend on institutions that act according to ad hoc compromises between the interests of special groups. Therefore, the central planning problem that institutions pose is, how can these various interests, which are prima facie in conflict, be transformed into, or subsumed within a universal interest to which all can subscribe, and that can then be directive of the planning process? This universal interest I refer to as the *public interest*.

THE IDENTIFICATION OF INTERESTS

Understanding of the problem posed by the need to replace a variety of interests by a unified public interest requires that the subsidiary interests be categorized in some way. What are the major and competing sources of interest that need reconciliation? For the present purpose, it is proposed that they be categorized as: personal, practical, organizational, and critical. This categorization is derived from the nature of the jurisdictions within which institutions exist.

First of all, jurisdictions exist to enable those who inhabit them to pursue their own interests more effectively. We can, therefore, define a personal interest that expresses the aims and values of those members of a jurisdiction who, considered individually, have a stake in, or are affected by, a particular institution, and see a potential for conflict between their own aims and values and those embodied in the institution. In relation to curriculum, these will be principally the students, or prospective students, but also teachers, administrators, and others whose lives are directly affected by contact with concrete aspects of the institution. In one sense, there are as many personal interests as there are individuals affected by curriculum. But, looked at another way, the personal interest can be seen as a general expression of the conflict between personal preferences and practical, organizational, or revisionary demands.

The personal interest, then evokes the primacy of the concerns of the individual citizen over those of the institution. It raises the possibility that, in so far as the institution acts in the interests of collectivities, it may, in fact, work against the interests of individuals. The legitimacy of the personal interest is based on the idea that institutions exist to serve individuals, and not vice-versa.

The practical interest resides in practitioners who think of their work as professional and are now, more often than not, employed by institutions whose authority and standards are derived from other, sometimes conflicting sources. It expresses the aims and values of those practices that are essential to the purposes of an institution, as the practice of teaching is to curriculum. This interest focuses on how ideals of practice, which are general, can be translated into actions adapted to the requirements of specific individuals and contexts.

Like the personal interest, the practical interest can be thought of as potentially in conflict with institutional aims and values, since it promotes ethically directed action, in response to unique circumstance, over general directives or prescriptions. The practical interest has legitimacy because it supplies a moral dimension to the actions of institutions, without which their claims on public trust and support might lack credibility.

Though the values of practice can be seen to be in conflict with the values of institutions, their survival requires the support of institutions, since these supply the organizational frameworks that ensure the administrative, logistic, and financial backing required by practices operating in complex, technologically advanced societies.

The organizational interest, then, stands for the promotion and preservation of established agencies such as ministries, school boards, committees, and inspectorates, which guarantee the continuity and predictability of institutional activity. In the main, it reflects the views of administrators. The organizational interest has legitimacy since the curriculum, understood as programs of learning, depends on the existence of structures that can reliably maintain the schooling system in a state of stability, while also providing the means through which new initiatives can be translated into action.

The final interest is the critical, or revisionary interest, which represents the thinking of those groups and individuals who, on the basis of a theoretically or practically based critique—rather than on the ground that some personal, practical, or organizational interest is being violated—raise challenges to the claims of institutions to legitimacy or effectiveness. The critical interest is the voice of principled reform that, though having adherents within the institution, is most often articulated by outside observers, usually academics or politicians.

The critical interest has legitimacy because institutions, as well as promoting and stabilizing internal action in relation to existing states of affairs, also need a capacity for identifying and accommodating change in the society in which they serve.

Though personal, practical, organizational, and critical interests are in some ways mutually supportive, in others they are in conflict. If institutions are to be maintained and improved, it is necessary that this situation of commonality-combined-with-conflict be deliberatively resolved through identification of a universal interest, which, while taking account of subsidiary interests, and building on their diversity, understands that they do not, in themselves, represent a satisfactory basis for action. Planning and policymaking that takes places within and for institutions must discover this universal, or public interest.

RELATIONSHIPS OF THE INTERESTS

Personal, practical, organizational, and critical interests can be seen as occupying congruent or opposing positions on questions of attitudes adopted toward two key dimensions of the nature of institutions.

The first key dimension refers to the question of whether actions and purposes are to be understood in specific and individual, or general and universal terms. The personal and the practical interests relate actions and purposes to specific people and contexts. The question those guided by personal interest ask about institutions is, "how can they be shaped to advance the individual interests of those who are the clients of practice?" While those guided by practical interests ask, "how can they guarantee freedom of response to those wishing to treat specific cases in what they understand to be a professional manner?" On the other hand, organizational and critical interests share a concern to relate actions and purposes to common structures and general principles. Those guided by organizational interests ask, "how can institutions maintain organizational clarity and consistency?" While those guided by critical interests ask, "how can the failings of institutions be identified and remedied by the application of general ideas and principles?"

The four interest groups offer radically different accounts of how action and purpose should be determined (and therefore how planning and policymaking should be conducted). However, the accounts given by personal and practical interests, on the one hand, and organizational and critical interests, on the other, share some common ground: the former begin from the specific and judge the merits of institutions in terms of tactics; the latter begin from generalities and judge them strategically.

The second key dimension refers to the question of whether institutions are to be thought of as inherently bad, or inherently good. Here the relationships between the interests fall into a different pattern. Personal and critical interests tend to stress the deficiencies and evils of institutional activity, while the practical and the organizational tend to represent it as benign, or praiseworthy. Emphasis on the personal interest leads almost inevitably to a perception that institutions are, at best, crosses to be borne, while investment in the critical interest presupposes that they are inherently flawed. On the other hand, the practical interest, while often critical of aspects of institutions, accepts that practice depends on institutional support, while the organizational interest is fully persuaded of the necessity for preserving institutions with as little change and interference as possible.

RECONCILING THE INTERESTS

Examination of the nature of the four interests suggests firstly that the differences between them are such that no overall public interest could be derived simply from an amalgamation of their points of view—potentiality for conflict is too great—but, secondly, that, on any particular issue, it is unlikely that no common ground will exist between two or more of them. It could therefore be supposed that the possibility of resolution exists, and that, as a result of such a resolution, a public interest, transcending subsidiary interests, might be recognized. How is this resolution to be brought about? Three types of resolution need to be discussed: political, dialogic, and deliberative.

Politics is a means of allocating and legitimating advantage and disadvantage within a jurisdiction. In the case under consideration, the issue seems to be: when all interests cannot be served, which shall have priority? Politics could be thought of as an appropriate means for resolving such a question. But though politics often appeals to a public interest, it is a poor means for creating one, since what it is best adapted to do is to favor existing interests, roughly according to the power they are perceived to command.

If these interests relate to individual citizens, or groups of citizens, this may be appropriate. If, for example, what has to be determined is how to allocate increases in taxation over various sections of the population, this could be a matter for political resolution. In the present case, however, what has to be considered is how to make plans, involving allocation, for an institution that exists to serve, and depends upon, its reflection of a public interest. Action must begin from an assumption of the integrity of the institution, which cannot be the case if action is to be based on politically determined priorities that largely represent the relative powers of interest groups.

When plans have to be made for actions that are seen to lie in the public domain, where the application of politics is restricted, resolution is sometimes sought through dialogue, within which we can include debates, commissions, hearings, and reviews.

The virtue of dialogue is that it can take place outside political structures, and therefore claim to address questions of policies and priorities in a way that can have regard to the special nature of public institutions, respecting evidence, rather than reflecting the relative weight of the interests concerned. Its possible defects are, first, that dialogue tends to be about making choices between already determined alternative actions, and, second, that its very claim to objectivity means that the conclusions it reaches may not engage those responsible for translating ideas into action. In so far as dialogue avoids those shortcomings, it assumes the character of deliberation.

Deliberation is contrasted to dialogue in that it describes not only a social process for determining decisions on practical action, but also a philosophical conception of how such decisions should be arrived at. While dialogue is initiated in hopes that ideas about practical interventions will be agreed upon, deliberation represents the means through which problems about states of affairs are naturally resolved.

The particular account that deliberation gives of the nature of practical action embodies morally and ethically grounded conceptions about the relation of theory to practice, about questions of who should deliberate and how, and about how decisions on practical action should be reached.

THE MORAL CHARACTER OF DELIBERATION

The deliberative model offers a morally grounded account of how practical problems affecting individuals and institutions should be resolved. Since it has this character, the practical process of deliberation has to be thought about as much in terms of virtues and vices, as techniques and organization.

Virtue is not only necessary to the process of deliberation because of the kinds of problems with which it deals, it is also integral to the method which it proposes. Resolutions of problems are made possible through the qualities of character displayed by those individually involved in deliberation—through their exercise of patience, humility, courage, sympathy, resourcefulness, and so on. Equally, deliberation may be hindered by corresponding vices such as impatience, arrogance, intolerance, cowardice, or recklessness.

Each of the subsidiary interests that come together to define the public interest also brings characteristic virtues as well as vices to the project. The personal interest brings concern for the welfare of the individual, the practical interest brings the ethical standards of professionalism, the organizational interest brings care for reliability and consistency, the critical interest brings honesty and regard for principle. But in order that these virtues can contribute to deliberation, the corresponding vices have to be subdued. The personal interest can descend into privatism, where personal concerns take on a selfish aspect, the practical interest can become sectarian, elevating the concerns of a subgroup above those of the institution, the organizational interest can adopt a dirigiste attitude, emphasizing the values and purposes of administration above the ends that administration is supposed to serve, the critical interest can manifest itself as nothing but subversion, so that the critique becomes an indulgence for the critics, rather than a means for enabling institutions to be objective about their failings.

Subjugation of the vices that impede deliberation depends on a variety of factors. The most efficient means of ensuring that deliberative judgments stem from virtuous engagement in the process, is the existence of a tradition of deliberation that embodies standards of conduct and offers instances of exemplary problem solving to those groups or individuals who are newly inducted into its processes. But traditions have to be created, and can only be created through efforts, however tentative, to promote the traits of character and setting on which they depend.

Where tradition is lacking, character and setting must be fostered both by looking to other exemplary models that can be invoked, and, more fundamentally, by using whatever resources of technique lie to hand for creating the circumstances in which the elements of a tradition can be set in place. Deliberation creates itself. It does not emerge from a recipe.

Tradition, example, and technique, in combinations appropriate to the circumstances of particular deliberations, will be the means of ensuring that the virtues of particular interests are given scope to work collaboratively toward the the definition of the public interest, and that this process is not vitiated by competition arising from their inherent vices.

The deliberative model of planning differs from administrative models in that it finds it not only desirable, but necessary, to discuss method and process in terms of virtue and character, as well as in terms of skill and technique. Thus it answers the question of how planning is to avoid conclusions that are morally objectionable in the most fundamental way—by insisting that the conduct of planning should itself be a morally grounded practice, rather than by subjecting the already flawed results of technically neutral processes to further screening, filtering, and revision.

NOTES

1. Westbury, I. (1994). Deliberation and the improvement of schooling. In J. T. Dillon (Ed.). *Deliberation in education and society.* Norwood, NJ: Ablex, p. 63.
2. Westbury in Dillon, *op. cit.*, pp. 37–65, provides cogent arguments for believing that it is indeed possible to envisage a deliberative process that "presumes deliberative choice making . . . that takes place within a framework that assigns different roles to different parts of both the overall education 'system' *and* the larger polity" (p. 62).
3. It can be argued, for example, that the English 19th-century commissions that I cited in "The evolution of educational constituencies" and "The institutional categories of schooling" operated on a deliberative model that was the natural one to use before the government became bureaucratized and administration subordinated to projects of scientific management.
4. See, Ong, Walter J. (1974). Agonistic structures. *Interchange, 5,* 1–12.

The Language of Deliberation: A Glossary

It is both an advantage and a disadvantage of deliberative theory that it does not consist of a set of propositions. Learnable propositions provide recipes for action that can, in some circumstances, lead to appropriate outcomes. Deliberative theory presents a disadvantage because it does not confront us with anything so straightforward. To engage with it, we have to tolerate—better still welcome—complexity and ambiguity. But complexity and ambiguity are bound to be fundamental to the nature of a theory of action intended to deal with problematic situations that are not of a universal character and treatable by instrumental means, but of a particular character and demanding morally justifiable resolutions. The advantage of deliberative theory is that it offers a method that can deal with situations of this kind. Mastery of the method involves, essentially, mastery of its language.

Propositional language presents its own difficulties, but, paradoxically, they are relatively easy to overcome. I say paradoxically because at first sight, propositional language (of which mathematical language is the archetype) looks to be far removed from natural language. However, it possesses an inner logic that can guide us in its correct use. The language of deliberation, on the other hand, is deceptive in that, on the surface, it appears to be very close to natural language. However, it uses the terms of natural language in a special way, so that appreciation of their meaning depends, not upon convergent skills of seeing how the scope of terms is curtailed by the context of their use, but on divergent skills of seeing how the resonance of terms is amplified by the whole universe of discourse of which they form a part.

Learning the language of deliberation can be compared to learning a foreign language at the point when competence has progressed beyond the stage of recognizing and using words as though they reflected a universal understanding of objects and states, and relationships between objects and states. Now it enters a stage where the learner begins to appreciate that the very existence of another language means that conceptions of objects and states are not universal after all, but embedded in unique cultures: when, for example, in our projects of international research, we come to realize "that 'skola' does not mean 'school,' and 'læreplan' does not mean 'curriculum.' "[1]

The project of learning and using a language at this level is an altogether different enterprise, which can be compared to Schwab's discussion of the "Impossible role of the teacher in progressive education," where he says:

> In Dewey's original statement, the members of a numerous set of terms were placed in new and fruitful relations to one another: time, fact-idea, change, freedom, organism-environment, experience, individual and society. In each epitome, on the other hand, only one or two of these terms appear, and conclusions about the character of education are drawn from them alone. Thus each epitome inflates what was a part of the original into an alleged whole.[2]

This illuminates the dangers that beset us when we launch ourselves into the realms of deliberative theory. Schwab chose very "deliberately" to subtitle his first "practical" paper "A *language* for curriculum," but then, having set his readers on their guard against assuming that they could select terms from his discussion and expand them into comprehensive statements about the nature of curriculum planning and decision making, he neglects to formally initiate them into the language he proposes for thinking about and resolving practical problems of curriculum.

I do not here attempt to repair this gap: only to make a beginning by commenting on some of the key terms of a discussion that was launched in the writings of Aristotle, elaborated through the work of the medieval commentators, adapted to 20th-century society through the contributions of Dewey and McKeon, and promoted by Schwab as a key to the understanding of how the problematics of curriculum should be addressed. In accordance with the preceding argument, discussion of each term is not self-contained, but is to be read in conjunction with discussion of all other terms.

Action—The language of deliberation aims to facilitate discussion of how we should act in order to resolve practical problems. It is not intended to solve theoretical puzzles. We have to have reasons to act, but these reasons will, in the face of uncertain practical problems, be persuasive rather then demonstrative. Therefore, the language of deliberation benefits from some sacrifice of precision in favor of imagination and inspiration. This is particularly the case because taking action will usually require the achievement of consensus among individuals and interests with varying aims and priorities. Action is undertaken to resolve an unsatisfactory situation, but action itself depends on the resolve of those who recommend it. The language of deliberation must be capable of securing this resolve.

Aims—Deliberation is purposeful and can therefore to said to be directed toward the realization of aims. However, it treats aims as something to be discovered, rather than as premises that should guide discussion. It also considers that, in situations of uncertainty, the pursuit of fixed and precise aims can be disadvantageous, and therefore shies away from use of terms like "objective," generally preferring to go in the other direction and discuss "ends-in-view."

Appreciation—How should the consideration of uncertain practical problems be approached? The first step is to engage in a process of appreciation—to look at the situation from a variety of viewpoints, to search widely for evidence, to entertain all kinds of possibilities. Use of the word appreciation acknowledges that feelings of dissatisfaction, leading to a sense that some problem requires resolution, are generally vague in nature. Often, however, this vagueness is not felt by those directly affected, who may leap to conclusions about who or what is to blame. By insisting that what is amiss may not be obvious, and that its discovery may require extended appreciation, deliberation diminishes the likelihood that eventual resolutions will be inappropriate, perhaps expensively so.

Arts—Today the word art tends to be confined to products or processes that are not seen as centrally involved in the economic or administrative aspects of society. Painting, sculpture, or poetry can be categorized as the work of artists, but not the organization of schooling, the planning of airports, or the running of federal agencies. The language of deliberation harks back to a time when the scope of the arts was much wider, embracing all manner of activities that were thought to require cultivated judgment and imaginative insight, as well as skill and technique. Schwab, following McKeon and others, suggests that a reappraisal is overdue, and that modern restriction of the medieval conception of "arts and methods" has led to impoverishment of our ability to design and manage social institutions.

Career—Deliberation views the contexts within which action has to be taken as dynamic. The people, the institutions, the beliefs and aspirations that make them up cannot be treated as items to be observed, measured, and classified. The concept of career encapsulates this idea. Applied to people, it emphasises that, at any given moment, as students, teachers, or administrators, they are on some kind of trajectory, and that understanding of where they have come from, and where they might be going, or wanting to go, is critical to decisions about taking action that affects them. But the conception is also applicable to other elements in the problematic context. Institutions, for example, can also be seen as having an historical career.

Character—What is it that determines whether deliberative resolution is successful? Other problem-solving methods tend to rely on the correct application of procedure. But deliberation starts from the premise that procedure, on its own, is inadequate for treating practical problems. If, then, there is no rule to show infallibly what should be done, how is the success of the process to be ensured? Deliberation puts the onus for this on the character of the participants. Instead of treating actors in decision making as neutral technicians, applying a procedure, it works on the assumption that good decisions come out of processes guided by the virtues, and bad decisions out of processes contaminated by the vices. If the object of deliberation is promotion of the general good—a moral end, then it seems only reasonable to believe that the route to achievement of the good must lie through virtuous conduct. Thus, the method of the practical has to take account of qualities of character, as well as skill and knowledge in those who engage in deliberation.

Commonplaces—Just as the processes of deliberation are not specifiable, so the evidence to which it should attend is not specifiable. The nature of uncertain problems is such that, in both instances, what to do must be a matter of judgment. But some set of working assumptions is needed in order to make the question of where to seek evidence a tractable one. The idea of the commonplaces provides just such a set of assumptions. The parallel is with the question of where we look for subject matter for a speech. The methods of classical rhetoric suggested that, for any given topic, there were "loca communa," or generally agreed-upon places where we should search. Thus, if the topic of our deliberation is within curriculum, then, perhaps, we should think of the "loca communa" as being students, teachers, subject matter, curriculum making, and the milieus. This is not to say that we should not look elsewhere as well, but, given constraints of time, we should at least check that these obvious commonplaces have been visited.

Community—Many features of the character of deliberation—its concern with character, its pursuit of the general good, its promotion of personal engagement—stem from the perception that it is being conducted within, and on behalf of, a community. Actors in deliberation are not seen as technical experts, employed to bring their specialist skills to bear on a problem that they are uniquely equipped to solve, but as constituting a representative subgroup of a community, entrusted to focus its attention on issues affecting the community as a whole. Therefore, they bear a special responsibility to understand their community, to consult its interests, and to trace out the consequences for the community of actions which they decide upon.

Consensus—Ideally, the deliberating group should, at critical points of its proceedings act as a consensual group, rather than as a collection of individuals. Recommended actions should be actions that the group supports, and not those that can command a majority vote, or that merely escape a veto. In this respect, as in the case of the commonplaces, deliberation follows a rhetorical model. Since the group is constituted of members with varying interests, it has to deploy persuasive powers to convince them of the significance of evidence, the force of arguments, and the desirability of actions. On the other hand, members have to be willing, in most circumstances, to allow the nature of the problem to be resolved, and the general (or public) interest to prevail over personal inclinations in order that consensus can be achieved on a decision for action.

Constituencies (see Publics)

Curriculum—Obviously, the character of curriculum deliberation is posited upon a particular interpretation of what a curriculum is. If a curriculum is thought to be a schedule of testable skills and knowledge, derived from specific objectives that can be logically determined, then we would not want to invoke deliberation as a means of designing it. What assumptions about the nature of a curriculum are inevitably linked to the proposition that, at least on some occasions, decisions about it must result from deliberation? First of all that it is the possession of a community: that questions of what we propose to teach, to whom, and in what way, are definitive of an identity that a community wants to claim for itself. Secondly, and following on from this, that a curriculum is about much more than the acquisition of skills and knowledge: at issue may be exposure to knowledge, attitudes to knowledge, and so on. Thirdly, that curriculum is an institution and not simply a schedule of content, and that decision making about it must therefore have regard to other institutions, such as the institution of schooling, to which it is intimately connected. If curriculum is seen in this way, it follows that at least some decisions about it must result from processes of deliberation. Deliberation is adapted to decision making that must take account of the aspirations of a community, and must confront subject matters that impinge on many varied and sometimes contradictory interests.

Curriculum making—Curriculum making figures as one of the list of commonplaces of curriculum deliberation, emphasising that making and deliberating are to be understood as two different things. Making refers to technical matters, or ability to appreciate specific situations, while deliberating covers a much wider field. But making is not something invoked at the point where a deliberative decision on action has been made. It contributes to that decision. Thus, while it may appear that deliberation downgrades the contribution of curriculum experts because what they do is subject to the contribution of many kinds of nonexpert people, in another way their contribution is elevated because they play a part on a wider stage where issues much broader than the content, style, or structure of a curriculum are at issue. It also assumes greater importance in that, in some formulations of deliberative theory, the curriculum-making function is seen as including the responsibility of organizing and guiding the whole course of the deliberation.

Deliberation—As a commonsense term, deliberation is close in meaning to discussion, implying, perhaps, that the discussion in question is serious and thoughtful rather than light-hearted and inconsequential. Within deliberative theory, however, deliberation takes on a philosophical sense. Deliberation is the method of the practical: that is, the method that must inevitably be used when uncertain questions of what action to take are considered. It is contrasted with induction or deduction that are the methods of theoretic: the methods employed when questions of the truth of empirically or logically based beliefs are at issue. If we accept the proposition that deliberation is the method of the practical, then debate is not about whether we should use it in the solution of uncertain practical problems, but how to use it well. Poor deliberation may result from lack of skill or understanding in circumstances where we correctly intend to deliberate, or from use of inappropriate strategies when we mistakenly believe that we are engaged in some radically different process.

Democracy—Support for deliberation is also, in some sense and to some degree, support for democracy. What kind of democracy depends on the place and the epoch. Clearly, Aristotle, as a deliberator, was a democrat. But his version of democracy would have excluded slaves. The basis of the connection between deliberation and democracy lies in the implications of deliberation for a conception of the relationship between theory and practice. Since deliberation is about action it has to be concerned about the nature of practice. But, equally, it is about the rational choice of action, and must therefore also have a conception of theory that shows it as capable of being connected to practice. The only conception of the relationship of theory to practice that fits the requirements of deliberation is one that sees both as manifestations of inquiry. This in turn implies that questions of practice are, in principle, questions for decision by all who can contribute to, or who are affected by their resolution. Thus, deliberative processes are intrinsically democratic. Extrapolating from that observation, we could go on to claim that, therefore, curricular proposals resulting from a deliberation should have a democratic character: that there is, in fact, an intrinsic relationship between process and product, such that each reflects the other.

Discovery—Deliberation aims to be a process of discovery. First of all, it does not assume that the problematics of a case are obvious. Appreciation is a form of discovery. Secondly, discovery is involved in the search for the evidence that allows the nature and extent of the identified problem to be exposed. Thirdly, and most importantly, the production of possible problem resolutions is seen as a matter of discovery. Deliberative resources are used not merely to adjudicate among actions that are already known, but to imagine, or invent actions that have not previously been proposed.

Eclectic (Arts of)—Though the focus of deliberation is on making decisions about action, it proceeds on the principle that better knowledge will produce better actions. Therefore, it is also concerned with the theoretic: for example, not just "how can we secure learning?", but "how does learning take place?" However, there can be many different accounts of how learning takes place. These might be physiological, psychological, sociological, and so on. As well, there can be many accounts of circumstances conducive to learning: economic, cultural, historical, biological. All of these accounts are produced within the parameters of an academic discipline. It is this that gives them their explanatory power. By confining themselves to the terms and concepts of their respective disciplines, theoreticians are enabled to produce self-consistent explanatory propositions. But deliberation, which seeks resolution in action, is unable to ally itself with any one discipline: to say, for example, that only psychological theory will be called in evidence when questions of how learning takes place are addressed. All the disciplines have to be treated as potentially credible witnesses. Then, for practical purposes, their evidence has to be, in some way, combined. The eclectic arts are arts that enable diverse theoretic propositions to be brought together in order that they can become consequential for decisions about action.

Ends (see Means)

Ends in view (see Aims)

Enquiry (see Inquiry)

Good (The)—Deliberation aims at improvement. But how do we understand improvement? If test scores on mathematics rise, is this improvement, or not? On the face of things, it represents improvement, but that is only the case if we make two assumptions: first, that the improvement does not entail any corresponding cost, and, second, that this particular item of improvement fits with some wider conception of what improvement means. These should not be difficulties for processes of deliberation because deliberation works with an idea of the general good. We take action, not simply because it seems intrinsically desirable, but because we have considered how it relates to the good, conceived as what is generally beneficial for a community or a society. First of all, we do not assume that actions can be considered in isolation. All actions have consequences, possibly of quite a complex nature. Deliberation aims, as far as possible, to trace out these consequences before recommending action. Secondly, deliberation also asserts that actions must be seen within the context of a community, and that a major part of deliberation must be directed toward understanding what constitutes the good for that community. Discovery of the good is not a theoretical exercise, but one undertaken through the direct participation of community members, and through their conjoint activities of appreciation and discovery.

Gradualism—As a recipe for curriculum planning, deliberation suffers from disadvantages of looking old-fashioned and slow moving. The modern taste in planning, as in other spheres, such as architecture, is for what is striking and what can be rapidly achieved. There are few takers for the idea that a century or more should be spent on building a cathedral that, superficially, looks like all other cathedrals. But a cathedral that truly reflects the complexity of the culture and beliefs of a community is not going to be a simple object. Nor, in fact, can it lack uniqueness; a uniqueness springing from the fact that, while its construction may follow a general pattern, its detail is immensely varied, precisely because it is the product of a community and not simply of a grand design (One of the best deliberative texts—though not intended as such—is John James' *Chartres: The Masons Who Built a Legend*[3]).

Should we then conclude that the gradualism of deliberation is fine when problems do not require immediate solution, but inappropriate when rapid action is called for? This assumption arises from a focus on a concomitant rather than a central characteristic of deliberation. What is central is not that large amounts of time should be spent on appreciating problems and inventing solutions to them, but that *the problem should control the process*. This being the case, and given that the problems to which we would want to apply deliberation will be complex in nature, it follows that investment of time, if possible, is always worthwhile. But what if time is not available? Extensive simulator research carried out in the 1980s by airlines in the United States established that in situations where about 20 minutes was available to remedy serious system failures, disaster was most likely to be avoided by crews who employed deliberative methods to deal with the problem. It is the nature of problems that determines whether deliberation can be effective, not the scope for gradualism.

Inquiry—The centrality of the concept of inquiry to deliberative theorists is shown by Schwab's concern about how to spell it. He says he tried to insist on the spelling "enquiry," because "In years centering on 1958, some educational psychologists became interested in the strategies children use to solve problems. The psychologists called this problem-solving 'inquiry.' To ensure that I would not be mistaken for one of these psychologists, I took to spelling 'inquiry' with an 'e.' "[4] Not myself being in competition with other claimants of the word, I am happy with inquiry, which, to my eye, looks better—although I am not consistent in using it.

Deliberative theory regards inquiry as a universal term denoting the means by which problems or puzzles get solved. We are all, as an inevitable consequence of being human, inquirers. But inquiry is a multifaceted tool, and what blade we should use depends on how we classify the material that must be worked upon. The key to deliberative method is the artful matching of the form of inquiry to our identification of the nature of the problem to which it is applied. To state the question of method in this way is significant because it suggests that, though the classification of problems (an aspect of problem appreciation) is a critical matter, we should also accept that classification is not easy. We always need to be aware of the total scope of inquiry processes because problems will not fit neatly into categories, and problem resolution will often require the application of different types of inquiry at different stages of the process. This is an argument for being careful about handing over problem solving to "experts" who may be conversant with only one kind of inquiry.

Institutions—One criticism levelled at Schwab's listing of the commonplaces of curriculum deliberation is that too great a burden is assigned to the commonplace of the milieus. This is connected to the charge that his vision of deliberation can be seen as having a private quality. Deliberators in the Chicago College of Education, or in university committees, needed to have regard to students, teachers, subject matter, and curriculum making, but, while some attention had to be paid to the milieus within which deliberation went on, this was not at the forefront of their minds. The university, as an institution, mandated them to carry out their task, and also, to a large extent, protected them against the intrusion of other institutions—state and federal authorities, educational organizations, professional associations. Once the translation of deliberative theory to the curriculum of schooling is undertaken, the situation is radically changed. This kind of curriculum deliberation has to be centrally concerned with its relationship to national and local institutions. Thus it has to address the question of the nature of institutions. How is the idea of institution different from that of organization? Schools, for example, are organizations, but schooling, as an institution, presents an altogether different constellation of publicly embodied values, attitudes and aspirations.

Interests—Deliberation brings together different people, ideas, and knowledge. This is its central function—to ensure that practical problems are considered from as wide a variety of angles as possible. But the bringers of ideas and knowledge do not come to deliberations simply as providers: they are, inevitably and usefully, representative of interests. The more that deliberation is seen as linked into society in the broadest possible way, the more this is true. Thus, deliberation has to confront the question of how it can be more than a process of adjudication between already articulated interests (which, I have suggested, can be construed as personal, practical, organizational, and critical). Politics is equipped to act as an adjudicator between such interests, but deliberation has to aspire to more than politics (though it cannot set politics aside). Deliberation must be centrally concerned with what it means to serve a public interest, and, therefore, with how the public interest can be defined as something different from the least common denominator of the various subinterests.

Judgment—The nature of the problems that deliberation deals with dictates that there can be no clear-cut answers in terms of how they are defined, discussed, or resolved. At every stage, skills of judgment have to be brought to bear. Actions resulting from judgment can never be proved to be correct, but they do have to be seen to be justifiable. This means that they must not only be shown to be based on evidence, but also to have emerged from a trustworthy process of judgment applied to that evidence. Deliberative judgment must be seen to result from the exercise of virtue and experience, as well as skill and knowledge.

Learners—Learners are perhaps the hardest commonplace to accommodate in deliberation. Deliberation requires knowledge about learners, but, to be effective, it must also treat learners as a source of knowledge. However, effective deliberation requires that the deliberating group be kept small. Given that learners represent perhaps the most diverse, and certainly the most ill-organized of the commonplaces, how is their participation to be effected? This is one of the endemic ambiguities that deliberation must face.

Literacy (see Orality)

Means—Methods of problem solving often work by separating means from ends. First a solution is envisaged, then, given this conception of where the problem-solving process should arrive, means can be devised for getting there. Maybe, even, we know already know what end we want to achieve—it is given as part of the problem. We want, perhaps to show that the angles of a triangle, given certain assumptions, will add up to 180 degrees. If that is our objective, then we can concentrate our thought on possible means that might enable us to achieve it. This kind of thinking is often applied to practical as well as theoretic problems. It offers the security of well-tested procedures and the comfort of being able to show that a predetermined goal has been reached. But deliberation is not happy with this kind of thinking. While admitting that there can sometimes be merit in making distinctions between ends and means, it considers that uncertain practical problems are too ramified to yield to these kinds of strategies. Much better to think of ends and means as interacting, or even as indistinguishable. Looked at one way, a given action may appear to be an end: looked at another it may appear to be a means. Throughout the deliberative process, there will be a constant toing and froing between means-focused and ends-focused thinking, each modifying the other.

Method—Method is a capacious term for describing a way of accomplishing a task. To talk of procedure suggests that what has to be done is not a matter of debate. We agree on what we want to achieve and we can therefore confidently choose a known and tested route to arrive there. Deliberation is the method of the practical, not the procedure of the practical because practical problems are inherently ambiguous and ways of resolving them must be discovered as we go along. But use of the word method also proclaims that what we do is not random and unconsidered. Method can deal with complexity and ambiguity, yet also be confident that it is acting rationally and appropriately.

Milieus—The milieus is the name given by Schwab to the commonplace that represents the sociopolitical, or sociocultural setting within which curricula are planned and enacted. Its presence marks the fact that curriculum deliberation cannot be a totally circumscribed process, referring only to its internal commonplaces (students, teachers, subject matter, curriculum making). Use of milieus (in preference to milieux, which, presumably, is less obviously plural) indicates that it is not appropriate to think of what surrounds curriculum making as a unified medium, but as a multiplicity of media. This is a commonplace that presents great difficulty in terms of how it is to be represented and consulted. The milieus are complex and various, but the nature of deliberation dictates that it should be conducted by small groups.

Orality—Much of the character and flavor of the notion of deliberation stems from the fact that it is an intrinsically oral activity. Decisions about action stem from face-to-face discussion; liberal use is made of rhetorical concepts, such as the commonplaces, which are rooted in the oral tradition. Thus, as a means of dealing with practical problems, deliberation (the method of the practical) is contrasted with the essentially literate procedures applied to theoretic questions. Yet deliberation is also a literate activity, in that it involves the use of arts and methods, which can only exist within a literate culture. Here, as in so many aspects of its nature, deliberation exhibits a fruitful ambiguity.

Policy—Deliberation is often criticized as a costly and time-consuming way of taking decisions. It is supposed, for example, that subscription to the method of the practical implies that all manner of dissatisfactions will have to be subjected to detailed research and discussion. This is not the case. Deliberation works with a notion of policy: if, as a result of past decisions, an understanding, or policy exists about how things should be done, then that is capable of handling day-to-day decision making until circumstances arise where applications of policy fail to prevent unsatisfactory states of affairs from arising. Only at that point, is renewed deliberation required.

Practical (The) (see The Theoretic)

Problems—The philosophy of deliberation is built around conceptions of the nature of problems. Classification of problems as practical or theoretic, certain or uncertain, or moral or procedural provides the ground on which propositions about appropriate action-oriented methodologies can be elaborated and defended. Thus the association of deliberation with a terminology of problematics is inescapable, but this inevitably leads to it being identified simply as a problem-oriented activity in the common sense use of the word problem. This is unfortunate because it tends to cast deliberation in the rather limited and negative role of a way of sorting out what went wrong. Deliberation is a way of creatively considering and improving states of affairs for the general good. It would be more appropriate to depict it as a way of capitalizing on opportunities, rather than treating problems.

Publics—Unpacking of the commonplace of the milieus leads to the discovery of subcategories such as publics. Curriculum deliberation has to take into account the publics that support curriculum, or that act as bearers of its meanings in its various manifestations, such as the subjects of the curriculum, the levels of schooling, and so on. Understanding of these publics is of critical importance for successful decision making on curriculum matters. Deliberation also has to be concerned to discover the public interest, a collective interest that transcends those of the subpublics, or subinterests.

Responsibility—Those who exercise judgment in the course of deliberation have to accept responsibility for the quality and the results of that judgment. While other methods or procedures involve their users as technical actors, so that errors and shortcomings can be put down to failures of the system, or to skill deficiencies, the character of deliberation requires that its participants assume a personal and moral responsibility for the choices they make.

Stages (see States)

States—Discussion and description of deliberation requires the making of distinctions between different kinds of activity: problem appreciation, collection of evidence, formulation of proposals, and so on. The obvious way to categorize these is as stages of the process. But this is to project deliberation as a sequenced procedure—which it is not. More appropriately the various activities can be seen as states of the deliberating group. It may start off in a problem appreciation state, then move to proposal formulation, but, at that point, revert back to problem appreciation, as discussion of proposals reveals aspects of the problem not previously considered. Since the logic of the process is determined by the nature of the problem, and by interactions between problem and method, transitions from one state to another are not sequentially determined. Sometimes, even, the different states can coexist.

Subject Matter—Subject matter is one of the curriculum commonplaces. To label it in this way is to give it the broadest possible definition. At the other extreme, some might want to talk about the commonplace of the disciplines, on the ground that deliberation should not be about absolutely anything that could be learned or experienced, but only those things to which a community can consensually assign an educational value. A way of stating this, while allowing that a curriculum can consist of more than just the disciplines, is to talk of subject matter as consisting of cultural achievements.

Teachers—To list teachers and learners as separate commonplaces makes it appear as though deliberation can address curriculum only in a very traditional way: that curriculum is simply what some people teach to others. But the commonplaces are not intended to identify distinct groups of people. Rather, they point to functions that generate the kinds of knowledge that curriculum deliberation should not ignore. That teachers and students should have indeterminate roles, being both givers and acquirers, or creators of knowledge at the same time, is an idea totally within the compass of curriculum deliberation. However, thinking about such an idea means drawing on experience generated through activities thought of as teaching and activities thought of as learning.

Theoretic (The)—Deliberative theory contrasts the theoretic with the practical as dual aspects of inquiry. The theoretic describes activities of solving puzzles arising from states of mind. That is, intellectual puzzles to which we would like to have an answer (is there life on Mars?), but that we are not compelled to answer. The practical, on the other hand, refers to the resolution of puzzles arising from states of affairs. That is, situations demanding action (should we vote in favor of dedicating public funds to a search for life on Mars?). Our resolution may consist of a decision to do nothing—but that is still a positive resolution of a practical dilemma.

Virtue—Exercise of good judgment in the course of deliberation depends on the possession of practical competence, but also of qualities of character. Deliberation requires the language of virtue. It needs to be able to discuss courage, honesty, responsibility, and humility in relation to decisions on action and on the taking of action.

EXAMPLES OF WORDS NOT FOUND IN THE LANGUAGE OF DELIBERATION

Behavioral objectives—Objectives, as a description of what deliberation might be directed toward, appears as far too precise and far too simple. And behavior, which here is understood as "what can be observed" would be thought to be a misleading end point. The activities that curriculum deliberation aspires to foster do not have meaning simply as behaviors. What is done assumes significance only in terms of a understanding of what led up to them, and within what context they occur.

Effectiveness—There is currently much discussion of how schools can be made more effective. This is not a word that fits well into the vocabulary of deliberation. Its use is to describe the outcome of the use of materials that are intended to produce uncomplicated and undifferentiated results. Weed killers are said to be effective. Deliberation promotes a conception of curricula that sees them as working in complex and subtle ways to promote the education of those who follow them.

Management—Development of the idea of management suggests that methodologies of planning and administration can be separated off from the specifics of the activities that are to benefit from their use. Deliberation insists that how affairs are conducted should be determined by the intrinsic nature of the affairs in question. The commonplaces of curriculum belong specifically to curriculum, and should be at the heart of any process that sets out to maintain what is good, or bring about improvements where deficiencies are identified.

NOTES

1. Reid, William A. (1998). Systems and structures or myths and fables? A cross-cultural perspective on curriculum content. In Bjørg B. Gundem & Stefan Hopmann (Eds.). *Didaktik and/or curriculum? An international dialogue.* New York: Peter Lang, p. 11.
2. Schwab, J. J. (1978). The "impossible" role of the teacher in progressive education. In I. Westbury & N. J. Wilkof (Eds.). *Science, curriculum, and liberal education.* Chicago: University of Chicago Press, p. 167.
3. James, John (1982). *Chartres: The masons who built a legend.* London: Routledge & Kegan Paul.
4. Westbury, I., & Wilkof, N. J. (1978). Introduction. In I. Westbury & N. J. Wilkof. *Op. cit.*, p. 3.

Author Index

Subject Index

A

Action, 7, 18, 23, 27, 36, 37, 47, 52-57, 59, 61, 67, 86, 87, 89, 91, 92, 97, 104, 108, 195-197, 200, 201, 205, 209, 212

Appreciation
see Problems

Arts, 11, 68, 69, 71, 76, 78, 176, 201, 205

C

Categories
commonplace, 29, 30, 112
institutional, 112, 143, 149, 150, 160, 164, 173-177, 180-183
organizational, 143, 160, 173, 181, 183, 190
of problems, 24

Character, 8, 11-13, 45, 47, 49, 197, 198, 202, 212

Classrooms, 42, 62, 93, 98, 112, 120, 122, 133, 152-154, 161, 165, 167, 168, 172, 174, 177, 178-180, 189, 192

Commonplaces, 94, 107, 109, 112, 202, 203, 207-212

Common sense, 25, 35, 64

Community, 14, 60, 75, 91, 94, 135, 136, 190, 202, 203, 206

Completion (of curriculum), 97, 110, 175, 188, 189

Constituencies (educational), 151-169

Curriculum
change/innovation, 27, 116-128, 133-137, 149, 151-155, 159-162, 167-169, 188
decisions/decision making, 22, 27, 30, 33-37, 109, 203, 204
deliberation, 10, 29, 33, 34, 42-49, 58, 89-92, 94, 104-110, 112, 124, 187, 191, 192, 197-212
design/planning, 16, 17, 22, 27, 28, 42, 46-49, 84-95, 117-119, 123, 134-137, 203, 204, 206
evaluation, 24, 54, 55
groups, *see* Deliberative groups
as practice, 14, 15, 35, 43, 45, 77, 94, 97, 98, 109, 120, 124, 125, 143, 147, 150, 188, 189, 190, 191, 194
problems, 17, 21-25, 33, 35-37, 42-43, 45, 46, 89-91, 103, 116
research, 50-65, 142, 150
theory/theorists, 16-17, 22, 33, 35, 37, 48, 86-88, 117, 118, 122-124, 137, 152-154, 188

D

Debate, 103, 112, 117

Deliberation, 10, 11,17-18, 25, 27, 28, 29, 30, 33, 34, 42-49, 58, 92, 94, 104, 106, 107, 109, 112, 113, 124, 187, 191, 192, 197, 198, 199-212

Deliberative groups, 14, 15, 27-30, 45, 46, 85, 91, 203, 211

Democracy, 72-76, 91, 103, 204, 205